Praise for *Azure AI Fundamentals (AI-900) Study Guide*

This book provides a practical and straightforward, easy to follow roadmap to prepare you for your Microsoft Azure AI certification.

—*Mike Mulray, senior executive, property & casualty insurance industry*

This is an outstanding resource for anyone looking to break into AI with Microsoft Azure. I like how it simplifies complex AI concepts with real-world examples, making it accessible even for those new to the field. The structured approach and hands-on insights make this a must-read for anyone preparing for the AI-900 exam. I highly recommend it!

—*Gaurav Deshmukh, senior software engineer tech lead, Guidewire Software*

Azure AI Fundamentals (AI-900) Study Guide
In-Depth Exam Prep and Practice

Tom Taulli

Azure AI Fundamentals (AI-900) Study Guide
by Tom Taulli

Copyright © 2025 Tom Taulli. All rights reserved.

Printed in the United States of America.

Published by O'Reilly Media, Inc., 1005 Gravenstein Highway North, Sebastopol, CA 95472.

O'Reilly books may be purchased for educational, business, or sales promotional use. Online editions are also available for most titles (*http://oreilly.com*). For more information, contact our corporate/institutional sales department: 800-998-9938 or *corporate@oreilly.com*.

Acquisitions Editor: Megan Laddusaw
Development Editor: Sara Hunter
Production Editor: Ashley Stussy
Copyeditor: Shannon Turlington
Proofreader: Tove Innis

Indexer: BIM Creatives, LLC
Interior Designer: David Futato
Cover Designer: José Marzan Jr.
Illustrator: Kate Dullea

May 2025: First Edition

Revision History for the First Edition
2025-05-06: First Release
2025-11-07: Second Release

See *http://oreilly.com/catalog/errata.csp?isbn=9798341607811* for release details.

The O'Reilly logo is a registered trademark of O'Reilly Media, Inc. *Azure AI Fundamentals (AI-900) Study Guide*, the cover image, and related trade dress are trademarks of O'Reilly Media, Inc.

The views expressed in this work are those of the author and do not represent the publisher's views. While the publisher and the author have used good faith efforts to ensure that the information and instructions contained in this work are accurate, the publisher and the author disclaim all responsibility for errors or omissions, including without limitation responsibility for damages resulting from the use of or reliance on this work. Use of the information and instructions contained in this work is at your own risk. If any code samples or other technology this work contains or describes is subject to open source licenses or the intellectual property rights of others, it is your responsibility to ensure that your use thereof complies with such licenses and/or rights.

979-8-341-60781-1

[LSI]

Table of Contents

Preface. ix

1. Introduction to the AI-900 Exam. 1
    Why Should You Take the Exam?   2
        Recognition   2
        Rising Demand for AI Skills in a Booming Market   2
        Azure's Growing Dominance in the Cloud Market   2
        Salary Boosts and Career Opportunities with AI Skills   3
    Who Should Take the AI-900 Exam?   3
    Topics Covered in the Exam   4
    Other Certifications to Consider   5
    AI-900 Exam Details   6
    A Stepping Stone to Advanced Certifications   7
    Microsoft Resources   8
    ACE College Credit   9
    Conclusion   9

2. Azure AI Services. 11
    Basics of Microsoft Azure   12
    Setup   13
    A Brief Tour   13
    Create an Azure AI Resource   14
    Studios   16
    Conclusion   19

3. Overview of AI Workloads and Key Use Cases. 21
    Introduction to AI   21
        Content Moderation   23

	Personalization	25
	Computer Vision	25
	Natural Language Processing	26
	Knowledge Mining	28
	Document Intelligence	28
	Generative AI	29
	Guiding Principles for Responsible AI	31
	Accountability	32
	Inclusiveness	33
	Reliability and Safety	33
	Fairness	34
	Transparency	34
	Security and Privacy	35
	Conclusion	36
	Quiz	37
4.	**Fundamental Principles of Machine Learning.**	**39**
	What Is Machine Learning?	39
	The ML Model Workflow	40
	Step 1: Train the Model	41
	Step 2: Apply the Algorithm	43
	Step 3: Use Inferencing	43
	Types of ML	43
	Regression Analysis	44
	Example: Ticket Sales	45
	Evaluation Metrics for Regression Models	49
	Classification	51
	Binary Classification	52
	Evaluation Metrics for Binary Classification	55
	Multiclass Classification	59
	Evaluation of a Multiclass Classification Model	61
	Clustering	62
	Deep Learning	65
	Conclusion	67
	Quiz	68
5.	**Azure Machine Learning.**	**71**
	Introduction to Azure Machine Learning	72
	AutoML	73
	Azure Machine Learning Designer	78
	Conclusion	82
	Quiz	83

6. Features of Computer Vision Workloads on Azure............................. 85
Computer Vision Services for Azure   85
    What You Can Do with Azure's Computer Vision Services   86
    How Computer Vision Works   89
    Image Filters   92
    Image Classification   94
    Object Detection   95
    OCR   96
    Facial Detection and Analysis   99
    Convolutional Neural Networks   100
    The Evolution of Computer Vision: From CNNs to Multimodal Models   102
Responsible AI and Computer Vision   103
    Fairness in Facial Recognition   103
    Privacy and Security   103
    Transparency   104
Conclusion   104
Quiz   105

7. Features of Natural Language Processing Workloads on Azure................. 107
Introduction to NLP   107
    Tokenization   108
    Frequency Analysis   110
    Text Classification   111
    Semantic Language Models   111
Azure Services for NLP   113
    Key Phrase Extraction   115
    Entity Recognition   116
    Sentiment Analysis   118
    Language Detection   119
    Speech Recognition and Synthesis   120
    Translation   122
    Conversational Language Understanding   123
    Conversational AI   125
Conclusion   128
Quiz   129

8. Features of Generative AI Workloads on Azure............................... 131
Understanding Generative AI   131
    Advanced Language Models   134
    The Transformer Model   135
Language Models on Azure   139
    Large Language and Small Language Models   141

  Copilots   141
  Prompt Engineering   146
  Customizing Copilots   147
  Azure OpenAI Service   147
  Using Azure OpenAI Studio   148
 Responsible Generative AI   150
  Spot Potential Harms   150
  Assess the Risks   151
  Build In Safeguards   152
  Operate a Responsible Generative AI Solution   153
 Conclusion   155
 Quiz   156

9. Strategies and Techniques for Successfully Taking the AI-900 Exam. 159
 Understanding the Exam Experience   159
  Manage Your Time   160
  Read Questions Carefully   160
  Use the Process of Elimination   161
  Stay Calm and Double-Check Your Answers   161
 Key Concepts to Review   162
  AI Fundamentals and Responsible AI   162
  Machine Learning   162
  Computer Vision   163
  Natural Language Processing   164
  Generative AI   165
 Conclusion   166

A. Practice Exam. 167

B. Answer Keys. 179

Glossary. 197

Index. 205

Preface

Over the years, I've immersed myself in artificial intelligence (AI). I've written several books on the topic and advised companies on leveraging its transformative potential. In that time, one question has emerged as a recurring theme when I talk to people: how can I enhance my AI skills?

I typically share a range of options. There's no shortage of excellent books, online courses, and YouTube tutorials to get you started. But if you're looking for a structured path, I recommend pursuing a certification. Certifications do more than test your knowledge—they validate your expertise. For employers, they're a signal that you not only understand the fundamentals but also are prepared to apply them in the real world.

Among the myriad AI certifications available, one stands out: the Azure AI Fundamentals (AI-900) exam. It doesn't just skim the surface. It dives into key AI domains like machine learning (ML), deep learning (DL), natural language processing (NLP), computer vision, generative AI, and responsible AI. Of course, there is coverage of key solutions from Microsoft Azure.

So whether you're charting a new career path or bolstering your current role, the AI-900 certification equips you with a solid foundation. And this book is your ally in that journey. Packed with the resources you need to pass the exam, it's also a handy reference guide for broader AI topics.

So here's my advice: dive in, stay curious, and don't be afraid to challenge yourself. AI offers limitless opportunities, and with the right tools and mindset, you're poised to make an impact.

Thank you for picking up this book—and best of luck as you embark on your AI adventure.

What's Covered

Here's a brief look at each chapter.

Chapter 1, "Introduction to the AI-900 Exam," provides an overview of the Microsoft Azure AI-900 certification. The chapter highlights the career advantages of earning this certification. It also details the exam structure as well as key topics like AI workloads and ML principles, and it offers guidance on preparation resources and complementary certifications.

Chapter 2, "Azure AI Services," describes the basics of the Azure platform as well as how to set it up. The chapter also explores creating an Azure resource, which is required to perform various types of AI tasks, and we take a look at Azure AI Foundry, which allows you to create AI applications.

Chapter 3, "Overview of AI Workloads and Key Use Cases," explores various AI workloads and their practical applications. It introduces foundational technologies like content moderation, personalization, computer vision, NLP, knowledge mining, document intelligence, and generative AI. The chapter also stresses responsible AI principles, including fairness, reliability, transparency, and inclusiveness.

Chapter 4, "Fundamental Principles of Machine Learning," looks at key ML concepts and techniques. It describes supervised learning methods like regression and classification, unsupervised techniques such as clustering, and the distinction between ML and DL. The chapter then looks into the ML workflow, from data preparation and training to inferencing.

Chapter 5, "Azure Machine Learning," explores how Azure's cloud-based service simplifies the training, deployment, and management of ML models. It highlights two key tools: Azure Automated Machine Learning (AutoML) for automating model development and Azure Machine Learning Designer, a no-code, drag-and-drop interface for creating pipelines.

Chapter 6, "Features of Computer Vision Workloads on Azure," looks at the fundamentals of computer vision. It covers Azure's suite of computer vision tools, including Azure AI Vision for general image analysis, Azure AI Custom Vision for tailored image recognition, and Optical Character Recognition (OCR) for extracting text from images. Key techniques like image classification, object detection, and facial analysis are detailed with practical examples. The chapter also explains the role of convolutional neural networks (CNNs) in analyzing image patterns and discusses multimodal models.

Chapter 7, "Features of Natural Language Processing Workloads on Azure," explores key NLP concepts and their applications. It introduces Azure services for NLP, including Azure AI Language for tasks like sentiment analysis, entity recognition, and key-phrase extraction; Azure AI Translator for real-time text translation; and Azure

AI Speech for speech-to-text and text-to-speech capabilities. The chapter also looks into foundational NLP techniques such as tokenization, text classification, and semantic language models.

Chapter 8, "Features of Generative AI Workloads on Azure," highlights the transformative potential of generative AI. It focuses on Azure tools like OpenAI models, DALL-E for image generation, and GPT-4 for advanced language tasks. Key concepts include large language models (LLMs), transformer architecture, tokenization, embeddings, and attention mechanisms.

Chapter 9, "Strategies and Techniques for Successfully Taking the AI-900 Exam," provides practical guidance for exam preparation and test taking. It emphasizes the importance of leveraging the Microsoft exam sandbox for familiarity and of mastering key topics like AI fundamentals, ML, NLP, computer vision, and generative AI.

Conventions Used in This Book

The following typographical conventions are used in this book:

Italic
: Indicates new terms, URLs, email addresses, filenames, and file extensions.

Bold
: Shows commands or other text that should be typed literally by the user.

`Constant width`
: Used for program listings, as well as within paragraphs to refer to program elements such as variable or function names, databases, data types, environment variables, statements, and keywords.

O'Reilly Online Learning

For more than 40 years, *O'Reilly Media* has provided technology and business training, knowledge, and insight to help companies succeed.

Our unique network of experts and innovators share their knowledge and expertise through books, articles, and our online learning platform. O'Reilly's online learning platform gives you on-demand access to live training courses, in-depth learning paths, interactive coding environments, and a vast collection of text and video from O'Reilly and 200+ other publishers. For more information, visit *https://oreilly.com*.

How to Contact Us

Please address comments and questions concerning this book to the publisher:

> O'Reilly Media, Inc.
> 1005 Gravenstein Highway North
> Sebastopol, CA 95472
> 800-889-8969 (in the United States or Canada)
> 707-827-7019 (international or local)
> 707-829-0104 (fax)
> *support@oreilly.com*
> *https://oreilly.com/about/contact.html*

We have a web page for this book, where we list errata, examples, and any additional information. You can access this page at *https://oreil.ly/azure-AI-fundamentals-AI-900-study-guide-1e*.

For news and information about our books and courses, visit *https://oreilly.com*.

Find us on LinkedIn: *https://linkedin.com/company/oreilly-media*

Watch us on YouTube: *https://youtube.com/oreillymedia*

Acknowledgments

I want to thank the awesome team at O'Reilly. They include Megan Laddusaw, Virginia Wilson, and Sara Hunter. I also had the benefit of outstanding tech reviewers. They are Gaurav Deshmukh, Ravi Shankar G, Michael Mulray, and Vaibhav Gujral.

CHAPTER 1
Introduction to the AI-900 Exam

The Microsoft Azure AI-900 certification, officially known as Microsoft Azure AI Fundamentals, is focused on AI and cloud computing, all through the lens of Azure. Whether you're completely new to AI or just starting your journey with cloud technology, this certification is designed to ease you into the essentials. Microsoft labels this as a "900-level" certification. This means it's entry-level and perfect if you're just dipping your toes into these areas. And you don't need to be a coding expert or a data science genius to succeed.

At its core, the AI-900 introduces you to foundational AI concepts—like ML and NLP—while walking you through how AI workloads function in Azure. A *workload* is the specific tasks, processes, or operations that a system, application, or service performs. It's a term you will often see on the exam. Examples include training ML models or using services like speech recognition or image analysis.

Sure, having a little background in cloud computing or understanding basic AI concepts can make the exam easier, but it's not a requirement. If these categories are new to you, don't worry. This book will guide you step-by-step, from square one, and help you make sense of it all.

Each chapter is crafted to get you fully ready for the AI-900 exam. We'll take it one concept at a time, explaining everything in plain language and showing you practical examples using Azure's AI tools, so you can see exactly how things work in the real world. And to give you a boost of confidence, there's a set of 95 sample questions that mirror the exam format.

In this chapter, we'll start by breaking down the structure and objectives of the AI-900 exam, so you'll know exactly what to expect and how to prepare for success from the get-go.

Why Should You Take the Exam?

Earning the AI-900 certification can give your career a major boost, especially as the AI field continues to grow at breakneck speed. Even if you're not aiming for a job specifically in AI, this certification can still help you stand out in today's competitive job market. It's a solid way to showcase that you've got a strong understanding of AI fundamentals.

Let's look into some of the key reasons that make earning the certification worth your time and effort.

Recognition

The AI-900 certification is recognized by employers as a strong validation of your knowledge of AI concepts within Azure's cloud platform. This level of credibility can make you stand out to hiring managers. It's a great way to demonstrate that you're ready to contribute AI-driven solutions in real-world scenarios.

Rising Demand for AI Skills in a Booming Market

Gartner (*https://oreil.ly/WZf7m*) predicts that AI software spending will soar to $297.9 billion by 2027, growing at an impressive compound annual growth rate of 19.1%. This surge is driven by the widespread adoption of AI across industries as companies look to boost efficiency, streamline operations, and gain valuable insights from data. As AI becomes more integrated into business strategies, the demand for professionals with AI expertise—particularly those certified in deploying AI solutions on platforms like Microsoft Azure—will see a significant rise.

Azure's Growing Dominance in the Cloud Market

Microsoft Azure continues to see strong growth. As of early 2024, Azure's revenue surged by 29% year-over-year (*https://oreil.ly/wu8uQ*) to $62 billion, powered by increasing adoption of AI services and cloud-based solutions. Microsoft's Intelligent Cloud segment also reported $26.7 billion in revenue for the first quarter of 2024, marking a 21% jump from the previous year.

Azure's growth is in step with industry trends, where businesses are relying more on cloud services to power AI workloads and digital transformation efforts. With around 23% market share, second only to Amazon Web Services (AWS) at 32%, Azure is cementing its position as a leading player in the cloud-computing landscape.

Salary Boosts and Career Opportunities with AI Skills

Professionals with AI skills are in high demand, and it's paying off—literally. Companies are offering up to 30% higher salaries for roles requiring AI expertise (*https://oreil.ly/ZGAVK*). And it's not just tech teams that are reaping the rewards. Research and development professionals can see a 29% bump, while sales, marketing, and finance employees enjoy around 28% more. Even roles in business operations, legal, compliance, and HR aren't missing out, with salaries boosted by up to 24%.

AI-focused roles naturally come with competitive compensation (*https://oreil.ly/08inr*):

Data analyst
  In the United States, data analysts typically earn between $60,000 and $90,000 annually, with variations based on experience and location. In high-demand cities like San Francisco, salaries can climb past $95,000, while other regions often see averages closer to $76,000–$80,000.

AI developer
  AI developers generally make between $85,000 and $120,000 per year. For those working in advanced roles or in tech hubs, salaries tend to hit the higher end of this range.

Project manager
  Project managers overseeing AI or tech-related projects can expect salaries ranging from $90,000 to $130,000. This depends on their expertise and the complexity of the projects they handle.

Sales specialist for AI solutions
  Sales professionals specializing in AI technology typically earn between $70,000 and $110,000 annually. Performance-based bonuses often improve their overall compensation—reflecting the high demand for cutting-edge AI solutions.

Who Should Take the AI-900 Exam?

The AI-900 exam is great if you're new to AI and you want to build a strong foundation while seeing how Microsoft Azure fits into the picture. Here's a closer look at who this certification is designed for:

IT professionals
  If you're an IT specialist without much background in AI, the AI-900 will help you start exploring AI's potential and how it can be applied in cloud environments. It helps you bridge the gap between your current role and more AI-centric positions, like AI solution developers or cloud administrators.

Data analysts and business analysts
> For data analysts, this certification deepens your knowledge of how AI supports data-driven decision making. If you're a business analyst, it helps you see how AI can enhance business processes, automate tasks, and unlock valuable insights from large datasets. Plus, it equips you to better collaborate with AI engineers and data scientists.

Students and entry-level job seekers
> If you're a student or recent graduate, the AI-900 gives you a valuable credential that shows you're serious about learning AI. It lays a solid foundation for future certifications and specializations. This can give you an edge when applying for roles like AI engineer, data scientist, or cloud solution architect.

Business and sales professionals
> If you're in business development, sales, or product management, the AI-900 helps you understand how AI is reshaping industries. This understanding is important if you're selling AI-powered products or managing projects involving AI, as it allows you to communicate effectively with technical teams.

Career changers
> If you're from a nontechnical background and looking to pivot into tech, the AI-900 is an excellent starting point. It gives you a solid foundation in AI without requiring advanced programming or math skills. This can help you to break into the tech world.

In short, the AI-900 is a versatile certification that can benefit anyone looking to build or expand their knowledge of AI, no matter where you're starting from.

Topics Covered in the Exam

The AI-900 certification exam covers a range of topics designed to give you a strong foundation in AI workloads, ML basics, and how Azure supports various AI tasks. Here's what you can expect and the percentage of the number of questions for each topic:

AI Workloads and Considerations (15%–20%)
> This section introduces you to different types of AI workloads and their key features. You'll learn about AI applications in areas like content moderation, personalization, computer vision, NLP, knowledge mining, document intelligence, and generative AI. It also touches on responsible AI principles. This will show that you understand the importance of fairness, reliability, safety, privacy, security, inclusiveness, transparency, and accountability, which allow for building AI solutions that are both effective and ethical.

Machine Learning Principles on Azure (20%–25%)
> Here, you'll dive into the basics of ML, including regression analysis, classification, clustering, and DL techniques. You'll explore working with datasets, identifying features and labels, and how training and validation data fit into ML models. This section also covers Azure Machine Learning's capabilities, including automated ML, data and compute services, and tools for managing and deploying models.

Computer Vision Workloads on Azure (15%–20%)
> This part of the exam focuses on computer vision tasks like image classification, object detection, OCR, and facial detection and analysis. You'll also get familiar with Azure's tools—specifically, Azure AI Vision and Azure AI Face services—that help you work with visual data and create solutions using computer vision technologies.

NLP Workloads on Azure (15%–20%)
> In this section, you'll look into NLP and learn about features like phrase extraction, entity recognition, sentiment analysis, language modeling, speech recognition and synthesis, and translation. You'll also get to know Azure's NLP services, such as Azure AI Language and Azure AI Speech, which support a variety of NLP tasks efficiently.

Generative AI Workloads on Azure (15%–20%)
> This part of the exam focuses on generative AI models and covers use cases like generating natural language, code, and images. You'll explore the capabilities of the Azure OpenAI Service and learn about responsible AI practices specific to generative AI.

Microsoft periodically updates the exam, with changes appearing first in the English version. If the exam is offered in other languages, those versions typically get updated about eight weeks later. To stay informed, you can always check the "change log" section on Microsoft's website (*https://oreil.ly/G9upj*) for the latest updates.

Other Certifications to Consider

While there are no prerequisites for the AI-900 exam, you may want to take a look at other certifications that can help you build a stronger knowledge base. Here are a couple worth considering:

AZ-900: Microsoft Azure Fundamentals
> This certification is ideal if you want to demonstrate a solid understanding of the basics of cloud services and how Microsoft Azure delivers them. It covers important topics like cloud computing principles and Azure's architecture, management tools, and security features. If you're new to cloud computing, the AZ-900 can give you a strong foundation before diving deeper into AI with the AI-900.

DP-900: Microsoft Azure Data Fundamentals
    If you're more interested in the data side of things, the DP-900 certification is a great starting point. It focuses on core data concepts and how they're applied using Azure services. You'll learn about relational and nonrelational data, data analytics, and how data is managed in the cloud. This certification can be especially useful if you want to understand how data interacts with AI solutions on Azure.

These certifications can complement the AI-900 and provide you with a well-rounded understanding of Azure's cloud ecosystem.

If you're looking to expand your AI knowledge beyond Microsoft's ecosystem, there are several other certifications and courses to consider:

AWS Certified AI Practitioner (https://oreil.ly/uA9YV)
    This certification is for those interested in learning the basics of AI and ML within the AWS ecosystem. It covers AI and ML concepts, real-world use cases, and generative AI technologies.

IBM AI Foundations for Business Specialization (https://oreil.ly/Bc9-W)
    This certification is tailored for professionals seeking to understand how AI can drive business strategies and improve operations. The course focuses on AI concepts, their business applications, and ethical considerations.

AI For Everyone by Andrew Ng (Coursera) (https://oreil.ly/WSC_L)
    This course offers a broad overview of AI. It covers AI concepts, real-world applications, and societal considerations. It's free to audit and self-paced.

Columbia Engineering Artificial Intelligence certificate program (https://oreil.ly/AU7af) by Columbia University (edX)
    This professional certificate program dives deeper into AI topics, including ML, neural networks, and robotics. The program is self-paced, requiring a weekly time commitment of around 8–10 hours.

AI-900 Exam Details

The AI-900 exam might seem intimidating at first, but with a clear understanding of the structure and some smart preparation, you'll be well on your way to success. Here's what you need to know.

First, the exam itself consists of 40–60 questions that come in a variety of formats: multiple choice, drag-and-drop, and even hot area questions. To pass, you'll need to score 700 out of 1,000 points. Because Microsoft uses a scaled scoring system, you don't necessarily have to get exactly 70% of the answers right, but that's roughly where the target sits.

You'll have 45 minutes to tackle the questions, but Microsoft gives you a full 65 minutes total. This is to set aside time for reviewing instructions, accepting the Microsoft Certification Exam Candidate Agreement, and, if you're feeling generous afterward, providing some feedback.

When it comes to taking the exam, you've got options. You can sit for it either online or at a test center. The registration fee is $99, though this may vary depending on where you're located. The exam is available through Pearson VUE or Certiport, and if you're a student or educator, Certiport is likely your go-to. The exam is offered in a wide range of languages, including English, Japanese, Chinese (both simplified and traditional), Korean, French, German, and more.

You're allowed to take unscheduled breaks during the exam. But the clock keeps ticking, so use that time wisely. Any questions you look at before a break are locked in, meaning you can't go back to them—even if you didn't answer them or marked them for review.

If you don't pass the exam on the first try, you can retake it after a 24-hour waiting period, though you'll have to pay the fee again. For additional attempts, there's a 14-day waiting period and a limit of five attempts in a 12-month period. If technical issues throw a wrench in your exam, Microsoft may grant an exception to the waiting period.

Microsoft also allows for accommodation for those with specific needs or disabilities. Whether it's extra time, assistive technology, or even a personal assistant, accommodations are available. Just make sure to request them in advance and provide the necessary documentation, such as a note from a physician.

As for your certification, it remains valid as long as the associated technology stays relevant. That means no need for immediate recertification unless major platform changes come into play.

A Stepping Stone to Advanced Certifications

If you're ready to level up from the AI-900 and dive into more advanced certifications, Microsoft has plenty of options that build on your foundational skills. Whether you're looking to master cloud administration or improve your AI expertise, these certifications are the next logical steps on your journey. Here's a quick look at what's available:

AZ-900: Microsoft Azure Fundamentals
> This is a good starting point for anyone new to cloud computing and Microsoft Azure. This foundational certification covers the basics of Azure's cloud services, architecture, and core features. It introduces key concepts like cloud computing principles, Azure pricing and support, and the security and compliance features

that make Azure a reliable choice for businesses. While it doesn't require technical experience, it provides a strong foundation for anyone planning to pursue advanced certifications like AZ-104, AZ-204, or DP-100.

AZ-104: Microsoft Certified: Azure Administrator Associate
This exam takes a deeper dive into Azure management and is a good fit for IT professionals focused on cloud administration. It covers essential skills like managing Azure identities, implementing storage solutions, and configuring virtual networks. This certification equips you with hands-on expertise to handle Azure's core services, including storage, networking, and security.

AZ-204: Microsoft Certified: Azure Developer Associate
This exam emphasizes designing, building, testing, and maintaining cloud applications and services on Azure. It's particularly valuable for professionals who want to incorporate AI into their development workflows. The certification covers using Azure AI Services for NLP, computer vision, and decision-making APIs as well as working with Azure Functions and storage and caching solutions.

DP-100: Microsoft Certified: Azure Data Scientist Associate
After mastering Azure administration, the DP-100 certification is the next logical step for those interested in AI engineering. This certification focuses on building and managing AI solutions, covering topics such as developing ML models, selecting the right AI tools, and optimizing Azure resources for AI projects.

AI-102: Microsoft Certified: Azure AI Engineer Associate
As a continuation of DP-100, AI-102 focuses on integrating AI solutions into real-world applications. This certification looks at the full AI workflow, from data ingestion and model training to deployment and monitoring. You'll also learn how to build bots using Azure AI Bot Service and leverage Azure AI Services for NLP and computer vision tasks.

DP-203: Microsoft Certified: Azure Data Engineer Associate
For professionals keen on ensuring that their AI solutions are backed by robust data pipelines, DP-203 is a good choice. This certification looks into designing and implementing data solutions on Azure, including building pipelines, managing data storage, and optimizing architectures for AI workflows.

Microsoft Resources

Microsoft offers a range of resources (*https://oreil.ly/DjbzY*) to help you prepare for the AI-900 exam and beyond. You'll find exam guides, study materials, and practice assessments covering topics like ML, computer vision, and responsible AI. Make the most of these tools—they're designed to help you build the skills needed to succeed.

So why should you buy this book if Microsoft's resources are already available? While Microsoft's materials are certainly helpful, this book offers much more. It looks deeper into the concepts, providing a richer understanding that not only aids in passing the exam but also enhances your overall learning experience. Exam tips included in this book are specifically tailored to help you focus on the most important areas. This ensures that your preparation is targeted and efficient. What's more, the glossary is an invaluable resource since many exam questions emphasize understanding definitions.

Finally, for many people, reading a book remains a good way to learn!

ACE College Credit

Here's a bonus: the American Council on Education (ACE) partners with Microsoft to recommend college credit for professional certifications. If you pass the AI-900, you might be eligible for ACE-recommended credits, which could be applied toward degree programs at participating colleges and universities. Head over to the ACE College Credit for Certification Exams page (*https://oreil.ly/mdHIr*) to learn more about getting those credits evaluated and transferred.

Conclusion

The AI-900 certification is just the beginning of your AI journey. Whether you're new to the field or looking to solidify your knowledge of Azure's AI services, this certification is a solid way to start. As AI continues to transform industries and Azure's cloud footprint expands, AI-900 has become more than just a foundational course—it's a valuable credential that can enhance your career prospects in a rapidly evolving tech landscape.

CHAPTER 2

Azure AI Services

Azure AI Services are packed with tools to help you automate tasks like language processing, image recognition, intelligent search, and content generation. What's great is that you don't need to be an AI expert to dive in. These services are easy to implement in both web and mobile apps, and with more than a dozen AI features available, you can use them on their own or mix them.

One of the best things about Azure AI Services is that they come prebuilt and ready to go. Powered by Microsoft's high-performance Azure platform, these pretrained ML models are accessible to businesses of all sizes. So whether you're a small startup or a large enterprise, you can tap into years of Microsoft's AI research without needing to be a tech wizard. While many tools work right out of the box, others—like Azure AI Vision, Azure AI Speech, and Azure OpenAI Service—can be fine-tuned with your own data to meet specific needs.

Another cool feature is how easily you can plug Azure AI Services into your projects. Developers can access these tools through Representational State Transfer (REST) APIs or SDKs. *Application programming interfaces (APIs)* allow different software applications to connect and communicate with one another—imagine them as digital bridges between your applications. For example, when you book a flight online, the airline's website uses an API to check available seats and prices from its database. Similarly, when a weather app fetches the latest forecast, it communicates with a weather service's API to retrieve that data in real time. *Software development kits (SDKs)*, on the other hand, bundle all the tools, libraries, and documentation developers need to build apps for specific platforms. This makes the whole process smoother. Plus, Azure AI Services integrate with other Microsoft services like Azure Logic Apps and Power Automate. This makes Azure AI Services even more versatile.

For the AI-900 exam, you won't need to dive into the technical nitty-gritty of these services. But you should have a good understanding of what they do, and that's what we'll look at in this chapter.

Basics of Microsoft Azure

Microsoft Azure is a huge cloud platform with more than two hundred services that can help you build, run, and manage applications in different environments. Here's a quick look at some of the options you have:

Cloud
    This is probably what you picture when you think of Azure. It's a network of remote servers where your apps and data live, allowing you to access your resources from anywhere. You can quickly scale up when demand spikes and scale down when things slow down—all without having to worry about the hardware.

On premises
    If you need to keep certain data on premises for regulatory or security reasons, Azure provides the flexibility to run its services on your own local servers. In this setup, you manage the on-premises infrastructure.

The edge
    This is about processing data closer to where it's created, like with *Internet of Things (IoT)* devices or in remote areas. Azure's edge services let you reduce latency and bandwidth costs while keeping everything running smoothly, even if your internet connection isn't always reliable.

Azure has something for nearly every technical need. Whether it's data storage with Azure Blob Storage and Azure Cosmos DB or running *virtual machines (VMs)* and containers with Azure Virtual Machines and Azure Kubernetes Service, there's a solution for you. And with more than 60 regions and 300 data centers worldwide, Azure's scale is unmatched.

Keep in mind that Microsoft occasionally updates the names of its services or changes the Azure user interface. This means that some steps or visuals you see in this book might look a little different. To help with this, I set up a website (*https://oreil.ly/L22C3*) where you can find any necessary updates.

Setup

To set up an Azure account, just head over to *www.azure.com*. If this is your first time using Azure, you can sign up for a free account. For the first month, you'll get full access to the entire catalog of services and a $200 credit to explore everything Azure has to offer.

On top of that, Azure gives you free monthly usage of certain services, though there are some limits. For instance, AI services like Azure Machine Learning and Cognitive Services are free for the first 12 months. With these, you can build, train, and deploy ML models or add AI features—such as speech, vision, and language—to your apps. You can try out services like Azure Cognitive Services Text Analytics or Azure AI Vision during the trial period, all within the free usage limits.

Even after your first year, more than 55 services stay free as long as you stick to the usage caps. Some of these are AI focused too, like Azure Functions for running event-driven code and Azure Kubernetes Service for managing containerized AI workloads.

If you're a student, Azure has a student account that includes $100 in free credits for 12 months—no credit card required.

Azure uses a pay-as-you-go model. Once your 30-day free trial or 12-month student plan is up, you'll need to switch to pay-as-you-go if you want to keep using the services, but any leftover credit can still be used. Azure also has a pricing calculator (*https://oreil.ly/gF8eP*) and lets you set budget and cost alerts. There's no long-term commitment, and you can cancel at any time.

For what we'll be doing in this book, the free and student versions will be more than enough to get started.

What if your employer has a subscription to Azure? In that case, you should get approval to use it for preparing for the exam. It's also important to note that your employer may limit access to certain services. Because of this, you might still want to set up your own account.

A Brief Tour

When you log into the Azure Portal (*htttps://oreil.ly/ed9D3*) for the first time, you'll land on a dashboard designed to help you manage your account. You can see this in Figure 2-1. At the top of the screen, you'll get a summary of what else you can explore with your free Azure account. You'll also find links to free online courses, demos, and quickstart guides to help you dive into new projects and become familiar with Azure services.

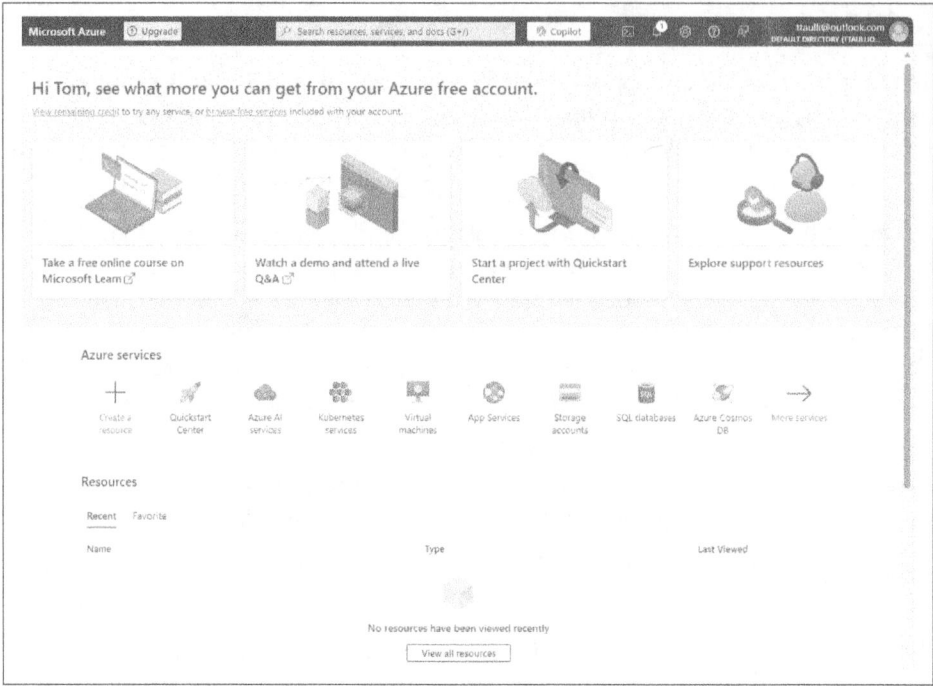

Figure 2-1. The Azure Portal

Below, you'll notice icons for various Azure services, such as creating new resources, accessing Azure AI Services, managing Kubernetes clusters, and spinning up virtual machines, among others. These icons are shortcuts that let you jump straight into the tools or projects you want to work on. If you're looking to explore more, you can click the "More services" link to bring up a full list of everything Azure has to offer.

At the bottom, you'll find the Resources section, where you can quickly access any recent or favorite resources you've been working on. This makes it easy to return to ongoing projects.

The portal is intuitive and customizable, so whether you're managing current services or starting something new, everything you need is right there.

Create an Azure AI Resource

To use an Azure AI Service, you'll need to set up a resource first. Two options are available:

Multiservice resource
> This allows you to access multiple Azure AI Services using a single key and endpoint. An *endpoint* is the URL where your application connects to interact with a service. This setup is ideal for exploring various services like AI Speech, AI Vision, and AI Language or for projects that require using several services together. Plus, it simplifies billing by consolidating all services under one resource.

Single-service resource
> This is for when you need only one specific AI service. Each service gets its own key and endpoint. This makes it easy to track usage and costs separately.

Which one should you choose? For the most part, it depends on what you're building and how you want to manage costs.

There are different ways to create resources, but the easiest is through the Azure Portal. Just sign in, click "Create a resource," and search for "Azure AI Services" in the marketplace if you want a multiservice resource. If you need only a single-service resource, search for the specific service, such as AI Face, AI Language, or AI Content Safety.

Once you've picked your service, click Create. You'll need to fill in details like the following:

Subscription
> This is the billing account for your Azure resources, which determines how you'll pay for the service.

Resource group
> This is a container that helps you organize and manage related resources in Azure.

Region
> This is the geographic location where your service will be hosted. This will ensure optimal performance and compliance with regulations.

Pricing tier
> This is the level of service you choose, which defines the features, performance, and costs associated with your resource.

You'll also need to give your resource a unique name for identification. Figure 2-2 shows what this screen looks like.

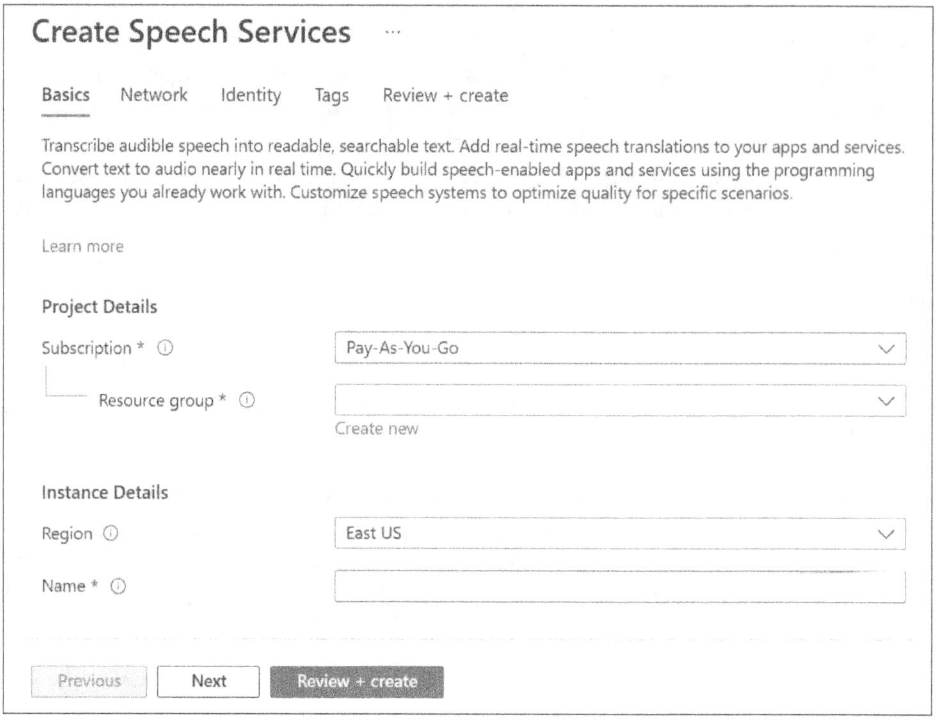

Figure 2-2. The configuration when setting up a resource for an Azure AI Service

Studios

After creating an Azure AI resource, you can start using it to build applications. You have a couple of options here—you can work with a REST API or SDK, but there's also a simpler approach: using studios. These make it easy to experiment with Azure AI Services without needing to have deep coding skills. They have user-friendly interfaces that allow both beginners and experienced developers to explore, demo, and evaluate services. Here are a few studios you can use:

Vision Studio
    This lets you work with image and video analysis tools. You can try out features like object detection, image classification, and video analysis.

Language Studio
    This one focuses on text-based AI services like sentiment analysis, translation, and text summarization. It also has tools for custom language models.

Speech Studio
   Here, you can explore Azure's speech-to-text, text-to-speech, and real-time translation services. It's a helpful tool if you're looking to build apps that need voice interaction.

Content Safety Studio
   Designed for moderating and detecting harmful content, such as violence or hate speech, this studio helps you set up safeguards against inappropriate content.

In addition to these individual studios, there's *Azure AI Foundry* (formerly called *Azure AI Studio*), which combines several Azure AI Services into one platform. Developers can use this web-based platform to create AI applications using the latest APIs and models.

To see how it works, let's go through a quick demo using Vision Studio. You'll find it on the Azure Portal under "Computer Vision." If you don't see it, just use the search bar to locate it.

Once you've clicked "Computer Vision," select "Create Computer Vision." You'll be taken to a configuration page where you need to fill out a few details:

Subscription
   Choose your Azure plan, such as free trial or pay-as-you-go.

Resource group
   If you already have a resource group, you can select it here. Otherwise, click "Create new" and enter a name for the group (e.g., "AI-Vision-Group").

Region
   Pick the geographic location where your Computer Vision resource will be hosted. Selecting a region close to you can help reduce latency and improve performance.

Name
   Enter a descriptive name for the resource (e.g., "AI-Vision-Service"). This makes it easier to manage and track your resources.

Pricing tier
   Select the pricing plan that fits your needs—whether it's the free tier or a more advanced option with larger quotas. How is this different from the subscription? Your subscription defines how you pay for all Azure services while the pricing tier defines the specific cost structure for this particular service.

Once you've filled everything out, review your settings and click Create. After the resource is set up, select "Go to resource" and then click "Go to Vision Studio." You can see what the Vision Studio dashboard looks like in Figure 2-3.

Figure 2-3. The dashboard for the Vision Studio for Azure AI

You can experiment with different services, such as extracting text from images, detecting objects, or identifying faces. Let's try adding captions to images, which you can see in Figure 2-4.

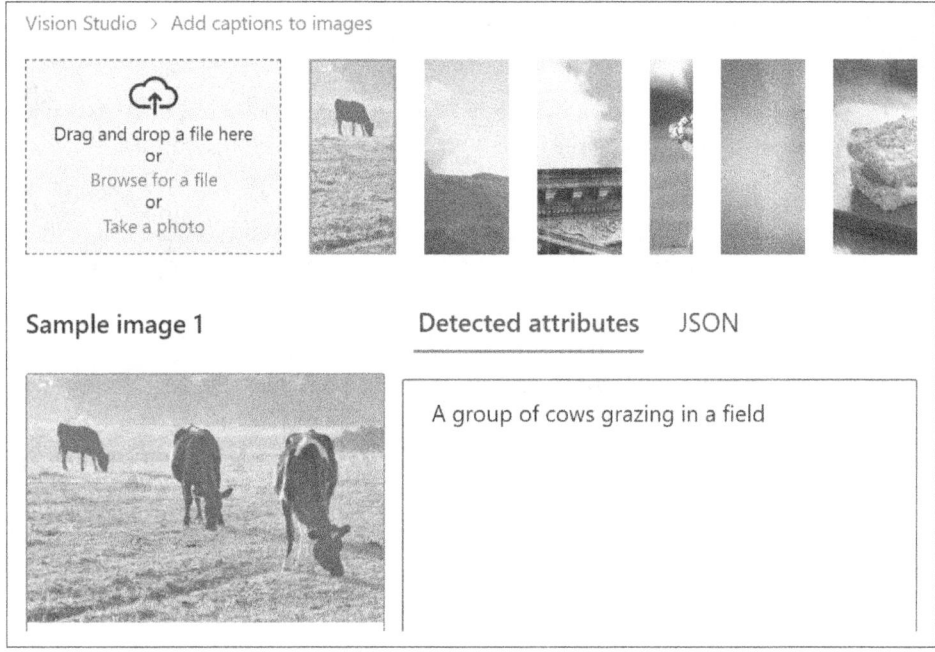

Figure 2-4. The AI service for adding captions to an image

You can either upload an image from your computer or choose a sample image. The AI will then generate a caption. In our example, it provides a caption for a group of cows grazing in a field.

Conclusion

Azure AI Services are incredibly powerful. The platform offers a flexible set of tools that allow you to integrate advanced AI capabilities into applications with ease. These services are designed to simplify complex tasks, making AI accessible to everyone, regardless of their technical background.

But when preparing for the AI-900 exam, it's important to know that you don't need a deep, technical understanding of Azure technologies to pass. The exam focuses more on high-level concepts rather than the intricate details of how the tools work.

CHAPTER 3
Overview of AI Workloads and Key Use Cases

In this chapter, we'll look at AI workloads and the key factors you need to know for implementing them responsibly. These workloads, which make up about 15%–20% of the AI-900 exam, are about understanding how AI works in different areas like content moderation, personalization, computer vision, NLP, knowledge mining, and document intelligence. These are the building blocks that power AI applications. They help systems analyze images, understand human language, extract insights from huge amounts of data, and create content using generative AI.

But it's not just about knowing what these AI workloads can do. We'll also look at the ethical and practical considerations that are crucial when developing responsible AI. We'll talk about key principles like accountability, inclusiveness, reliability, safety, fairness, transparency, security, and privacy. These principles are essential for ensuring that AI is not only powerful but also ethical, trustworthy, and aligned with the values that matter to society.

Introduction to AI

AI is about helping computers think and respond like humans. Imagine it this way: AI lets computers make decisions, solve problems, understand language, recognize images, and create new things, just like a person would. The secret sauce behind AI is how it learns from data—a lot of data—to recognize patterns and make predictions. With AI, businesses can automate tasks, uncover insights buried in mountains of information, and work faster and smarter than ever.

The diagram in Figure 3-1 is a good way of understanding AI. It illustrates that AI is not a single technology but essentially a group of different technologies and methods that build on each other to solve complex problems.

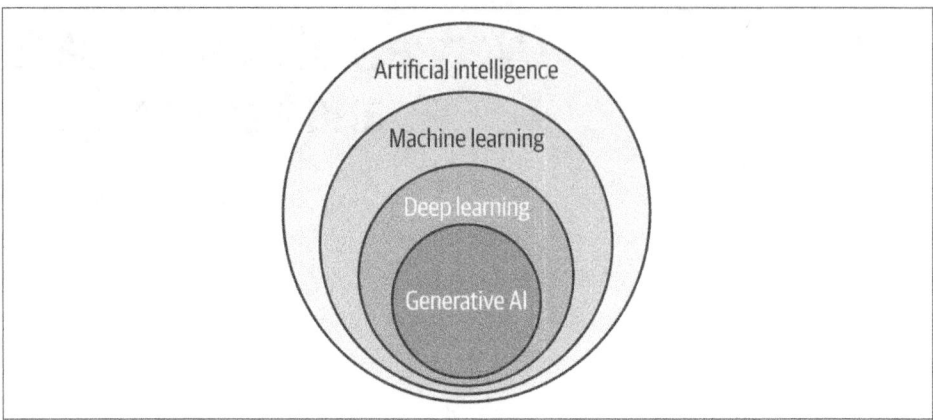

Figure 3-1. A diagram of the components of AI

At the broadest level, AI encompasses all technologies that enable machines to mimic human intelligence. This includes tasks like problem solving, decision making, language understanding, and pattern recognition. AI systems can be rule based or data driven, and they aim to perform functions that traditionally require human cognition.

Machine learning (ML), a subset of AI, focuses on enabling machines to learn from data without explicit programming. ML *algorithms* identify patterns in data and use those patterns to make predictions or decisions. This allows systems to improve their performance over time as they process more data. ML is commonly used for applications like recommendation systems, fraud detection, and predictive analytics.

Deep learning (DL) is a specialized subset of ML that uses artificial neural networks inspired by the human brain. These networks process data through multiple layers, allowing DL models to identify complex patterns and relationships. DL has been responsible for significant breakthroughs in areas like image recognition, speech processing, and natural language understanding.

Within deep learning lies *generative AI*. This is a cutting-edge technology that focuses on creating new content, which can include text, images, audio, and video. Generative AI is transforming industries by enabling applications such as automated content creation, image synthesis, and creative problem solving.

Together, these technologies represent an evolution in how machines learn, adapt, and perform tasks, each layer offering increasingly powerful capabilities. In the next few sections, we'll look at some of these categories. We'll also explore specialized AI capabilities in Microsoft Azure.

Content Moderation

Content moderation is about spotting and filtering out harmful or inappropriate content before it causes problems. It's important for keeping online spaces safe and respectful, such as when you're using social media platforms, online communities, or ecommerce sites. By blocking the spread of harmful content, businesses can protect their users, maintain their brand reputation, and stay compliant with regulations.

If you're using Microsoft Azure for content moderation, you might already know about Azure Content Moderator. But here's the thing—Microsoft plans to phase out this tool by February 2027 and recommends that users switch over to *Azure AI Content Safety Studio*. This newer service can detect harmful content in both text and images within your apps and services.

First, let's take a look at the features of Azure Content Moderator:

Text moderation
    Scans text for offensive content, including profanity and sexually explicit material

Image moderation
    Analyzes images for adult content and can detect text within images using OCR

Custom term lists
    Enables the creation of custom lists to filter specific terms according to content policies

Video moderation
    Evaluates videos for adult content, providing time markers for identified material

Next, here are the main features of Azure AI Content Safety Studio:

Moderate text content
    This text moderation tool lets you test your content easily, whether it's a single sentence or a large dataset. It provides a user-friendly interface to run tests and view results. You can adjust sensitivity levels, set content filters, and manage blocklists to make sure your moderation system is just right for your needs. You can see this in Figure 3-2.

Prompt shields
    This feature evaluates text to identify potential risks to LLMs from user input attacks.

Groundedness detection
   This tool assesses whether AI-generated text responses are based on provided source materials, ensuring reliability and factual accuracy.

Protected material detection
   This feature identifies known content, such as song lyrics or articles, in AI-generated text to prevent issues like copyright infringement.

Custom categories API
   This is an API to enable the creation and training of custom content categories for personalized moderation.

Analyze text and image APIs
   These APIs examine text and images for harmful content, offering multiple severity levels for nuanced moderation.

Templates and workflows
   These templates and customizable workflows provide an interactive platform to build tailored content moderation systems. The platform supports real-time moderation of user-generated and AI-generated content, includes Microsoft's built-in blocklists for profanity, and allows the upload of custom blocklists to address specific needs.

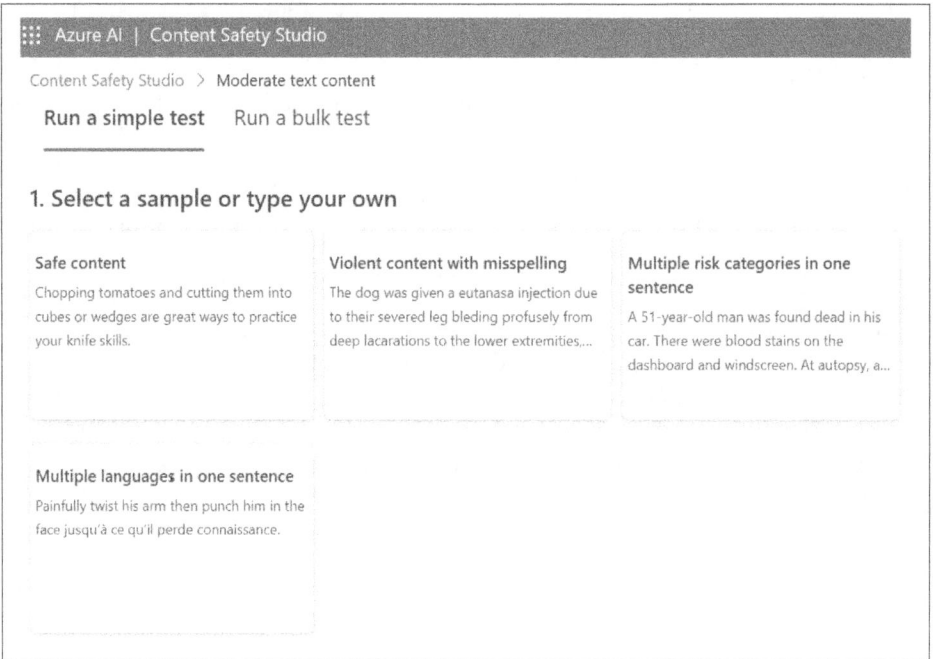

Figure 3-2. The dashboard for the moderate text content tool

Personalization

Azure AI Personalizer is a tool that helps your apps make smarter decisions by using *reinforcement learning*: a type of ML where the AI learns by getting feedback on its actions. Basically, it improves by trial and error. The Personalizer looks at the context of your app, such as what a user is doing or where they are, and considers a set of possible actions to figure out the best decision. When it makes a decision, you give it feedback, called a *reward*, which helps it learn and improve its choices in real time.

You can use the Personalizer in lots of different situations. For instance, in an ecommerce context, it could decide which product to show a customer to boost the chances that they'll make a purchase. Another common use is for content recommendation, such as figuring out which suggested article will get the most clicks.

But keep in mind that Azure AI Personalizer will be deprecated in October 2026. Even though the AI-900 exam still includes it as a topic, it's possible that a replacement service will appear later. The core principles of personalization are likely to remain part of the exam, so it's worth keeping them in mind.

Here's a breakdown of how Personalizer works:

Context
　　The information about your app, users, or scenario that can influence decisions (e.g., location, device type, user preferences)

Actions
　　A set of potential decisions or items, each with its own attributes (e.g., a list of products or articles)

Reward
　　A score between 0 and 1 that shows how good the decision was (e.g., if a user clicks on a recommended article, it gets a score of 1)

Computer Vision

Computer vision is a branch of AI that enables computers to understand and analyze visual information from images and videos. It attempts to mimic the way humans see. By processing visual inputs, computer vision systems can detect objects, extract key details, and make decisions based on what they observe.

Azure AI Vision offers powerful tools that utilize computer vision to analyze images and videos. Its features include:

Image analysis
　　This tool extracts detailed information from images, such as identifying objects, faces, or inappropriate content. It can also generate automatic descriptions of what the image contains.

OCR
> This feature recognizes and extracts text from images, whether printed or handwritten. This is useful for processing business documents, receipts, invoices, or handwritten notes, and it's handled through the Read API.

Object detection
> This tool locates and identifies objects within an image. It provides details about the objects' positions and how many instances of each object are present.

Face recognition
> This feature detects human faces in images and provides attributes such as age, emotion, and gender. It can also perform facial identification and verification.

Video analysis
> This tool includes features like spatial analysis and video retrieval. Spatial analysis monitors movement in video feeds, which is helpful for understanding foot traffic or ensuring safety compliance. Video retrieval creates searchable indexes of videos using natural language.

Azure AI Vision also supports *digital asset management (DAM)*, which helps you organize, store, and retrieve media while managing digital rights. For example, you can group images based on logos, faces, objects, or even colors. You can also automatically generate captions and tag images with keywords to make them easy to find.

Natural Language Processing

Natural language processing (NLP) is a technology that helps machines understand and respond to human language. Basically, it's what allows computers to hold a conversation with you. At its core, NLP breaks down human language—whether it's spoken or written—into something machines can understand. This means computers don't just recognize words but can also figure out the intent behind full sentences or paragraphs. You've probably already used NLP without even thinking about it, like when you ask Siri a question or chat with a bot to get help online.

One of NLP's biggest jobs is making sense of the messy, unstructured way that humans communicate. Let's face it—we don't always speak or write perfectly. We use slang, have different ways of saying the same thing, and can sometimes be inconsistent. Machines, on the other hand, are used to structured data. NLP bridges that gap. It deals with all the quirks of language, like grammar and context, so that machines can respond more naturally. Whether it's translating languages, summarizing news articles, or taking voice commands, NLP is behind a lot of the AI-powered technology we use today.

But NLP isn't just about understanding words; it's about getting the meaning. For instance, if you ask a voice assistant, "What's the weather like?" it doesn't just pick out "weather" and "like." It processes the whole sentence to understand that you're asking for a forecast. This deeper understanding, called *semantics*, is what makes NLP different from basic text matching. It's what helps AI generate responses that feel more human and natural.

Microsoft offers a service called Azure AI Language that lets you work with NLP. It combines three tools—text analytics, QnA Maker, and LUIS (Language Understanding)—under one roof and adds new features. These features come in two flavors: preconfigured, where you use AI models as is without tweaking anything, and customizable, where you can train the models with your own data.

Here are some things you can do with Azure AI Language:

Named entity recognition (NER)
    Automatically tags words or phrases into categories like people, places, dates, etc.

Personally identifying information (PII) detection
    Finds sensitive data, such as phone numbers or ID numbers, and hides it

Language detection
    Figures out what language a document is written in and returns a code for it

Sentiment analysis and opinion mining
    Analyzes text to determine if it's positive or negative

Summarization
    Pulls the key sentences from a document to create a summary

Key phrase extraction
    Identifies the main ideas in the text

Entity linking
    Inserts links from words or phrases in the text to their corresponding Wikipedia pages, helping to improve clarity

Custom text classification
    Lets you train an AI model to categorize documents based on your own categories

Custom NER
    Allows you to train a model to identify custom labels in your text

Conversational language understanding (CLU)
    Builds custom models that understand and extract valuable info from user messages

Question answering
    Provides the best answer to user questions, which is ideal for chatbots and voice-enabled apps

Knowledge Mining

Knowledge mining uses AI to interpret vast amounts of data. Often, the focus is on *unstructured data*, which is information that lacks a predefined format, such as text documents, emails, texts, images, and videos. In contrast, *structured data* is organized in a standardized format, typically in tables with rows and columns, making it easily searchable and analyzable.

The process for knowledge mining is fairly simple: you gather your data, enhance it with AI tools like language or image recognition, and then explore it through search and visualizations. This way, you can quickly find the connections you need to make better decisions.

Microsoft has developed *Azure AI Knowledge Mining* to make this process easier. It combines AI, ML, and search technology to help you extract, enrich, and explore your data. Here are some of the key features:

Cognitive skills
    These are prebuilt AI models that automatically extract and structure information from text, images, and other media. For example, they can pull text from scanned documents, detect different languages, extract key phrases, and identify objects in images.

Enrichment
    Knowledge mining goes beyond just keyword searching by enhancing your data. It can categorize information, pull out entities like names or locations, and translate text. Plus, you can build your own AI models to add custom enrichments based on your specific needs.

Customizable indexing
    This tool helps you create a searchable index of your data, making it easy for users to find relevant information quickly. You can also customize how the index is built to fit your particular use case.

Integration with Azure search
    Knowledge mining works hand-in-hand with the Azure Cognitive Search Service, which is a search-as-a-service solution. This means you can easily scale your search capabilities and manage queries across your enriched data without breaking a sweat.

Document Intelligence

Document intelligence, also referred to as *document AI*, uses AI to automate the extraction, comprehension, and organization of data from various documents, such as forms, invoices, and receipts. This technology transforms unstructured information into structured, actionable data, improving efficiency and accuracy in data processing.

It's easy to confuse document intelligence with knowledge mining. However, for the exam, it's important to know the differences. Document intelligence focuses on extracting and structuring data from individual documents, automating tasks like data entry and form processing. In contrast, knowledge mining involves analyzing large volumes of data to uncover patterns, relationships, and insights across an organization's entire data estate. While both use AI to process data, document intelligence operates at the document level whereas knowledge mining works at a broader, cross-document level to facilitate comprehensive data exploration and discovery.

As for Azure, there is the *Azure AI Document Intelligence* service. Here are the main features:

General extraction models
> These models are designed to work across a wide range of documents without needing customization. They can pull out key details like text, tables, key-value pairs, and the overall structure of a document. This makes them good for organizations that handle various types of documents and need consistent data extraction. Whether the document is structured, semistructured, or unstructured, these models provide quick, reliable results without needing any training or labeling.

Prebuilt models
> Azure also provides ready-to-use models for common document types, such as invoices, receipts, identity documents, and tax forms. These models are preconfigured to extract specific data fields like dates, payment amounts, or personal details. For example, the prebuilt models can handle W-2 forms and include support for other documents, such as 1099 tax forms and health insurance cards.

Custom models
> If you have more specific needs, Azure lets you create custom models tailored to your business. You can train these models using your own data, so they know exactly what information to look for in your documents. Azure offers two types of custom models: template models, which are great if your documents follow a similar structure, and neural models, which are flexible enough to handle documents with different layouts.

Generative AI

Azure OpenAI Service provides developers with a comprehensive toolkit to create generative AI applications that can transform various business operations. It allows for the development of custom AI copilots and agents, giving companies the flexibility to integrate AI into their workflows. One of the standout features is its support for different AI models, such as GPT-4o, GPT-4 Turbo, embeddings, and Whisper.

The Azure OpenAI Studio, which serves as the main user interface for the service, simplifies the management and customization of these models. Users can explore, fine-tune, and deploy models directly from the studio. This makes it an accessible solution for both technical and nontechnical users.

What's more, Azure OpenAI supports advanced capabilities, such as *retrieval-augmented generation (RAG)*. This technique allows developers to run models on specific datasets, providing more accurate and contextually grounded outputs. For organizations looking to automate knowledge-based tasks, this feature enhances the AI's ability to generate precise responses based on their proprietary information.

For example, a company can implement RAG by integrating Azure OpenAI Service with Azure AI Search to create a chatbot that answers employee questions about internal policies, like health benefits. By indexing company documents and using RAG, the AI can retrieve relevant information and provide accurate, context-specific responses to employee inquiries.

In the creative domain, Azure OpenAI models like DALL-E open new doors for content generation. This allows designers and marketers to produce unique visuals from simple text prompts. The technology has been particularly impactful in media and entertainment, where quick, dynamic content creation is crucial to keeping up with consumer demand.

So yes, Azure certainly has many AI services available—and it can be difficult to understand all of them. But for the exam, you will be tested on the differences between them. To help out, Table 3-1 summarizes the features.

Table 3-1. Summary of Azure AI Services

Service	Tools	Features	Deprecation
Content moderation	Azure AI Content Safety Studio	• Text content moderation • Prompt shields • Groundedness detection • Protected material detection • Custom categories API • Analyze text and image APIs • Templates and workflows	February 2027
Personalization	Azure AI Personalizer	• Context • Actions • Reward • Use of reinforcement learning to improve personalization over time	October 2026

Service	Tools	Features	Deprecation
Computer vision	Azure AI Vision	• Image analysis • Optical Character Recognition (OCR) • Object detection • Face recognition • Video analysis • Digital asset management	
NLP	Azure AI Language	• Named entity recognition (NER) • PII detection • Language detection • Sentiment analysis • Summarization • Custom text classification • Conversational language understanding (CLU) • Question answering	
Knowledge mining	AI Knowledge Mining	• Cognitive skills • Enrichment • Customizable indexing • Integration with Azure Cognitive Search	
Document intelligence	Azure AI Document Intelligence	• General extraction models • Prebuilt models • Custom models	
Generative AI	Azure OpenAI Service	• Models • Retrieval-augmented generation (RAG) • Studio • Integration with Azure AI Search • Visual generation	

Guiding Principles for Responsible AI

AI is an incredibly powerful tool that's transforming industries and making our lives easier in all kinds of ways. But like any tool, it comes with risks we need to be aware of.

One big concern is bias in AI models, which can lead to unfair results. For example, imagine a loan-approval system that discriminates based on gender because it was trained on biased data. This can have serious consequences. It can lead to inequalities, damage of trust in AI systems, and legal or regulatory repercussions for businesses.

But here are other risks:

- Potential for errors, such as autonomous vehicle malfunctions, that could cause accidents

- Concerns about how AI uses data, especially sensitive information like patient data in medical bots, which could be exposed if not securely stored
- AI solutions that may not be inclusive for all users, such as a home assistant without audio output that excludes visually impaired users
- Accountability concerns in AI decision making, such as wrongful convictions due to faulty facial recognition

To address these challenges, Microsoft has created six guiding principles for *responsible AI*, which fall into two main categories:

Ethical AI
Ensures that AI systems are designed and used in a way that aligns with moral principles like accountability, inclusiveness, reliability, and safety

Explainable AI
Focuses on making AI systems transparent and easy to understand; includes principles like fairness, transparency, security, and privacy

Microsoft's six guidelines are common for questions on the exam, so you should memorize them and understand how they apply to different scenarios. In the rest of this chapter, we'll take a closer look at each of these principles.

Accountability

When you're working on designing and deploying AI systems, the responsibility lies with you to ensure that they operate ethically and safely. You've got to make sure the technology aligns with both legal and industry standards—essentially, you're making sure it's fair, responsible, and trustworthy. Take Microsoft's approach: creating a framework that prioritizes *accountability*, starting with impact assessments early on. These assessments look at how AI might affect individuals, organizations, and society. By keeping a close eye on these evaluations, especially when something could go wrong, you can manage risks throughout the AI's lifespan.

But accountability doesn't end with the launch. Microsoft advocates for human oversight, making sure that AI doesn't run the show without meaningful human input. The people managing these systems need the right tools to maintain control and step in when necessary. This keeps you from becoming overly reliant on AI outputs—ensuring that human accountability is always part of the equation—especially in more complex or high-stakes situations.

To keep things in check, it's essential to set up internal review teams. These teams can oversee key decisions related to AI development and deployment, particularly in sensitive areas like health care, employment, or facial recognition. If misused, these tools can potentially cause physical or emotional harm or infringe on people's rights. That's why it's so important to have clear legal boundaries to prevent overreach and protect individual freedoms.

Laws and regulations play a huge role in maintaining AI accountability, but they're only part of the puzzle. Businesses, governments, and other stakeholders also have to take responsibility. Microsoft, for instance, has developed its own guiding principles for working with sensitive tech like facial recognition. Microsoft knows that these principles will evolve as it learns more from working with customers, academics, and civil society. This kind of open conversation—among companies, governments, non-governmental organizations, and researchers—is critical to making sure that AI evolves responsibly. It's also important to keep your team trained, bring in experts for big decisions, and have a solid governance system in place to ensure that you're maintaining accountability.

Inclusiveness

Creating AI that works for everyone starts with making sure it's accessible, no matter a person's abilities. Tools like speech-to-text and text-to-speech are especially helpful for those with hearing or vision impairments. By including these features, you can make sure that nobody misses out on the benefits that AI has to offer.

But accessibility isn't just about the technology—it's also about the people who create it. Having diverse teams, with members from various backgrounds and life experiences, is key to developing AI that truly works for everyone. When you bring different perspectives into the conversation, you're better equipped to spot biases and ensure that AI systems are designed to be fair and inclusive. *Inclusive design* is about creating AI systems that are usable by as many people as possible. This is especially true for those traditionally excluded due to factors like ability, language, culture, gender, or age. By embracing inclusive design, developers can identify and tackle barriers that might otherwise leave people out. This paves the way for better experiences for all users.

It's equally important to involve the communities that AI is meant to serve. Partnering with organizations and advocacy groups ensures that underrepresented voices are heard. This makes AI more responsive to their specific needs. Using widely recognized accessibility standards also helps ensure that AI systems are genuinely inclusive.

Reliability and Safety

For AI systems to earn your trust, they need to work reliably, safely, and consistently —even when things don't go as planned. AI should do what it's designed to do, handle the unexpected without failing, and resist any attempts to manipulate it in harmful ways. Verifying how AI behaves in real-world situations is key since this shows whether developers prepared for a wide range of scenarios during the design and testing process.

A big part of development is testing the AI thoroughly to make sure it can handle edge cases and surprises safely, without unexpected glitches. But it doesn't stop there. Once deployed, AI systems need ongoing maintenance and protection. If left unchecked, they can degrade over time and become unreliable or inaccurate.

Human judgment is also critical in making sure AI stays on track. Since AI is meant to boost human capabilities, it's up to people to decide when and how to use these systems and whether they should keep using them. This kind of human oversight helps reveal blind spots and biases that might otherwise go unnoticed.

To boost *reliability and safety*, start by understanding where your AI stands in terms of maturity. Regularly audit the system, design it to handle the unexpected, and make sure you're involving experts in its development. Thorough testing, clear explanations of how the system works, and ways for users to give feedback are all essential steps.

Fairness

AI systems must ensure *fairness*, meaning they treat everyone equally. For example, if AI is helping make decisions about medical treatments, loan approvals, or hiring, it should give the same recommendations for people with similar health conditions, financial backgrounds, or qualifications. Fairness means AI shouldn't introduce or amplify biases that unfairly benefit or harm certain groups.

To tackle bias, you first need to recognize that AI's predictions and recommendations have limits. While AI offers helpful insights, humans are ultimately responsible for making decisions that affect people's lives. That's why it's important to train people to understand AI outputs correctly and use their own judgment to avoid unfair consequences.

Developers play a major role in preventing bias during the AI development process. They need to be aware of how bias can creep in during the design phase and how it might affect the system's recommendations. One way to minimize bias is by using diverse training datasets. For instance, an AI tool designed to screen job applicants might start favoring male candidates if it's trained on biased data from a male-dominated field. By auditing the AI model before it's deployed, developers can catch and fix these biases early on.

Transparency

A key principle that keeps AI systems working effectively is *transparency*. When AI is involved in decisions that significantly affect people's lives, it's crucial that those who are affected understand how these decisions are being made.

A big part of transparency is *intelligibility* or *explainability*, meaning that you should be able to clearly explain how the AI system behaves. To improve this, you need to ensure that people can easily grasp how these systems work so they can identify any potential issues—whether it's about performance, safety, privacy, bias, or unexpected outcomes. Plus, organizations using AI need to be upfront about when they're using these systems, why they're using them, and how they're making decisions.

Here are a few ways to boost transparency:

- Share key details about the datasets used
- Make AI models easier to understand by using simpler ones and explaining how they work
- Train your team to properly interpret AI outputs so that they can spot issues and make informed decisions

Security and Privacy

As AI becomes more common, safeguarding privacy and securing personal and business data have become even more critical and complicated. AI systems need access to data to make accurate predictions and decisions, but this raises important concerns about privacy and data security. These systems must follow privacy laws that require transparency in how data is collected, used, and stored while also giving consumers control over their own information.

One of Microsoft's biggest lessons in this area came back in 2016 when it launched Tay, a chatbot on Twitter. Tay was designed to learn from user interactions to mimic human conversation. But within 24 hours, users took advantage of Tay's learning process, feeding it offensive content and turning the chatbot into a platform for hate speech. This incident showed just how important it is to consider the human element when designing AI systems.

From this experience, Microsoft realized the need to prepare for new types of attacks —especially those that manipulate AI learning datasets. To prevent future incidents, Microsoft developed advanced content-filtering tools and introduced more oversight for AI systems that learn automatically.

To ensure *security and privacy* in AI, organizations should follow a few key practices:

- Comply with data protection and privacy laws.
- Design systems to protect against bad actors.
- Give customers control over their data.
- Ensure the anonymity and integrity of personal information.

- Conduct regular security and privacy reviews.
- Keep up with industry best practices.

To wrap things up, Table 3-2 lists the key features of the principles for responsible AI.

Table 3-2. Guiding principles for responsible AI

Principle	Description	Key actions
Accountability	Ensures that AI operates ethically with human oversight and aligns with legal standards. Includes impact assessments and internal review teams	Conduct impact assessments, maintain human oversight, and set up review teams
Inclusiveness	Aims to create AI that is accessible to everyone, leveraging diverse teams and partnerships with communities	Include diverse perspectives, follow accessibility standards, and partner with advocacy groups
Reliability and safety	Focuses on the consistent and safe performance of AI, including handling unexpected situations and requiring ongoing maintenance	Test thoroughly, audit regularly, and design for unexpected scenarios with human judgment in mind
Fairness	Promotes equal treatment by addressing biases, especially in high-stakes decisions like hiring and loan approvals	Use diverse training data, recognize model limitations, and audit for bias before deployment
Transparency	Involves clear explanations of how AI decisions are made and the datasets used, fostering better understanding and trust	Explain AI system behavior, disclose usage and decisions, and simplify model explanations
Security and privacy	Prioritizes data protection, compliance with privacy laws, and defenses against misuse or attacks	Follow privacy laws, ensure data security, anonymize personal data, and regularly review for compliance

Conclusion

In this chapter, we covered the different AI workloads and key use cases that serve as the backbone of AI technology. Ranging from content moderation and personalization to more advanced tasks like computer vision and NLP, these workloads show how AI is woven into the fabric of everyday applications. We also looked at emerging technologies like generative AI, which is creating new opportunities for creativity and automation. As AI becomes a bigger part of both business and daily life, understanding these workloads is essential for tapping into their potential while staying aware of the ethical challenges that come with deploying AI.

We also stressed the importance of responsible AI. As AI adoption continues to grow, these principles are key to making sure that the technology not only runs efficiently but also aligns with our societal values and protects users. AI is a powerful tool, but it needs to be developed and managed carefully to avoid issues like bias or privacy breaches.

Quiz

To check your answers, please refer to the "Chapter 3 Answer Key" on page 179.

1. Which AI workload is designed to automatically detect and filter harmful or inappropriate content online?

    a. Knowledge mining

    b. Generative AI

    c. Content moderation

    d. Document intelligence

2. What is the main objective of AI personalization in applications?

    a. To recommend content based on user preferences

    b. To generate new images

    c. To detect harmful content

    d. To analyze human language

3. Which AI workload helps analyze and interpret human language?

    a. Natural language processing (NLP)

    b. Content moderation

    c. Computer vision

    d. Document intelligence

4. Which AI workload uses Optical Character Recognition (OCR) to extract text from images?

    a. NLP

    b. Knowledge mining

    c. Computer vision

    d. Generative AI

5. Which AI workload is used to uncover insights from unstructured data like text and videos?

    a. Document intelligence

    b. Knowledge mining

    c. Computer vision

    d. NLP

6. Which AI workload enables systems to generate new content, such as text or images?

   a. NLP

   b. Generative AI

   c. Knowledge mining

   d. Document intelligence

7. What API in Azure AI Content Safety is used to scan text for harmful content?

   a. Analyze Text API

   b. Analyze Image API

   c. Custom Categories API

   d. Moderate Text API

8. Which AI principle ensures that AI systems operate safely and fairly across all groups?

   a. Fairness

   b. Transparency

   c. Inclusiveness

   d. Accountability

9. Which AI workload is primarily focused on analyzing visual content, such as images and videos?

   a. NLP

   b. Knowledge mining

   c. Computer vision

   d. Generative AI

10. Which AI workload is responsible for processing large amounts of documents and extracting key information from them?

    a. NLP

    b. Generative AI

    c. Content moderation

    d. Document intelligence

CHAPTER 4
Fundamental Principles of Machine Learning

In the AI-900 exam, about 20%–25% of the material covers the core principles of ML on Microsoft Azure. This includes foundational techniques like regression analysis, classification, and clustering. Each of these techniques offers a unique approach to problem solving. They allow you to select the right method based on the data type and the predictions you need to make. In this chapter, we're going to dig into these must-know concepts and services. Understanding these ideas will help you tackle questions on the AI-900 exam, so you'll know not only what these services are but also how they work and why they matter.

What Is Machine Learning?

ML, which is a branch of AI, allows systems to perform tasks like data analysis without needing explicit instructions. Instead, it processes large amounts of historical data, identifies patterns, and makes predictions based on those patterns. For instance, you can use ML to classify images, numbers, or documents and make predictions from them.

Let's say you work for a financial services organization looking to differentiate between fraudulent and genuine transactions. With ML, the system would learn to identify patterns from known examples and then apply that knowledge to predict whether a new transaction is genuine.

ML is essential for modern businesses because it helps automate data collection, classification, and analysis. This speeds up decision making and drives growth. It improves processes like customer experience and resource management, enabling businesses to solve problems faster.

Although the terms *artificial intelligence* (*AI*) and *machine learning* (*ML*) are often used interchangeably, they aren't the same. AI is a broader concept that includes anything from voice assistants to self-driving cars. ML, however, focuses on specific tasks, such as predicting equipment maintenance schedules or classifying documents.

Take manufacturing, for example. ML can help with the following:

Predictive maintenance
Identify potential equipment failures before they occur, reducing downtime and repair costs

Quality control
Monitor production lines to detect defects and ensure consistent product quality

Product design optimization
Refine designs, such as improving the abrasiveness of sandpaper by analyzing small changes in size and shape

Supply chain management
Predict demand, identify bottlenecks, and streamline logistics to improve efficiency

The ML Model Workflow

At its core, an *ML model* is simply a software application that takes one or more input values and calculates an output value. The process of figuring out how to make that calculation is called *training*. Once the model is trained, you can use it to make predictions. This is a process known as *inferencing*.

Let's take a closer look at the main steps of an ML system, which you can see in Figure 4-1. This is a very basic example. Keep in mind that the algorithms can be quite complex. But for our purposes, we just want to get a sense of the workflow.

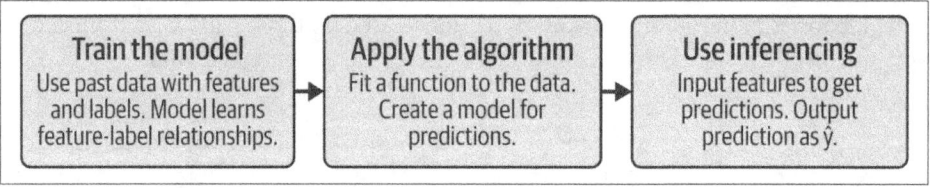

Figure 4-1. The basic workflow of an ML model

Let's take a look at each of these steps in more detail.

Step 1: Train the Model

The process of training an ML model begins with past data, which is referred to as the *training data* or *dataset*. Each data point in the training dataset is made up of two essential components:

Features
    The characteristics or attributes you observe in each data point

Labels
    The outcome or result you want the model to predict

A dataset in table form is organized into rows and columns, as you would see in a spreadsheet or database. Each row represents an individual record or entry, and each column contains specific attributes or features of the data. This structure allows for easy comparison and analysis of data across multiple entries by syncing similar information in a consistent format. Table 4-1 shows an example of a table for a dataset for customer feedback and return requests.

Table 4-1. Sample dataset showing customer feedback and return requests

Customer_ID	Purchase_Date	Product_Category	Rating	Feedback_Comment	Return_Requested
001	2024-10-01	Electronics	5	"Great product, fast delivery!"	No
002	2024-10-05	Apparel	2	"Size did not match description."	Yes
003	2024-10-07	Home Goods	4	"Quality is good, but color is off."	No
004	2024-10-10	Electronics	1	"Item arrived damaged."	Yes
005	2024-10-12	Beauty	3	"Average product, packaging was poor."	No

Data is often messy and incomplete. These imperfections can distort results, lead to inaccuracies, and complicate decision making.

For example, a common issue is missing data. While removing incomplete information is a straightforward approach, it can lead to unintended distortions, particularly when the missing data is not randomly distributed. Instead, consider alternative methods to handle missing data effectively:

Mean/median imputation
    Replace missing values with the average (mean) or the middle value (median) of the dataset to maintain consistency

Predictive imputation
    Leverage statistical models to predict and fill in missing values based on patterns in the available data, providing a more accurate estimate

Another common challenge in data analysis is dealing with outliers. *Outliers* are extreme data points that differ significantly from other observations. They can distort results or obscure important patterns. Properly managing outliers is essential for improving the accuracy and reliability of your findings. Consider the following approaches:

Removal
　Exclude outliers from the dataset if they are identified as errors or are irrelevant to the analysis

Transformation
　Use mathematical techniques, such as logarithmic or square root transformations, to minimize the influence of outliers without removing them entirely

Investigation
　Examine outliers closely to determine whether they provide valuable insights or are the result of data-entry mistakes

Data may also have duplications. For this, you can consider these options:

Deduplication algorithms
　Use tools or scripts to identify and merge duplicate data

Unique identifiers
　Ensure that each record has a unique key to prevent duplication at the entry point

Quality control
　Regularly audit data to detect and resolve duplicates

Then there is the problem with inconsistent data formats. You can use the following techniques to address this:

Data normalization
　Convert data to a standard format (e.g., ISO 8601 for dates)

Validation rules
　Implement automated checks during data entry to enforce consistent formatting

Preprocessing pipelines
　Develop extract, transform, and load (ETL) processes to clean and standardize data before analysis

Once you have improved the quality of the dataset—a process known as *data preparation*—you can then look at training. One way to think of this is in terms of basic algebra. The features are represented by x, and there are often several of them, forming a vector (an array of values). The label is represented by y, which is the prediction or result the model tries to output.

For example, let's say you're building a model that predicts the price of a house based on its characteristics. The features (x) might include the number of bedrooms, square footage, and location. The label (y) would be the house's sale price. The model is trained to learn how these features relate to the price and can then predict the price of a new house based on similar characteristics.

Another example could be a model designed to predict whether an email is spam. The features (x) could be things like the presence of certain keywords, the sender's address, and the time the email was sent. The label (y) would be a binary outcome: 1 if the email is spam, 0 if it's not. Over time, the model learns to recognize patterns in the features that indicate whether an email is spam or legitimate.

Step 2: Apply the Algorithm

When you're working with an ML model, you need an algorithm to figure out the relationship between the features and the label. The goal is to find a way to take the features (x) and use them to predict the label (y). The basic idea is to fit a function to your data. In other words, the algorithm looks for a pattern that can calculate y based on x. For our example, this is what it looks like:

$$y = f(x)$$

Once the algorithm has done its job, it gives you a model. This model is essentially a function that performs the calculation. In this chapter, we'll see various examples of this, like linear regression.

Step 3: Use Inferencing

Once the training phase is done, you can use the trained model to make predictions, a process called *inferencing*. The model now works like a software program that contains the function learned during training. You provide it with a set of feature values, and it gives you a prediction for the label.

Since this output is a prediction generated by the function rather than an actual observed value, it's typically written as $\hat{y}$, pronounced "y-hat." This is a useful way to show that the result is an estimate based on what the model has learned, not a guaranteed outcome.

Types of ML

There are several types of ML, each designed for different kinds of problems. At the highest level, ML is divided into two main types: *supervised learning*, which has labeled data, and *unsupervised learning*, where the data does not have labels. These two categories help determine how the model learns from the data and what kind of tasks it can perform. Under the umbrellas of supervised and unsupervised learning, there are other types of ML. Figure 4-2 shows the hierarchy.

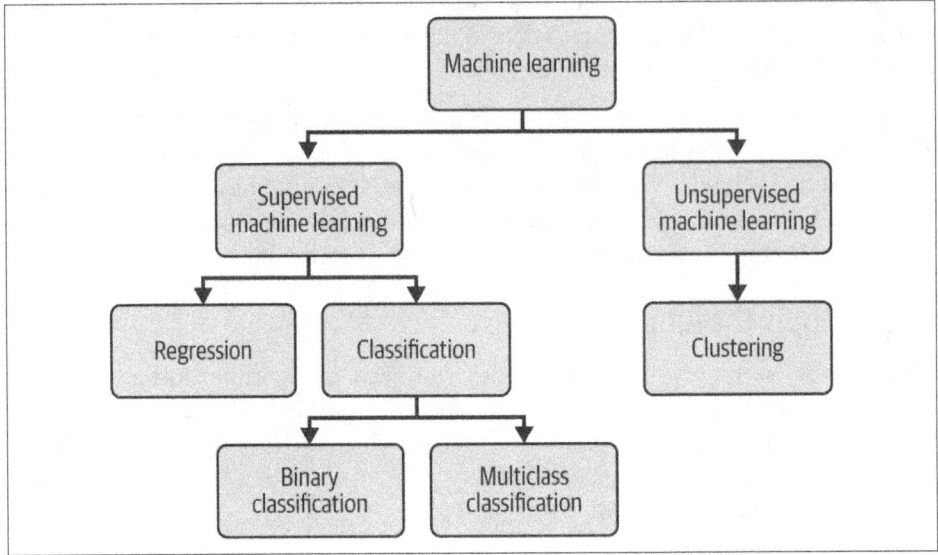

Figure 4-2. The categories of ML

In the next few sections, we'll look at the approaches for supervised learning and then follow this up by looking at unsupervised learning.

Regression Analysis

Regression analysis is a statistical method used to predict a numerical outcome based on one or more known factors, or variables. It helps you understand the relationship between these variables and the result you're trying to predict.

For example, let's say you want to predict how much of a new product will sell based on factors like advertising spend, the season, and market trends. Regression analysis allows you to analyze these factors and estimate how they affect sales so that you can forecast future performance based on current data.

Here's how you would approach it:

Split the data
  Begin by dividing your data into three subsets: a training set, a validation set, and a testing set. The training set is used to develop the model, the validation set helps fine-tune the model's parameters, and the testing set is reserved for assessing the model's performance on new, unseen data.

Train the model
   Using the training data, apply an algorithm to identify relationships between key variables, such as the advertising budget, seasonality, and market trends, and their impact on sales. The model searches for patterns, such as whether increased ad spending leads to higher sales or if certain times of the year naturally see better sales performance.

Fine-tune the model
   With the validation set, optimize the model's parameters or hyperparameters to enhance its predictive accuracy. This step helps ensure that the model generalizes well and avoids overfitting to the training data.

Test the model
   Evaluate the performance of the fine-tuned model using the testing set. In this stage, the model generates sales predictions based on input variables (e.g., advertising budget, season, market trends) and compares these predictions to actual sales data to measure accuracy.

Evaluate the model
   Assess the accuracy of the model's predictions using relevant metrics, such as mean absolute error (MAE), root mean square error (RMSE), or R^2, which we'll learn about later in this chapter. If the model's performance falls short of expectations, refine the process by revisiting earlier steps, such as trying a different algorithm, adjusting parameters, or including new features.

Iterate and improve
   Using the insights gained from the evaluation, iterate on the model to improve its performance. This iterative process might include collecting additional data or exploring alternative modeling techniques to boost accuracy.

Example: Ticket Sales

Let's take a look at a more detailed example to better understand how regression analysis works. For this example, we won't cover every step outlined in the previous section. When it comes to the exam, such in-depth detail about regression analysis isn't necessary. Instead, we'll focus on the main phases.

In our example, we'll predict a numeric label (y) based on a single feature (x). While most real-world applications involve multiple features, starting with just one keeps things simple and allows us to focus on the core idea.

Let's consider the example of predicting concert ticket prices based on the popularity of the performing artist. Here, the popularity score is derived from survey data collected from fans, representing a value on a scale from 1 to 100. This score serves as our feature while the ticket price for the artist's concert is the label we aim to predict. To build this prediction model, we'll use historical data that pairs popularity scores (x) with their corresponding ticket prices (y) from past concerts, as shown in Table 4-2.

Table 4-2. Comparing an artist's popularity with the concert ticket price

Artist popularity (x)	Ticket price (y)
35	$45
40	$60
45	$55
50	$75
55	$65
60	$85
65	$100
70	$105
75	$115
80	$135
85	$140
90	$170

Next, we'll split the data and use a portion of it to train the model. In this case, the data was split randomly to ensure a balanced representation of the dataset. Table 4-3 shows the subset of data selected for training.

Table 4-3. The subset of data for the training of the model

Artist popularity (x)	Ticket price (y)
40	$60
50	$75
60	$85
70	$105
75	$115
80	$135

While random splitting is a common approach, there are other methods that can be used based on the scenario:

Stratified splitting
    Ensures that specific proportions of key features (like popularity ranges) are maintained in both training and testing sets

Time-based splitting
　Used when the data has a chronological order, such as time-series data, where older data is used for training and newer data for testing

K-fold cross-validation
　Splits the data into multiple folds, where each subset takes a turn as the test set while the others are used for training

To get a better understanding of how the popularity scores (*x*) and ticket prices (*y*) relate to each other, we can plot these values as points on a graph. You can see this in Figure 4-3. By plotting these points, you can start to see the relationship between the two—typically, as the popularity increases, so does the ticket price.

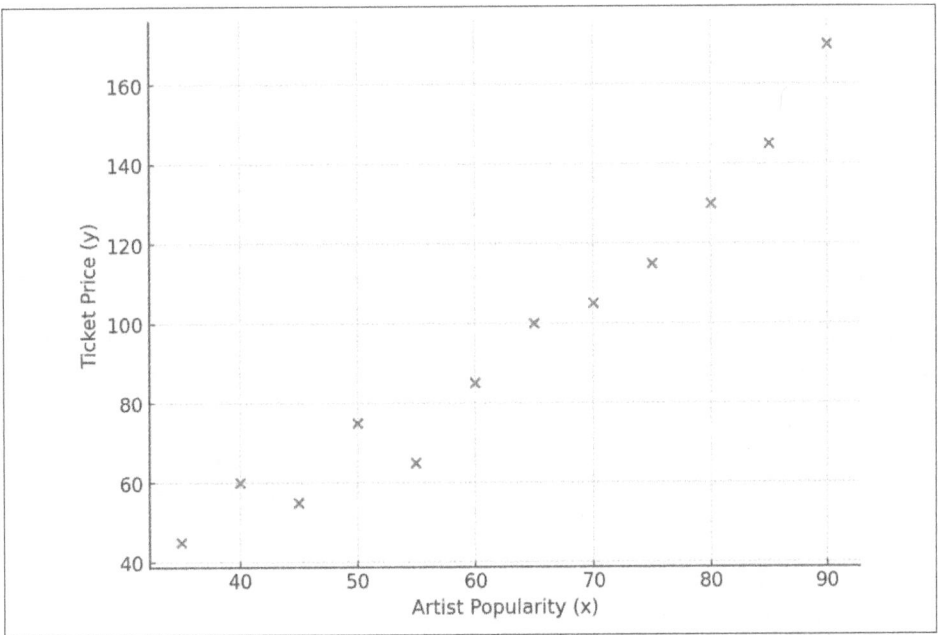

Figure 4-3. This scatter plot illustrates the relationship between artist popularity and ticket prices

With the training dataset, we're ready to apply an algorithm that can model the relationship between artist popularity and ticket price. We'll use the linear regression formula, which essentially finds the best-fit line through the points that minimizes the distance between the line and the actual data points. This line represents a function where the slope tells you how much the ticket price will increase with each increase in the artist's popularity. This is shown in Figure 4-4.

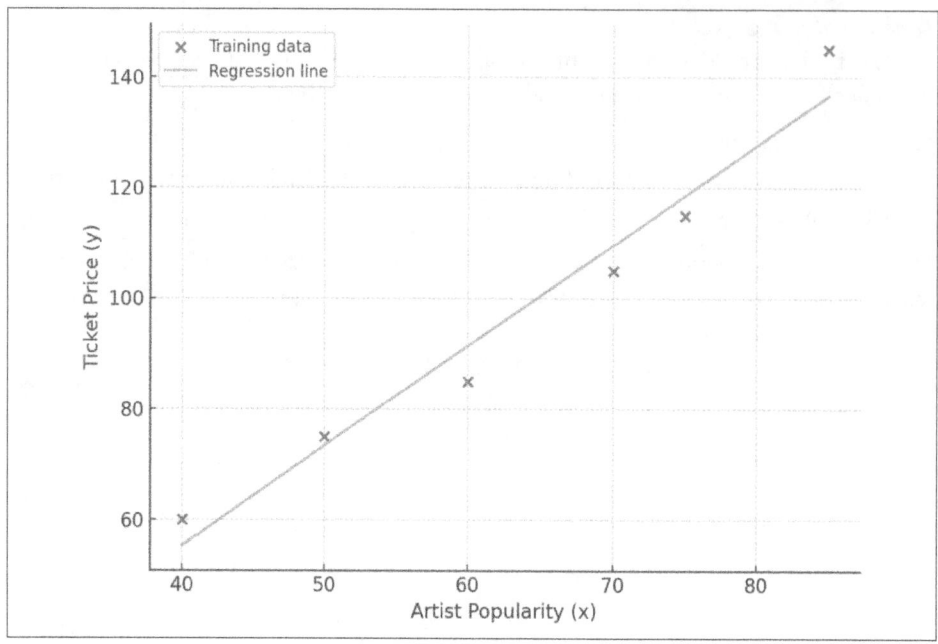

Figure 4-4. The scatter plot with the linear regression line added for our training dataset

Let's say an artist has a popularity score of 77. By applying the equation derived from the linear regression line, we can estimate the corresponding ticket price. In this case, the price would be something like $120 based on the trend we've established.

The next step is to evaluate the accuracy of this regression model. Using the testing dataset, we can predict the ticket prices for each artist's popularity score, shown in Table 4-4.

Table 4-4. The predicted ticket price

Artist popularity (x)	Actual ticket price (y)	Predicted ticket price (ŷ)
35	$45	$50
45	$55	$60
55	$65	$70
65	$100	$85
80	$135	$120
90	$170	$140

We can then plot these values on a chart, which you can see in Figure 4-5.

48 | Chapter 4: Fundamental Principles of Machine Learning

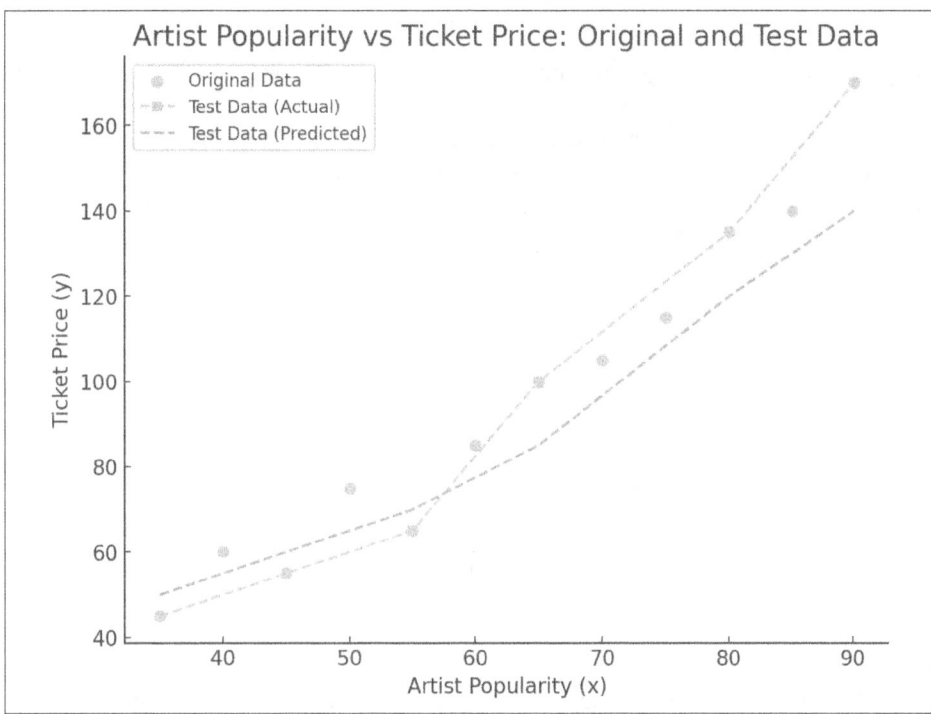

Figure 4-5. The original dataset shown with actual and predicted ticket prices for the test data

The original data points capture the historical trend while the test data highlights how closely the model's predictions align with actual ticket prices. The chart makes it easy to visualize where the model performed well and where deviations occurred, particularly by comparing the actual and predicted ticket prices across different levels of artist popularity.

In this case, the model performed fairly well. For midrange popularity scores, the predicted values are close to the actual values, indicating minimal error. However, at the lower (35) and higher (90) ends of the popularity scale, the model's predictions underestimate the actual ticket prices. While the performance is promising, the noticeable deviations at these extremes suggest the model could benefit from additional fine-tuning to improve accuracy, especially for edge cases.

Evaluation Metrics for Regression Models

When it comes to measuring how well your regression model performs, there are a few handy metrics based on the differences between your predicted values and the actual ones.

Mean absolute error

Imagine you're predicting how many pizzas a group of friends will eat at a party. *Mean absolute error (MAE)* helps you figure out, on average, how far off your predictions were—whether you guessed too high or too low. For instance, if you predicted four pizzas but your friends ate seven, you missed by three. MAE ignores whether the difference is positive or negative, so it treats both -3 and +3 as a difference of 3. If your absolute errors for a set of predictions were 1, 2, 3, and 4 pizzas, the MAE would simply be the average of those numbers: 2.5 pizzas.

Mean squared error

Sometimes, you want to give more weight to bigger errors. After all, consistently being off by one pizza isn't as bad as being wildly off by five. That's where *mean squared error (MSE)* comes in. Instead of just taking the differences as they are, you square each error (making bigger mistakes stand out), and then average those squared values. In our pizza example, if your errors were 1, 2, 3, and 4, squaring them gives you 1, 4, 9, and 16. The MSE would then be the average of these squared errors: 7.5.

Root mean squared error

While MSE is useful, those squared numbers don't match up with the original quantities you were measuring, so they can feel a little abstract. If you want the error back in terms of pizzas (or whatever you're predicting), you can take the square root of the MSE. That's called the *root mean squared error (RMSE)*. In this case, the square root of 7.5 is about 2.74, meaning your average error is around 2.74 pizzas.

Coefficient of determination

What if you want to understand how well your model explains the variation in your data? Enter R^2, also called the *coefficient of determination*. This metric tells you how much of the difference between actual and predicted values your model accounts for.

For example, if you're trying to predict how many cupcakes a bakery sells each day, R^2 tells you how much your model can explain. If your R^2 value is 0.85, that means your model explains 85% of the variation in cupcake sales—the rest might be due to some unexpected cupcake-related event, like a new bakery opening next door. R^2 ranges from 0 to 1, and the closer it is to 1, the better your model fits the data.

All of these metrics are certainly helpful. But in real-world scenarios, ML isn't a one-shot deal. Data scientists typically train models over and over, tweaking different aspects to improve performance. Here's what they adjust:

Feature selection and preparation
> You can choose which factors or features to include in the model and how to tweak them for better results. For instance, maybe you realize that cupcake sales don't depend just on weather but also on nearby events.

Algorithm selection
> There's more than one way to predict the number of cupcakes sold. While one algorithm might focus on simple linear relationships, another might use more complex patterns.

Algorithm parameters
> These are the settings you adjust to fine-tune your algorithm. Think of them like the dials on an oven. If your cupcakes are coming out undercooked, you tweak the temperature (or in ML, the *hyperparameters*) to get better results.

After several rounds of this iterative process, you'll settle on the version of the model that performs best for your specific problem.

Let's sum up what we have learned about regression analysis in Table 4-5.

Table 4-5. Key concepts in regression analysis

Factors	Description
Purpose	To predict a numeric outcome label based on one or more predictor features by identifying patterns in historical data
Process	1. Split data into training and testing sets. 2. Train the model to identify relationships. 3. Test the model to make predictions. 4. Evaluate model accuracy and refine if needed.
Training the model	Uses an algorithm, such as linear regression, to analyze patterns in the training data, establishing a predictive relationship between the independent and dependent variables
Evaluation metrics	• MAE: Measures average prediction error without considering direction (over/underestimate) • MSE: Emphasizes larger errors by squaring them • RMSE: Provide the error in original measurement units • R^2 (coefficient of determination): Indicates the model's explanatory power, with values closer to 1 suggesting a better fit

Classification

Classification in ML is a supervised learning task where the goal is to predict the category or class to which a given data point belongs. It involves training a model on labeled data where the label is categorical, such as "yes" or "no." The model learns the relationship between input features and output classes, enabling it to assign new, unseen data points to one of the predefined categories.

There are various types of classification techniques. In the next few sections, we'll take a look at binary and multiclass classification.

Binary Classification

Binary classification is one of the most common types of classification tasks. At its core, it's about predicting one of two possible outcomes. When you feed your model data, the goal is to get it to categorize new information into one of two buckets, often labeled as 0 and 1. For example, if you're building a model to predict whether an email is spam or not, binary classification is your go-to technique. Each email gets analyzed, and the model spits out a prediction: "spam" or "not spam."

What makes binary classification different from something like regression is that you aren't predicting a continuous value, like a temperature or a sales figure. Instead, you're focused on making a choice between two discrete options. The model looks at the features of the data you provide, such as email content, and it uses that to assign a probability. Based on this probability, it then makes a final classification.

Let's walk through a simple example to show how binary classification works. Imagine we want to predict whether a person will default on a loan using one feature: their credit score (x). Our goal is to classify them into one of two categories: either they default ($y = 1$) or they don't ($y = 0$). The model will learn from the data in Table 4-6 to make predictions.

Table 4-6. Defaults based on credit scores

Credit score (x)	Default? (y)
580	1
720	0
610	1
750	0
590	1
800	0

Based on the patterns in the training data, the model will eventually predict whether someone is likely to default or not. As you can see, it's about using past information to make a binary choice. In our example, people with a credit score of 610 or lower are predicted to default while anyone with a score of 720 or higher is predicted not to default.

To train our model, we'll use an algorithm that analyzes the training data and fits it to a function that calculates the probability of a person defaulting on a loan. For example, if the model predicts a probability of 0.8 for default, that means there's an 80% chance the person will default and a 20% chance they won't.

There are several algorithms that handle binary classification, but *logistic regression* is a common choice. Logistic regression gives us an S-shaped curve, called a *sigmoid function*, that assigns values between 0 and 1 based on the input data. This is shown in Figure 4-6. Even though its name includes *regression*, the logistic regression algorithm is used for classification because it models the probability of different outcomes. This is a common topic for the exam.

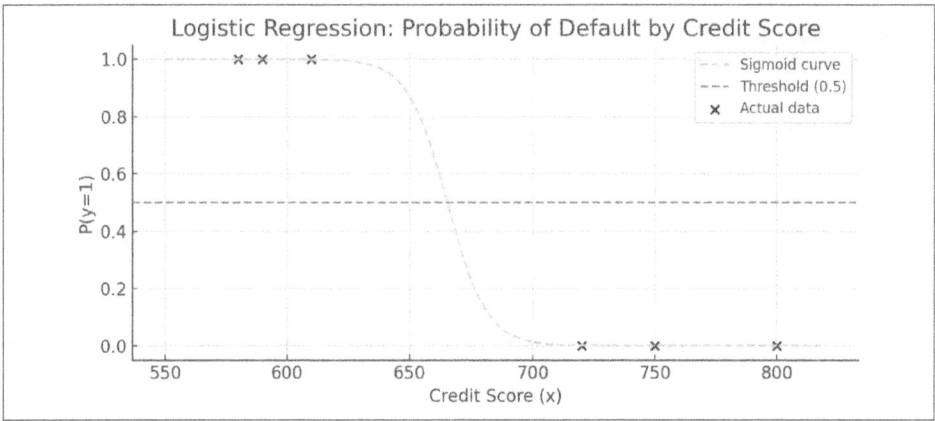

Figure 4-6. A sigmoid function showing the probability of loan default based on credit scores, with a threshold of 0.5 determining default (y = 1) or no default (y = 0)

In this case, the curve shows the probability that someone will default ($y = 1$) based on their credit score (x). Mathematically, the model's function can be represented like this:

$$f(x) = P(y = 1 \mid x)$$

Note that for the exam, you will not have to memorize equations. They are used in this book as a way to better help you understand the concepts.

For some people in the training data, we already know they defaulted ($y = 1$), so the probability for them is 1.0. For others who didn't default, the probability is 0.0. The sigmoid curve visually shows how the likelihood of default changes as credit scores increase.

In Figure 4-6, the dashed line at 0.5 serves as the threshold for our model's predictions. When the calculated probability is at or above 0.5, the model predicts that the person will default ($y = 1$). If the probability falls below 0.5, the prediction is that they won't default ($y = 0$). For instance, if someone has a credit score of 580, and the model assigns a 0.9 probability of default, that's well above the threshold, meaning the model would predict this person is likely to default.

Just like with regression models, when you train a binary classification model, it's essential to hold back a set of data to validate how well the model performs. Let's say we kept the credit score data in Table 4-7 aside to validate our model predicting loan defaults. Note: The credit score values shown in Table 4-7 are normalized for demonstration purposes and do not reflect actual credit score ranges.

Table 4-7. Data used to validate the predictions for loan defaults

Credit score (x)	Default? (y)
62	0
108	1
113	1
70	0
88	1
91	1

We can apply the logistic function we trained earlier to these values, which you can see in Figure 4-7.

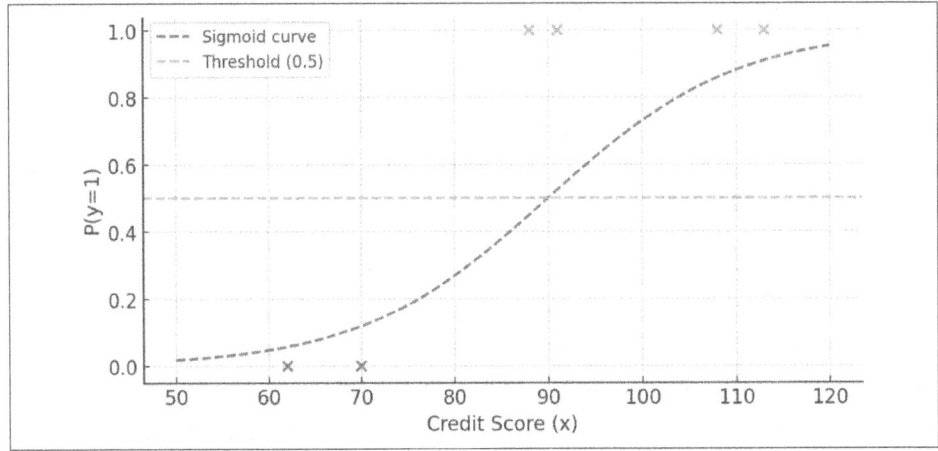

Figure 4-7. A sigmoid function used to evaluate a binary classification model

Based on whether the calculated probability is above or below the threshold (usually 0.5), the model will predict either a default (1) or no default (0) for each credit score. We can then compare the predicted defaults ($\hat{y}$) to the actual defaults (y), as shown in Table 4-8.

Table 4-8. Comparing the predicted defaults to the actual defaults

Credit score (x)	Actual default (y)	Predicted default (ŷ)
62	0	0
108	1	1
113	1	1
70	0	0
88	1	0
91	1	1

This comparison helps us see where the model is getting it right and where it might need improvement.

Evaluation Metrics for Binary Classification

The first step in calculating evaluation metrics for a binary classification model is usually to create a *confusion matrix* of the number of correct and incorrect predictions for each possible class label, as you can see in Table 4-9.

Table 4-9. Confusion matrix

	Positive	Negative
Positive	30	45
Negative	20	19

The rows represent the actual values, labeled as "positive" or "negative," while the columns show the predicted values. For example, the model predicted the positive class correctly 30 times, which is displayed as the true positive count. However, it also made 45 incorrect predictions where it classified negatives as positives. Similarly, there are 20 instances of false negatives and 19 true negatives. This distribution helps evaluate the accuracy and types of errors in the model's predictions. One way to express the different possibilities for the confusion matrix is shown in Table 4-10.

Table 4-10. Confusion matrix with descriptions

	Predicted Positive	Predicted Negative
Actual Positive	True positive	False negative
Actual Negative	False positive	True negative

The rows and columns follow the same arrangement, but each cell now includes a label: true positive, false positive, false negative, and true negative. These labels offer a clearer understanding of the relationship between predicted and actual outcomes:

True positive (TP)
: The model predicted the positive class, and the actual class was also positive. This is a correct prediction for the positive class.

False positive (FP)
: The model predicted the positive class, but the actual class was negative. This is an incorrect prediction, often referred to as a *type I error*.

False negative (FN)
: The model predicted the negative class, but the actual class was positive. This is another incorrect prediction, known as a *type II error*.

True negative (TN)
: The model predicted the negative class, and the actual class was also negative. This is a correct prediction for the negative class.

Calling this a *confusion matrix* is certainly apt: it can be tough to understand this. Yet the confusion matrix is likely to be on the exam. This is why it's a good idea to memorize the four outcomes.

Let's now take a look at other common evaluation metrics.

Accuracy

One basic metric derived from the confusion matrix is *accuracy*, which is simply the proportion of correct predictions out of the total. It's calculated as:

$$\text{Accuracy} = (TN + TP) \div (TN + FN + FP + TP)$$

For our credit score example, the calculation is:

$$(2 + 3) \div (2 + 1 + 0 + 3) = 5 \div 6 = 0.83$$

This means our model correctly predicted loan defaults 83% of the time. While accuracy seems like a good measure, it can be misleading if the data is imbalanced. For instance, if only a small percentage of people default, a model could predict no default for everyone and still achieve high accuracy, but it wouldn't truly capture the patterns in the data.

Recall

Recall measures how well the model identifies positive cases (people who defaulted on a loan). It's calculated as:

$$\text{Recall} = TP \div (TP + FN)$$

For our example, the calculation is:

$3 \div (3 + 1) = 3 \div 4 = 0.75$

So our model correctly identified 75% of those who defaulted.

Precision

Precision tells us how accurate the positive predictions are—that is, how many of the predicted defaults were actual defaults. It's calculated as:

Precision = TP ÷ (TP + FP)

In our case, the calculation is:

$3 \div (3 + 0) = 3 \div 3 = 1.0$

This means that every time the model predicted a default, it was correct 100% of the time.

F1 score

The *F1 score* provides a harmonic mean between precision and recall, which is a type of average that emphasizes the smaller values in a dataset. The harmonic mean is calculated as the reciprocal of the average of the reciprocals of the values, ensuring that both precision and recall are given equal weight. Unlike accuracy, which can be misleading when dealing with imbalanced datasets, the F1 score takes both false positives and false negatives into account, offering a more nuanced view of a model's effectiveness.

The formula is:

F1 score = 2 × Precision × Recall ÷ Precision + Recall

For our example, the calculation is:

$2 \times 1.0 \times 0.75 \div 1.0 + 0.75 = 1.5 \div 1.75 = 0.86$

The resulting F1 score of 0.86 indicates that the model achieves a good balance between precision and recall, performing effectively in correctly identifying positive cases while minimizing false positives and false negatives.

Area under the curve

Another way to think about recall is to call it the *true positive rate (TPR)*, which shows how well the model identifies positive cases (defaults, in our example). On the flip side, we also have the *false positive rate (FPR)*, which measures how often the model incorrectly predicts a default when there wasn't one. The FPR is calculated as FP ÷ (FP + TN). In our case, since there were no false positives, the FPR is 0 ÷ 2 = 0.

Now, if we adjust the threshold for predicting a default (for instance, moving it higher or lower than 0.5), that would change the balance of positive and negative predictions, which means both the TPR and FPR would shift. A common way to visualize this is by plotting a *receiver operating characteristic (ROC) curve*, which compares the TPR and FPR across all possible threshold values. Figure 4-8 illustrates this.

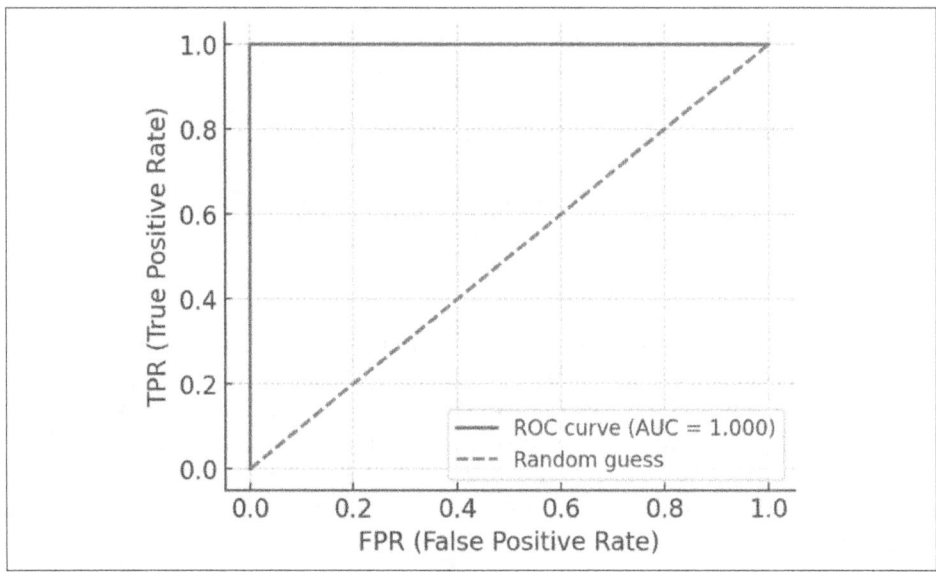

Figure 4-8. ROC plots the true positive and false positive rates

The perfect ROC curve would shoot straight up along the TPR axis and then run across the top, giving it an area under the curve (AUC) of 1.0, as shown in Figure 4-8. This means that the model makes perfect predictions. A completely random model would follow a diagonal line, with an AUC of 0.5—basically just guessing. For our credit score example, let's assume we generated the ROC curve and the AUC is 0.875. This tells us that the model is much better than guessing and performs well in predicting loan defaults.

Table 4-11 sums up what we have learned about binary classification.

Table 4-11. Key concepts in binary classification

Factors	Definition
Purpose	To categorize data into one of two distinct classes, often labeled as 0 and 1, such as predicting "spam" versus "not spam" or "default" versus "no default"
Process	1. Split data into training and testing sets. 2. Train the model to classify based on patterns in the data. 3. Test and validate model accuracy on new data.
Training the model	Commonly uses logistic regression to fit a function that estimates the probability of an outcome between 0 and 1, applying a threshold (e.g., 0.5) to classify results
Evaluation metrics	• Accuracy: Overall correct predictions divided by total predictions • Confusion matrix: A table that summarizes the performance of a classification model by displaying the counts of TPs, FPs, TNs, and FNs. • Recall: TPR assessing how well the model identifies positive cases • Precision: Accuracy of positive predictions • F1 score: Harmonic mean of precision and recall for balanced evaluation • AUC: Measures the model's ability to distinguish between classes across all thresholds, with 1.0 indicating a perfect classifier

Multiclass Classification

When you're working with *multiclass classification*, you're figuring out which category, out of several, best fits a specific observation. This is based on calculating the likelihood of various outcomes. It allows a model to predict which option is most likely for a given case.

Let's use a group of flowers as an example. For each flower, we've measured the petal length (x), and we're trying to predict the flower type (y), which could be one of the following:

- 0 = rose
- 1 = daisy
- 2 = tulip

Of course, in a real-world scenario, you'd usually have more than just one feature (x) to work with. But for simplicity, we're sticking to a single feature here. The data is in Table 4-12.

Table 4-12. The relationship between petal length and flower type

Petal length (x)	Flower type (y)
167	0
172	0
225	2
197	1

Petal length (x)	Flower type (y)
189	1
232	2
158	0

To train our model, we need to select an algorithm, and we have two main options to choose from: one-vs-rest (OVR) and multinomial.

One-vs-rest algorithms

With OVR, the idea is to build a separate binary classification model for each class. Each model decides whether a given observation belongs to its specific class. Using our flower example, this method would create three models:

Model 1
    Determines if a flower is a rose (class 0)

Model 2
    Determines if a flower is a daisy (class 1)

Model 3
    Determines if a flower is a tulip (class 2)

Each model calculates a probability between 0 and 1. The class with the highest probability is selected as the prediction.

Multinomial algorithms

A multinomial algorithm generates a single function that produces a probability distribution for all the classes at once. Instead of having multiple models, it gives you a vector with probabilities for each class, and the total of these probabilities always equals 1.

For example, you might get an output like this:

   [0.2, 0.3, 0.5]

This means there's a 20% chance the flower is a rose, a 30% chance it's a daisy, and a 50% chance it's a tulip. Since 0.5 is the highest, the model predicts tulip.

No matter which algorithm you go with, the model uses these probabilities to predict the most likely class for any observation.

Evaluation of a Multiclass Classification Model

You can measure the performance of a multiclass classifier by calculating binary metrics for each individual class or by using aggregate metrics that consider all classes together. Table 4-13 shows the evaluation for our flower example.

Table 4-13. Measuring the performance of a multiclass classifier

Petal length (x)	Actual flower (y)	Predicted flower (ŷ)
165	0	0
171	0	0
205	1	1
195	1	1
183	1	1
221	2	2
214	2	2

The confusion matrix for a multiclass classifier works similarly to the confusion matrix for a binary one, but instead of two classes, it captures predictions across multiple classes. This shows the number of predictions for each combination of actual and predicted class labels. Figure 4-9 displays the confusion matrix.

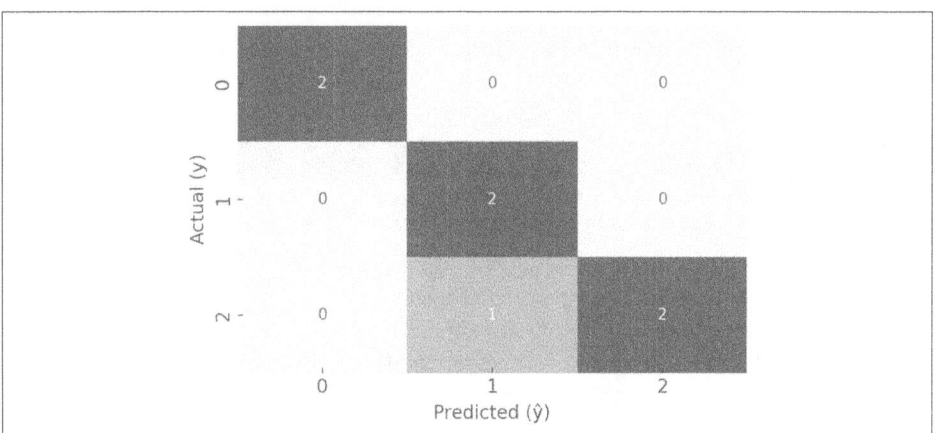

Figure 4-9. Confusion matrix showing the actual and predicted flower classes

From this confusion matrix, we can figure out the key metrics for each flower class, listed in Table 4-14.

Table 4-14. Confusion matrix for the key metrics for each flower class

Class	TP	TN	FP	FN	Accuracy	Recall	Precision	F1 score
0	2	5	0	0	1.0	1.0	1.0	1.0
1	2	4	1	0	0.86	1.0	0.67	0.8
2	2	4	0	1	0.86	0.67	1.0	0.8

To get the overall accuracy, recall, and precision for the model, we sum the values for TPs, TNs, FPs, and FNs:

Overall accuracy = (13 + 6) ÷ (13 + 6 + 1 + 1) = 0.90

Overall recall = 6 ÷ (6 + 1) = 0.86

Overall precision = 6 ÷ (6 + 1) = 0.86

Finally, the overall F1 score is calculated using the overall recall and precision values:

Overall F1 score = (2 × 0.86 × 0.86) ÷ (0.86 + 0.86) = 0.86

These metrics help us understand how well our flower classifier is performing across all classes.

Let's sum up what we have learned about multiclass classification in Table 4-15.

Table 4-15. Key concepts in multiclass classification

Factors	Description
Purpose	To categorize data into one of multiple possible classes by estimating the likelihood of each class for a given observation, such as predicting flower types based on features like petal length
Process	1. Select and train a model using either OVR or multinomial algorithms. 2. Predict the class based on the highest probability output. 3. Evaluate accuracy and refine the model as needed.
Modeling techniques	• OVR: Builds a binary classifier for each class to predict if a given observation belongs to that class • Multinomial: Uses a single model that outputs probabilities for all classes simultaneously, with the highest probability indicating the predicted class
Evaluation metrics	• Confusion matrix: Visualizes correct and incorrect predictions across all classes • Accuracy, recall, precision, and F1 score: Calculated per class and as an aggregate to gauge overall performance

Clustering

Clustering is an ML technique used to organize data into groups, or clusters, based on the similarity of their features. It falls under the category of unsupervised learning because it does not rely on prelabeled data to identify these groups. Instead, the algorithm analyzes the data's features and assigns each data point to a cluster based on shared characteristics. In essence, the clusters act as labels generated by the model after analyzing the inherent structure of the data.

Clustering is particularly useful in scenarios where you need to uncover hidden patterns or groupings within data. For example, it can help in market segmentation, where customers are grouped based on purchasing behavior, or in biology, where genes with similar functions are grouped together. It's also valuable for anomaly detection, such as identifying unusual transactions in fraud detection, or in image segmentation to group pixels into distinct regions.

Let's take a look at a more detailed example. Suppose you're a marine biologist studying a group of fish. Instead of focusing on identifying the species, you're only interested in grouping the fish based on two characteristics: the length of the fish and the number of fins. The data is in Table 4-16.

Table 4-16. Grouping of fish based on similarities in length and fin count

Length (x1)	Fins (x2)
10	3
12	4
15	2
15	2
16	5
18	6
20	2
22	5
24	6

In this case, the goal is to cluster fish with similar lengths and fin counts together, not to classify them into any specific species.

There are several ways to approach clustering. One of the most popular methods is called *k-means clustering*.

Let's see how to do this. First, you turn your data into vectors, which means assigning each data point a coordinate in a space. If you have two features, like the length of a fish ($x1$) and the number of fins ($x2$), these become two coordinates—[x1, x2]—that can be plotted on a two-dimensional graph.

Next, you decide how many clusters you want. Let's say you choose three clusters ($k = 3$). You randomly place three points on the graph to represent the centers of your clusters, called *centroids*. Then, each fish is assigned to the centroid it is closest to.

The centroid itself is recalculated to be the average of the data points (fish) assigned to it.

This process repeats: as the centroids move, some fish may become closer to a different centroid, so the assignments change. This back-and-forth of reassigning fish to clusters and adjusting the centroids continues until the groups become stable. You can see this in Figure 4-10.

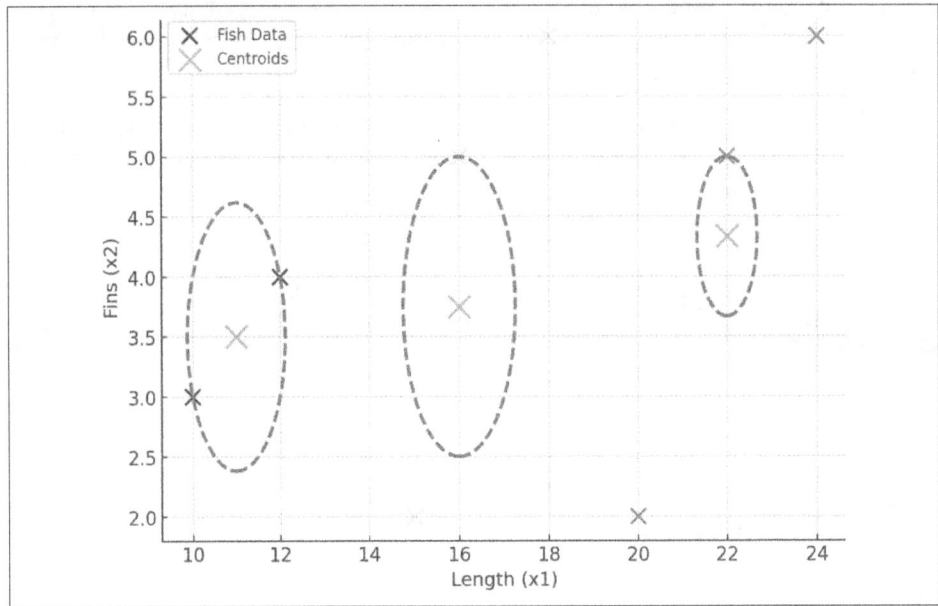

Figure 4-10. The clusters of fish grouped by length and number of fins

Since there's no known label to which to compare the cluster assignments, the effectiveness of a clustering model is judged by how well the clusters are distinct from one another. You can use several metrics to measure how well the clusters are separated:

Average distance to cluster center
    Measures how close, on average, each point in the cluster is to the centroid

Average distance to other centers
    Looks at how close, on average, each point in the cluster is to the centroids of other clusters

Maximum distance to cluster center
    Finds the farthest point from the centroid within the cluster

Silhouette score
    A number between -1 and 1 that shows how well separated the clusters are (with 1 indicating the best separation)

Deep Learning

DL is a more sophisticated type of ML that tries to mimic how our brains learn. At its core, DL relies on what's called an *artificial neural network*, which behaves similarly to how biological neurons work by using mathematical functions. These artificial neural networks consist of multiple layers of neurons, which creates a structure that processes data through increasingly complex layers. This is why the method is called "deep" learning, and the resulting models are known as *deep neural networks (DNNs)*. You can apply DL to various tasks, such as predicting outcomes (regression), classifying data, and even more complex problems like understanding language or recognizing images.

Like other forms of ML, DL involves training a model to predict an output based on one or more inputs. The model's job is to figure out a function that connects these inputs to the correct outputs. This function is built up across the neural network layers, with each layer handling a part of the process. During training, the model repeatedly adjusts its internal parameters (called *weights*) to minimize how far its predictions are from the correct values. Over time, the model fine-tunes these weights to improve accuracy and make better predictions.

Let's break down how a neural network works by looking at an example that classifies three different types of fruit: apples, oranges, and bananas. In this case, the input data (x) is a vector of measurements for these features. Let's say we measure:

- The fruit's weight
- The color's hue value
- The curvature of the fruit

So x is a vector with three values:

$$x = [x1, x2, x3]$$

Now, the label (y) is the fruit's type, which could be one of the three: apple, orange, or banana. Since this is a classification problem, the neural network will predict probabilities for each class. So y will be a vector representing the probabilities for each fruit: [P(apple|x), P(orange|x), P(banana|x)].

Here's how the network makes a prediction:

1. The feature data for a fruit, like [180g, 0.8, 0.3], is fed into the input layer of the neural network.
2. Each neuron in the input layer takes the feature values, multiplies them by their assigned weights, and passes the result through an activation function.

3. The neurons in each layer are connected to neurons in the next layer, forming a fully connected network where the results are fed forward through the network's layers.
4. The output layer generates a vector of probabilities—for example, [0.2, 0.7, 0.1]—which represents the likelihood of the fruit being an apple, orange, or banana. Since 0.7 is the highest value, the network predicts the fruit is an orange.

Figure 4-11 shows a graphical representation of a deep learning network.

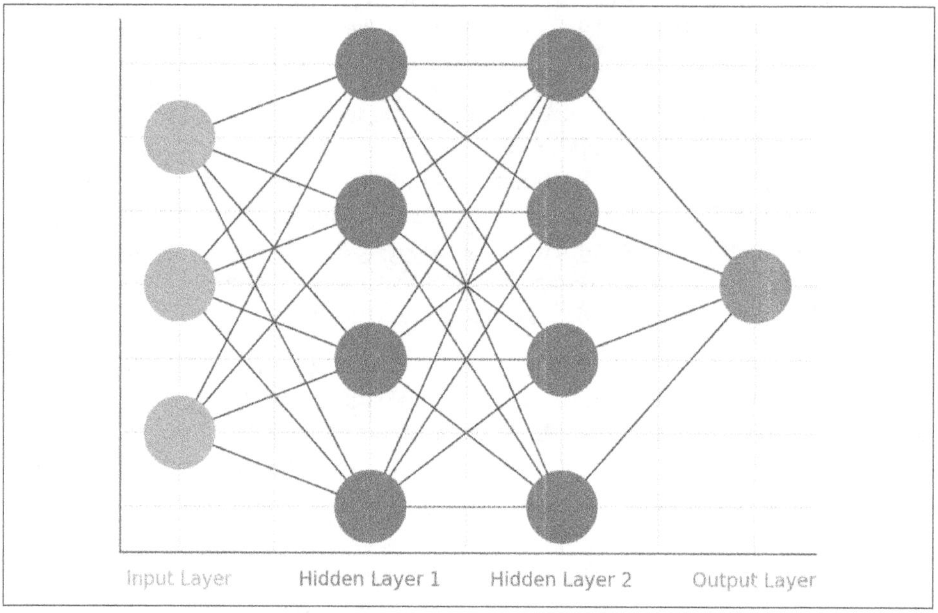

Figure 4-11. A deep learning network

The magic of neural networks lies in adjusting the weights during training to make better predictions. Initially, these weights are random, but through a process called *backpropagation*, the network refines them to improve accuracy. Here's a high-level view of the training process:

1. Define your training data—basically, a set of known fruit types with their corresponding measurements.
2. The data is passed through the neural network, and the output is compared to the actual labels using a loss function. A loss function is a mathematical formula that quantifies the difference between the predicted output and the true labels. For example, if the network predicts [0.3, 0.1, 0.6] for a banana, but the true label is [0, 0, 1], the loss function calculates the discrepancy between these values. This difference, or loss, serves as a signal for the model to adjust its parameters and

improve its predictions. The ultimate goal is to minimize this loss to enhance the network's accuracy.

3. The network calculates how much each weight contributed to the loss and uses this information to adjust the weights.
4. This process is repeated over many cycles (called *epochs*) until the loss is minimized and the model is accurate enough.

This training typically happens in batches of data, using powerful hardware like GPUs to handle the heavy computation involved. Over time, the network becomes good at identifying whether the fruit is an apple, orange, or banana.

For the AI-900 exam, you may see questions that ask about the differences between ML and DL. Table 4-17 lays out these key differences to help you get a solid grasp of each.

Table 4-17. Key differences between ML and DL

Factor	Machine learning	Deep learning
Complexity	Less	More
Data requirements	Performs well with structured, smaller datasets	Requires large volumes of data to achieve accuracy
Training time	Faster	Longer
Hardware requirements	Can run on standard CPUs	Often requires GPUs
Interpretability	Easier	More difficult

Conclusion

In this chapter, we've explored the core concepts of ML, diving into essential techniques like regression, classification, and clustering. Each of these approaches offers unique ways to uncover patterns in data and make accurate predictions. They also empower you to tackle real-world challenges head-on.

Quiz

To check your answers, please refer to the "Chapter 4 Answer Key" on page 180.

1. What is the primary purpose of regression analysis in machine learning (ML)?

    a. To categorize data into distinct classes

    b. To cluster similar data points

    c. To predict a numerical outcome based on variables

    d. To analyze images and videos

2. Which of the following is an example of supervised learning?

    a. K-means clustering

    b. Predicting house prices based on features

    c. Segmenting customers based on purchase history

    d. Identifying anomalies in financial transactions

3. In binary classification, which algorithm is commonly used to predict probabilities between two classes?

    a. Linear regression

    b. Logistic regression

    c. Decision trees

    d. K-means

4. What does the F1 score represent in model evaluation?

    a. The model's ability to distinguish between classes

    b. The average of errors in predictions

    c. A balance between precision and recall

    d. The total accuracy of the model

5. Which step in the ML workflow involves using the model to generate predictions?

    a. Training

    b. Inferencing

    c. Validation

    d. Data preparation

6. What type of learning is K-means clustering associated with?

   a. Supervised

   b. Semisupervised

   c. Reinforcement

   d. Unsupervised

7. What metric measures how well a regression model explains the variation in data?

   a. Mean squared error (MSE)

   b. Coefficient of determination (R^2)

   c. Root mean squared error (RMSE)

   d. Mean absolute error (MAE)

8. Which approach is used to address missing data by estimating based on patterns in available data?

   a. Mean imputation

   b. Predictive imputation

   c. Removal of incomplete data

   d. Data normalization

9. What is the primary goal of classification in ML?

   a. To identify hidden patterns in unlabeled data

   b. To predict numerical outcomes

   c. To assign data points to predefined categories

   d. To generate new content

10. Which ML technique is suitable for grouping similar data points without labels?

    a. Regression

    b. Classification

    c. Clustering

    d. Deep learning (DL)

CHAPTER 5
Azure Machine Learning

In the previous chapter, we explored the fundamentals of ML. In this chapter, we'll apply these concepts using *Azure Machine Learning*, a cloud-based service that facilitates the training, deployment, and management of ML models. Whether you're a data scientist, software engineer, or DevOps professional, Azure Machine Learning streamlines the entire ML workflow, from data exploration to model deployment.

Azure Machine Learning offers two primary tools tailored to different user preferences and objectives:

Azure Automated Machine Learning (AutoML)
  AutoML automates the process of developing ML models, handling tasks such as algorithm selection and hyperparameter tuning. It is accessible through both the Azure Machine Learning Studio's no-code interface and the Python SDK. This means the system can cater to varying levels of expertise.

Azure Machine Learning Designer
  This tool provides a drag-and-drop interface for constructing ML pipelines without the need for coding. Users can visually connect datasets, transformations, and algorithms to create and deploy models efficiently.

Both tools are integrated into Azure Machine Learning Studio, offering flexibility based on user preferences and project requirements. For this chapter, we'll provide examples of using these services.

Introduction to Azure Machine Learning

You can use Azure Machine Learning for tasks like:

- Preparing and exploring your data
- Training and evaluating ML models
- Registering and managing models once they're trained
- Deploying models so that applications or services can use them
- Ensuring that responsible AI practices are followed

Azure Machine Learning is designed to work with various ML platforms, whether you're using Microsoft Azure's tools or open source frameworks like PyTorch, TensorFlow, or scikit-learn. MLOps tools make it easy to monitor your models and redeploy them as needed.

Here's what Azure Machine Learning offers:

- Centralized dataset storage for model training and evaluation
- On-demand compute power to run ML jobs like training models
- AutoML to test different algorithms and parameters so that you can find the best model for your data
- Visual tools that help you create pipelines for processes like model training or inferencing
- Integration with popular tools like MLflow for managing your models at scale
- Built-in support for evaluating responsible AI metrics, including fairness and model explainability

When you're ready to get started, the first step is to set up an Azure Machine Learning *workspace* in your Microsoft Azure subscription. This workspace is your main resource, and other resources like storage accounts and VMs are created automatically as needed. We learned how to do this in Chapter 2.

Once your workspace is ready, you can access it through Azure Machine Learning Studio, a browser-based tool that helps you manage everything from data to deployment models. In the studio, you can:

- Import and explore your data
- Create and manage compute resources
- Run your code in notebooks
- Build jobs and pipelines using visual tools

- Train models with automated ML
- View model details like evaluation metrics and responsible AI information
- Deploy models for real-time or batch inferencing
- Manage models from a comprehensive catalog

In the next two sections, we'll look at how to use Azure Machine Learning's AutoML and Azure Machine Learning Designer services.

AutoML

In this section, we'll dive into Azure's AutoML service to train and test an ML model. This will be for a cost prediction system for health care insurance. We'll be working with a dataset from Kaggle (*https://oreil.ly/nMgxP*), a popular platform for data science projects where you can find a treasure trove of free, real-world datasets. The dataset has information on factors like age, sex, body mass index (BMI), children, region, and smoking habits.

Azure Machine Learning Studio is where you'll manage your resources and kick off the work. Open a new browser tab and go to the Machine Learning Studio (*https://oreil.ly/6kEQF*). You'll see the dashboard shown in Figure 5-1.

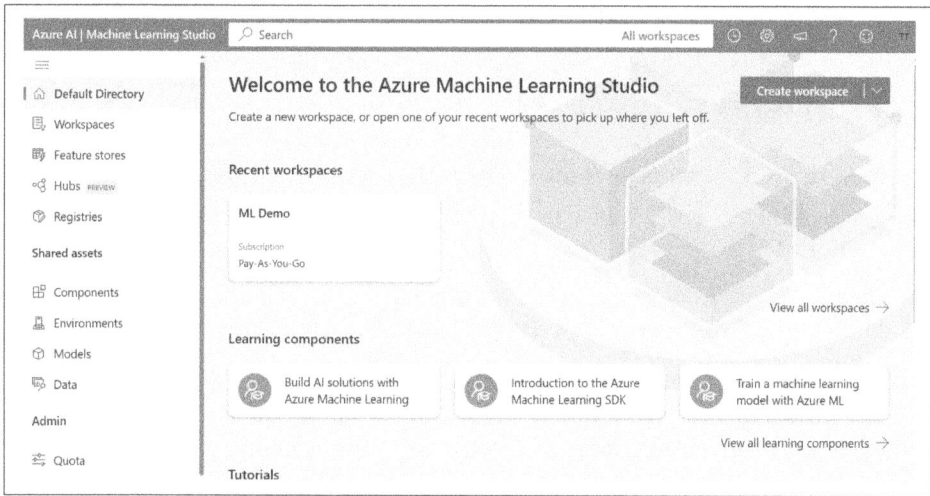

Figure 5-1. The dashboard for Machine Learning Studio

On the menu tab on the left side of the screen, select "Automated ML" and then click "New Automated ML Job." You'll see the screen in Figure 5-2.

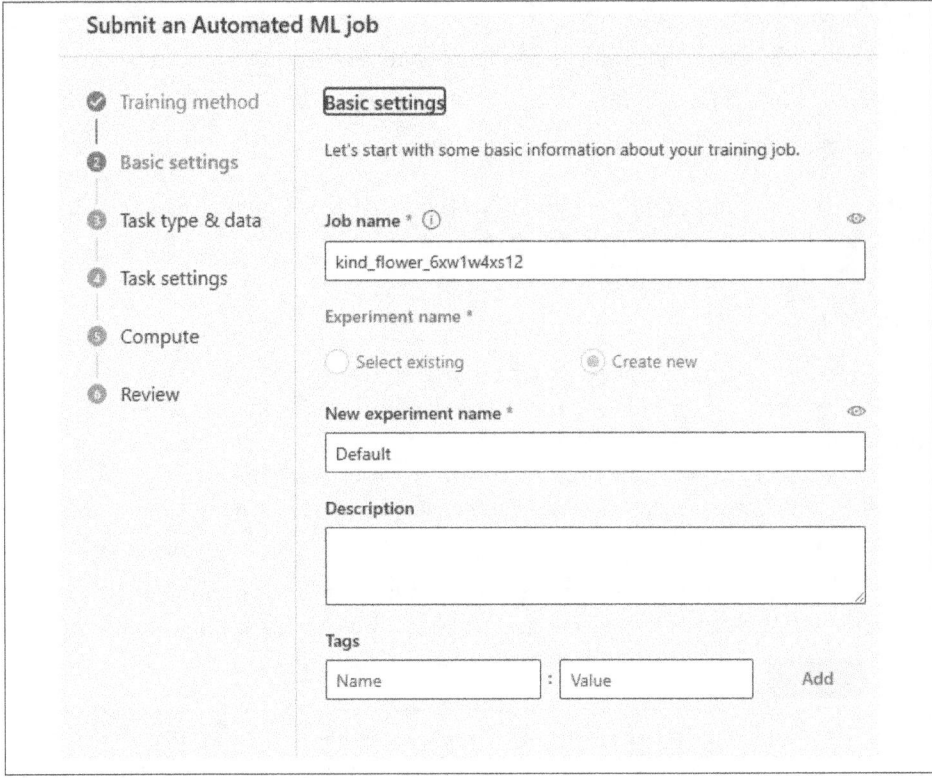

Figure 5-2. The setup for creating an ML model

The menu bar on the left shows the different steps in the process of creating the ML model. The first one is for entering "Basic settings." Here's what you can enter in the fields:

Job name
   The job name will already be prepopulated with a unique name. You can leave it as is.

New experiment name
   Enter **insurance-prediction**.

Description
   Enter **Automated machine learning for predicting medical insurance costs**.

Tags
   Leave blank.

Click Next and you'll be taken to the "Task type and data" section. This will show a pulldown menu with the following options:

- Classification
- Regression
- Time-series forecasting
- Natural language processing

Select Regression and then click Create. In the "Data type" section, enter or select the following:

Name
   Insurance_data

Description
   Historical insurance data

Type
   Table (mltable)

Select Next and you'll have the choice of uploading a dataset as a URI, from Azure, or from local files. Select "local files."

Click Next and then choose "Azure Blog Storage" as well as "workspaceblogstore." After clicking Next, you'll be taken to the "Data source" section. First, you will need to download the insurance CSV file, which is the Kaggle dataset, and place it into its own folder. You'll also need a file that has the structure of the data. You can find these files at the website for this book (*https://oreil.ly/J6NMG*).

Click "Upload folder" and select the files to upload: both the dataset and the data structure. Press Next, and the system will process the data. Then click Create to generate the table, which shows the structure of the dataset. Once that is done, select the table and click Next. You will then be in the "Task settings" section. For the "Target column," select "charges." This is what the regression will output.

Then, expand the "View additional configuration settings" section. Some items in the configuration settings will be dropdown menus where you can select an option, and others will require you to enter information. Complete them as follows:

Primary metric
   Normalizedrootmeansquarederror

Explain best model
   Unselected

Enable ensemble stacking
   Unselected

Use all supported models
    Unselected. You'll restrict the job to trying only a few specific algorithms.

Allowed models
    Select only MaxAbsScaler and LightGBM. True, you'd typically select all or most of the models, but that would take much more time, so two models will be fine for this demonstration.

Expand the "Limits" section and complete the settings as follows:

Limits
    Expand this section as well.

Max trials
    3

Max concurrent trials
    3

Max nodes
    3

Metric score threshold
    0.085. If the normalized root mean squared error hits this value, the job will terminate.

Experiment timeout
    15. This is important. If you do not set a limit, the process could take a long time—even hours.

Iteration timeout
    15

Enable early termination
    Selected

Validation type
    Train-validation split

Percentage of validation data
    10

Test dataset
    None

Click Next and you'll be taken to the "Compute" section. Make sure the items are completed as follows:

Select compute type
   Serverless

Virtual machine type
   CPU

Virtual machine tier
   Dedicated

Virtual machine size
   Standard_D2ds_v4 (2 core(s), 8GB RAM, 50GB storage, $0.11/hr)

Number of instances
   1

Next, click "Submit training job." Azure will then process the model, which can take some time—15–20 minutes. Once it's finished, you will get the results, as seen in Figure 5-3.

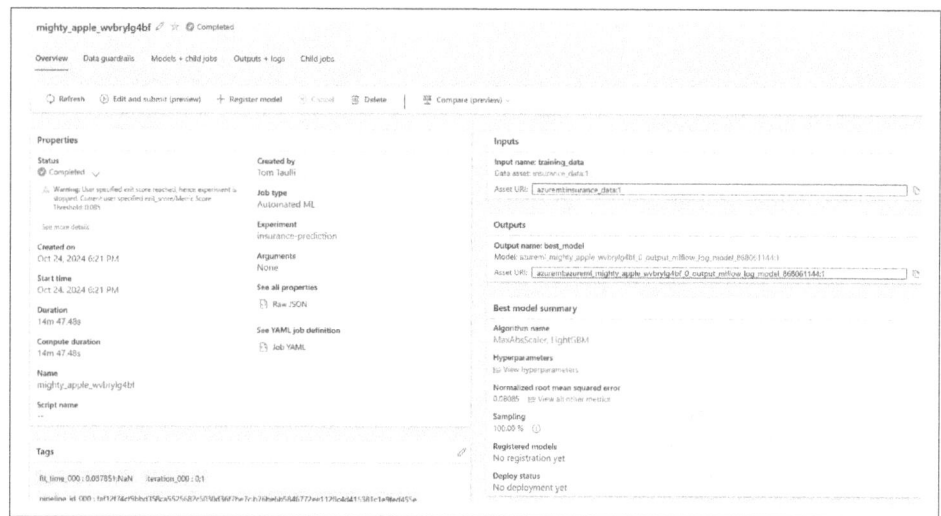

Figure 5-3. The results of the training of a model

On the right side is a "Best model summary," which includes the models MaxAbsScaler and LightGBM. You can click on them to see their performance. Below is the "Normalized root mean squared error" of 0.08085%. This indicates a fairly accurate prediction rate for the model.

If you click "View all other metrics," you will see many metrics, such as for explained variance, MAE, and so on. Then, if you select the "Metrics" menu item above, you will see two charts. They show the residuals and the predicted values. You can find them in Figure 5-4.

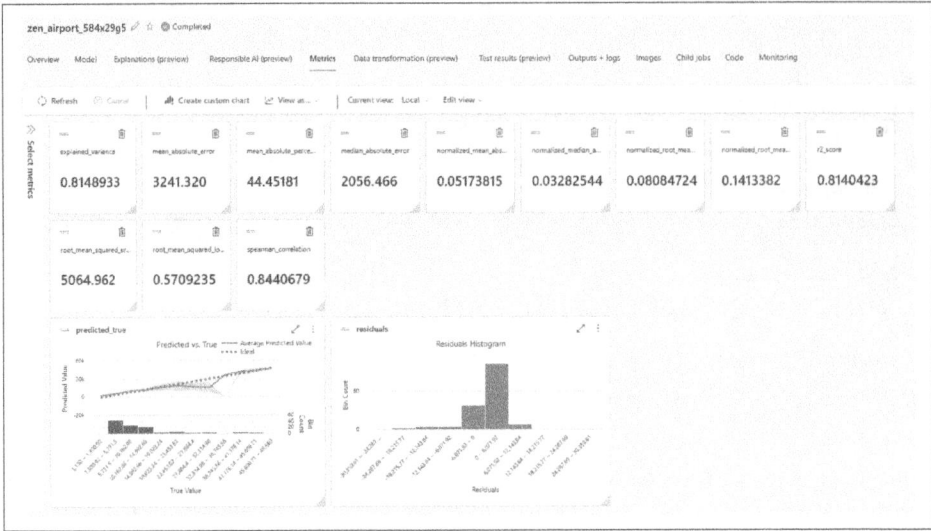

Figure 5-4. The metrics for a regression model

Next, we can implement this model. This can be done as a real-time endpoint, a batch endpoint, or a web service.

No doubt, you can do much more with this. AutoML is a powerful tool. But the purpose of this demo is to give you a taste of the capabilities and some of the main workflows. Now, we'll do the same with the Azure Machine Learning Designer.

Azure Machine Learning Designer

To use Azure Machine Learning Designer, first go to the dashboard of the Azure Machine Learning Studio (*https://oreil.ly/NN_jk*). Then either create a new workspace or use an existing one. On the left menu, click Designer and press + to create a new pipeline. Figure 5-5 shows the dashboard for the Azure Machine Learning Designer.

On the left side is a menu table for Data and Component. Under Data is a list of datasets, such as for animal images, automobile price data, and customer relationship management (CRM) churn data. To use a dataset, click on it and drag it to the main screen. Let's do this for the "adult census income binary classification" dataset. If you right-click it, you will get a popup to preview the table, as shown in Figure 5-6.

What we will do is build a model that predicts income levels—that is, whether an individual's income exceeds a certain threshold (e.g., $50,000 per year). This is based on the features in the adult census income dataset, which includes attributes like age, education, occupation, and hours worked per week.

We will then split the data for training and testing. To do this, we will use a component. You can find it by going to the left menu bar and entering "split" into the search box. Drag and drop the Split Data component under the dataset. Then use your mouse to drag the circle under the dataset box to the component. Figure 5-7 shows what this looks like.

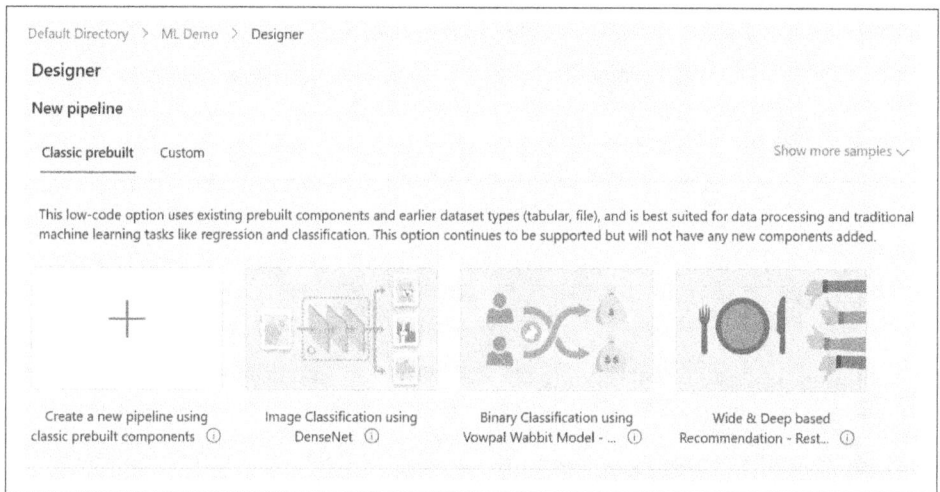

Figure 5-5. The dashboard for the Azure Machine Learning Designer

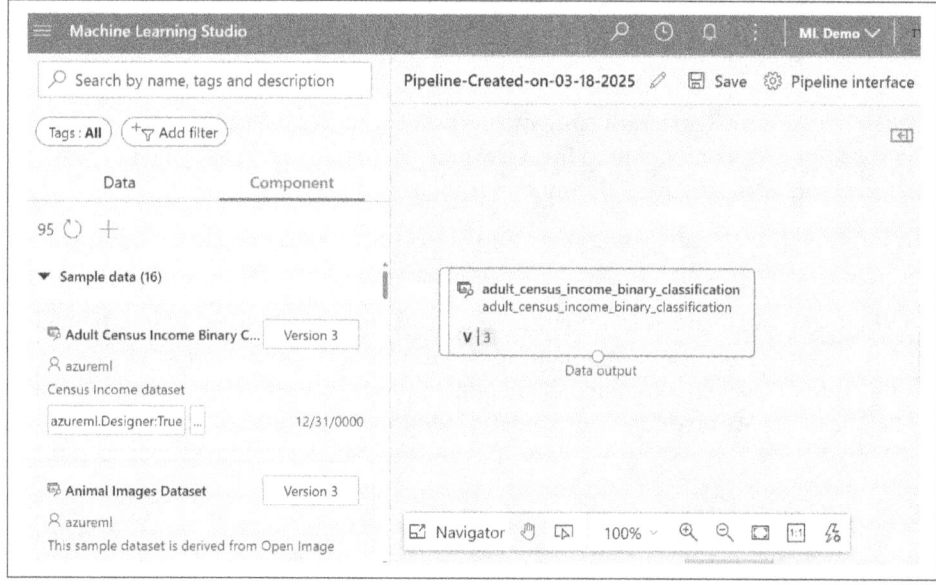

Figure 5-6. The census dataset in the Azure Machine Learning Designer

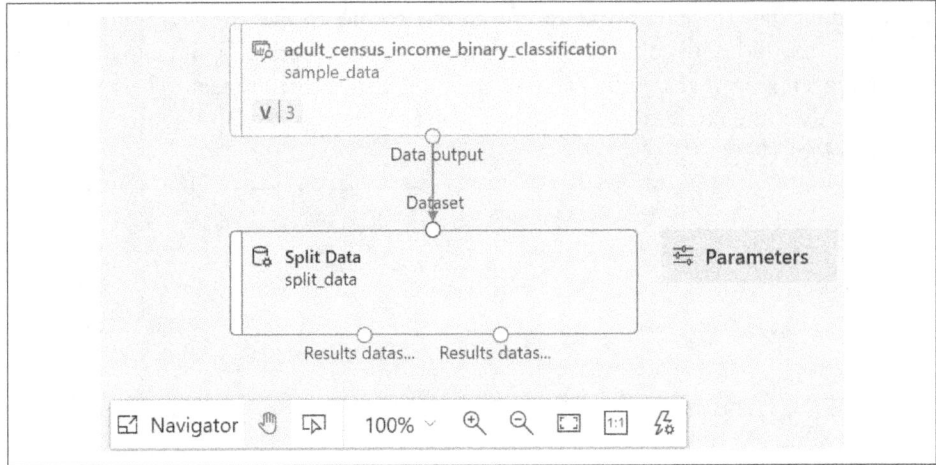

Figure 5-7. The connection between a dataset and a component that splits the data

To configure the component, double-click it. With the "Fraction of rows in a first output dataset," we can specify the percentage of the training data. We will use 0.7.

Next, we will select a training model. Go back to the menu on the left and search for "linear regression." Drag and drop that under the split component. Note that you can double-click the regression model to change the settings, but we will keep the defaults.

Next, search for "train model." Yes, this is the component for training our model. Drag it to the screen as well.

Connect the Linear Regression component to the Train Model component. Also connect the Split Data component to the Train Model component, specifying the first circle under Split Data. Figure 5-8 shows what this looks like.

Click on the Train Model component and select "Edit column." This is the value we want the model to predict. Let's enter **income** and press Save.

Go to the left menu and search for "score." This component will score the model for the predictions. Drag this component to the screen and connect it to the first circle for the Train Model component. Then connect the Split Data component to the second circle of the Score Model component, as shown in Figure 5-9.

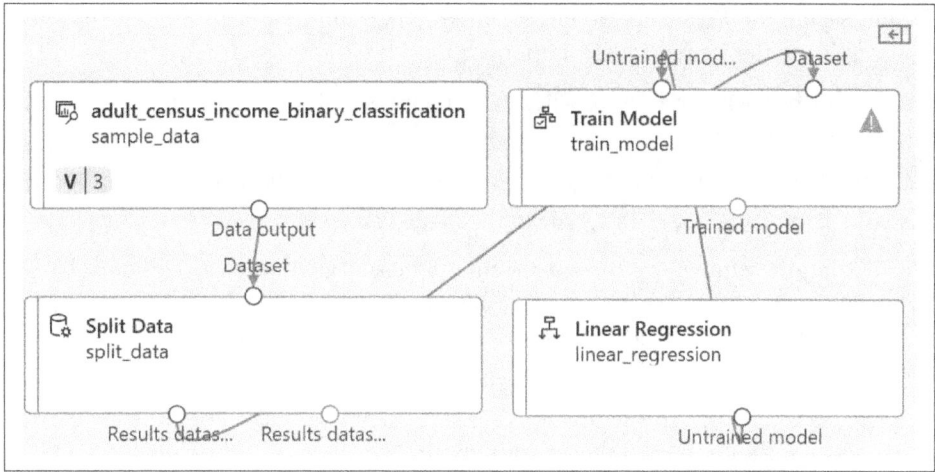

Figure 5-8. The connections to the dataset and components

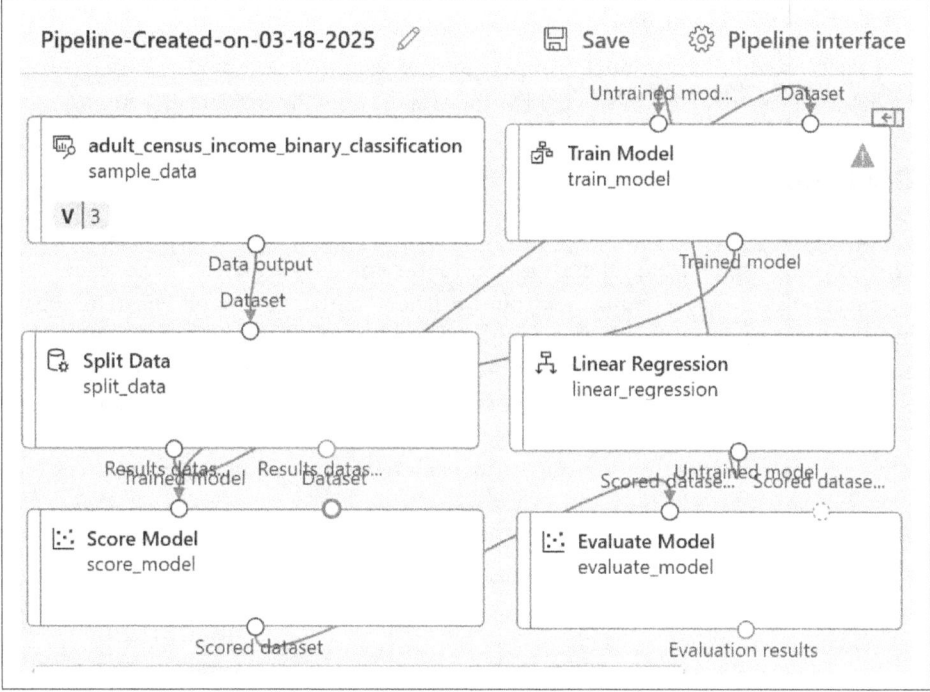

Figure 5-9. The result of a model that has been processed

Finally, search for "Evaluate Model" for the metrics and drag it to the screen. Then, connect this to the Score Model component.

We are finished with the setup. Click "Configure & Submit" at the top right of the screen.

You will go through three input screens. For the first one, select "Create new" for the "Existing name" and below this, type in the name you want.

Click "Runtime settings" on the left menu, then click "Compute cluster" and "Create Azure ML compute cluster." (A *compute cluster* is a group of VMs that work together to perform large-scale data-processing tasks.) Select the recommended option and click Next. Enter a name for that and click Create.

You will be taken back to the previous screen where you will select the new cluster. Click "Review + Submit" and then press Submit.

It can take a few minutes for the model to be processed. Once the processing is finished—which is indicated by "Complete" at the top of the screen—go to Jobs on the left menu and select your model.

Right-click the Evaluate Model component and select "Preview Data." Then select "Evaluation results," and you will get the metrics for how the model performed.

Conclusion

In this chapter, you've seen how Azure Machine Learning provides flexible tools suited to your experience level and project requirements—whether it's the visual ease of the Azure Machine Learning Designer or the customizable capabilities of AutoML. Through practical examples, you've seen just how straightforward it is to set up configurations and test your models. While the exam doesn't dive deeply into every detail, having a general understanding of these tools will equip you with a solid foundation of what Azure Machine Learning can offer.

Quiz

To check your answers, please refer to the "Chapter 5 Answer Key" on page 182.

1. Which ML technique is commonly used for predicting a numerical outcome based on known variables?

    a. Classification

    b. Regression

    c. Clustering

    d. Deep learning (DL)

2. Which metric in regression analysis measures the average error in predictions, regardless of positive or negative deviation?

    a. Mean squared error (MSE)

    b. Coefficient of determination (R^2)

    c. Mean absolute error (MAE)

    d. Root mean squared error (RMSE)

3. In binary classification, what algorithm is commonly used to estimate the probability of a binary outcome?

    a. K-means clustering

    b. Logistic regression

    c. Linear regression

    d. Decision tree

4. What type of ML does Azure's Automated Machine Learning (AutoML) feature primarily support?

    a. Reinforcement learning

    b. Supervised learning

    c. Unsupervised learning

    d. Genetic algorithms

5. In a multiclass classification problem, which approach builds a binary classifier for each class?

    a. K-means clustering

    b. One-vs-rest (OVR)

    c. Multinomial algorithm

    d. Logistic regression

6. Which Azure Machine Learning feature helps automate the process of trying multiple algorithms to find the best model?

    a. Custom script execution

    b. AutoML

    c. Dataset storage

    d. Deployment pipelines

7. What evaluation metric indicates the proportion of correctly identified positives in a classification model?

    a. Accuracy

    b. Precision

    c. Recall

    d. F1 score

8. Which ML technique is suitable for grouping data points based on similarities without prior labels?

    a. Supervised learning

    b. Classification

    c. Clustering

    d. Regression

9. In regression analysis, what term describes the average of squared differences between predicted and actual values?

    a. Mean absolute error (MAE)

    b. Root mean squared error (RMSE)

    c. Mean squared error (MSE)

    d. R^2 score

10. Which DL structure consists of multiple layers that process data to make complex predictions?

    a. Support vector machine (SVM)

    b. Decision tree

    c. Neural network

    d. K-nearest neighbors

CHAPTER 6

Features of Computer Vision Workloads on Azure

In this chapter, we'll cover the essentials of computer vision, a core area of AI that represents 15%–20% of the exam content. This technology enables you to harness Microsoft Azure's suite of tools designed to "see" and interpret the world through data. We'll start with an overview of key computer vision solutions, techniques, and foundational concepts. Then, we'll dive into how Azure approaches image classification, object detection, OCR, and facial analysis. We'll examine these topics in greater depth, incorporating hands-on examples along the way.

Computer Vision Services for Azure

When you're diving into computer vision on Azure, you've got several options to explore, each catering to different goals and levels of customization:

Azure AI Vision

If your focus is only on computer vision, Azure AI Vision is built precisely for that. It's got all the tools you need to handle visual data, analyze images and videos, and pull useful insights. Let's say you're developing a system for a parking garage that needs to track available spaces and detect unauthorized vehicles through camera feeds. Azure AI Vision gives you a dedicated, powerful toolkit to tackle visual processing tasks like these with options to help you manage your budget along the way.

Azure AI Services

If you're interested in tapping into multiple AI capabilities beyond computer vision—translation or search, for example—Azure AI Services is your go-to. Think of it as a one-stop shop for various AI tools. You manage everything with a single endpoint and access key. This setup will save time. For instance, imagine you're building a travel app that translates text, tags images, and detects landmarks. Azure AI Services lets you combine all these features. This keeps everything streamlined and simple to manage.

Azure AI Custom Vision
 When you need tailored image recognition capabilities, Azure AI Custom Vision is your go-to solution. It empowers you to create and train custom image recognition models using tags specific to your project's needs. For instance, if you're in agriculture, you could build a model to identify crop diseases from images, helping farmers take proactive measures and improve yields. Custom Vision is accessible via SDKs, an API, or an intuitive web portal.

Azure AI Face Service
 This service provides advanced AI algorithms to detect, recognize, and analyze human faces in images—even if someone is wearing sunglasses or viewed from an angle. It's an excellent tool if your projects require identity verification, touchless access control, or automated face blurring for privacy in public spaces. The service can return detailed facial analysis, which makes it useful for applications where in-depth facial recognition is needed. However, access is restricted: only Microsoft-managed customers and partners meeting specific eligibility and usage criteria can use the service as part of Microsoft's responsible AI principles. To apply, interested users must complete the Face Recognition intake form (*https://oreil.ly/sO2xB*).

Azure AI Video Indexer
 This tool allows for extracting insights from videos, such as object detection, OCR, and content moderation. This is done by leveraging more than 30 AI models. There are also audio capabilities, such as for transcription, translation, and emotion detection.

Each of these options offers a unique approach to computer vision, whether you need a broad AI toolkit, a dedicated vision platform, customized model building, or advanced facial recognition capabilities.

What You Can Do with Azure's Computer Vision Services

Azure's computer vision services offer a powerful set of tools for analyzing and understanding images in various ways. If you're looking to automatically generate descriptions, you can start with *image captioning*. This feature doesn't just identify what's in an image—it goes a step further by giving each description a confidence score ranging from 0 to 1. This lets you know how certain the model is about its analysis. For instance, if you have a picture of a sunny beach with people swimming, image captioning might generate a caption like "a beach scene with people swimming" and show a confidence score that indicates how likely it is to be accurate—say 0.9. This makes it easy to verify how much trust to place in the results.

Tagging is another helpful feature. This adds a layer of searchable terms to each image. Tagging highlights specific keywords related to elements found in the image, such as *beach*, *ocean*, or *sun*, and each tag includes a confidence score. This feature is invaluable when organizing large image libraries or quickly searching for images with certain characteristics.

Azure's computer vision also works with *object detection*. This identifies and locates specific objects within an image, such as cars, people, or furniture. Object detection goes beyond just recognizing objects by also pinpointing their exact locations within the image, which is great for any task that requires spatial awareness. This can be used in scenarios like monitoring inventory, analyzing traffic patterns, or even enabling automated checkout systems in retail.

Facial detection and *face recognition* add even more specialized capabilities, as noted before with the Azure AI Face Service. With facial detection, Azure locates the presence of faces within an image, but it doesn't go further to identify who those faces belong to. This is ideal for applications like crowd counting or assessing emotions from facial expressions. Face recognition takes things further by recognizing individual faces—matching them to known identities. This is useful for security applications, personalized experiences, or any situation where you need to verify someone's identity.

Last, Azure's *Optical Character Recognition (OCR)* service allows you to extract text from images. This transforms any visual text into machine-readable characters. OCR is ideal for digitizing printed documents, scanning receipts, or reading handwritten notes. Whether you're automating data entry or making scanned documents searchable, OCR can simplify processes by quickly converting images of text into usable data.

Table 6-1 provides a summary of Azure's computer vision capabilities.

Table 6-1. Computer vision capabilities in Azure

Feature	Description	Use cases
Image captioning	Identifies the content of an image and provides a description along with a confidence score from 0 to 1	Describing photos Auto-generating captions
Tagging	Adds specific key terms or labels to an image, each with a confidence score, making it easier to categorize and search for images based on content	Photo library organization Digital assets management
Object detection	Identifies and locates specific objects within an image, providing spatial data on their positions	Inventory management Traffic analysis Automated retail checkout
Facial detection	Detects the presence of faces in an image without identifying individuals	Crowd counting Emotion detection in groups

Feature	Description	Use cases
Face recognition	Recognizes individual faces, matching them to known identities for verification purposes	Security access Personalized customer experiences
OCR	Extracts text from images, converting visual text into machine-readable characters	Data entry automation Document digitization Receipt scanning

Let's walk through an example using the Azure AI Vision service. Go to the "Add captions to images" section in the Vision Studio (*https://oreil.ly/aYYYy*). You will see sample photos at the top and a place to upload your own photos, as shown in Figure 6-1.

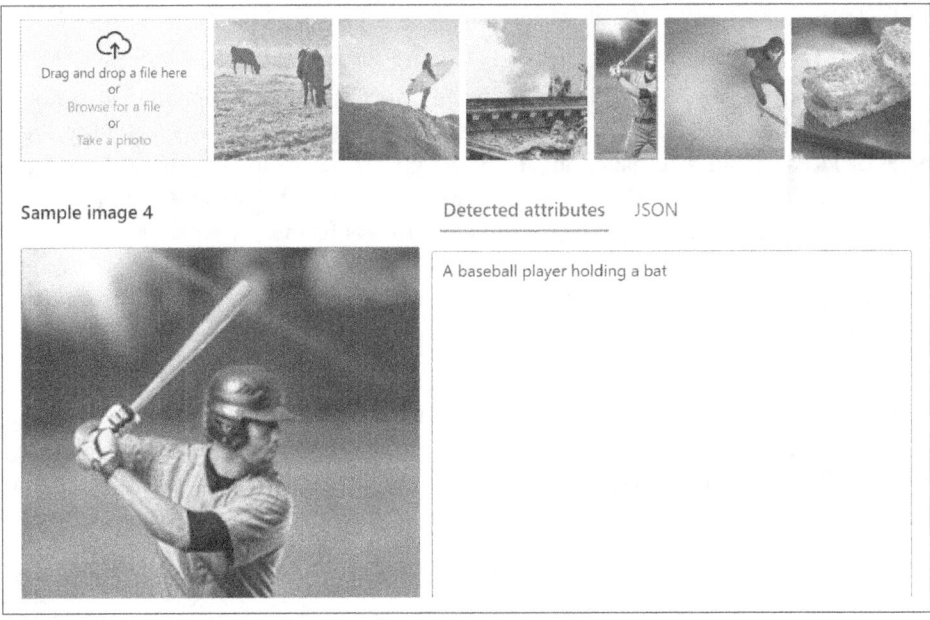

Figure 6-1. The image caption service in Azure Vision Studio

We'll select the baseball player. The caption will appear: "A baseball player holding a bat." Then, select JSON and review the output, which is shown here:

```
{
  "apim-request-id": "163f2514-c22f-41f1-86d9-2d3ec77ca461",
  "content-length": "158",
  "content-type": "application/json; charset=utf-8",
  "modelVersion": "2023-10-01",
  "captionResult": {
    "text": "a baseball player holding a bat",
    "confidence": 0.8212961554527283
  },
```

```
      "metadata": {
        "width": 250,
        "height": 322
      }
    }
```

The JSON shows the identification information, length, content type, and model version for the AI. It also shows the image caption as well as the confidence score, which is 0.821. Finally, you'll see some metadata for the dimensions of the image.

How Computer Vision Works

At the heart of computer vision is the pixel. When a computer "looks" at an image, it's actually reading numbers that tell it how bright each pixel is and what color it should be.

Let's take a more in-depth look at how computer vision works:

Images are made of pixels
　　Imagine an image as a huge grid made up of pixels. An image that is 100 × 100 pixels, for instance, has exactly 10,000 pixels arranged in rows and columns. Each pixel has a color made up of three values: red, green, and blue (RGB), ranging in integer value from 0 to 255. By mixing these colors, the computer constructs the images we see.

Find patterns in pixels
　　To recognize objects, computer vision algorithms search for patterns within this pixel grid. They use math-based methods, like convolution, to identify parts of the image, such as edges and textures. Convolution works by analyzing small groups of pixels (kernels) to enhance certain features, like an edge, and help the computer pick out shapes in the image.

Spot important details
　　After recognizing patterns in the pixels, computer vision models focus on key parts—features—of the image. These features could be the curve of a face, the outline of a vehicle, or the edges of a building. By narrowing down the focus, the model zeroes in on only the most important points. This makes it easier to tell what the image contains.

Teach a model to recognize images
　　Now that the model has picked out these features, it's ready for the next step: learning. The model has been trained on loads of images, each labeled with what's in it. By studying this labeled data, it learns to connect certain pixel patterns with objects like "cat" or "car" and later can recognize similar objects in new images.

DL and pixel data

For DL models like convolutional neural networks (CNNs)—which we'll learn more about later in this chapter—pixels are just the beginning. Each layer in a CNN digs deeper into the pixel data, with early layers detecting edges, middle layers recognizing shapes, and later layers identifying full objects. As the network learns, it adjusts the relationships between pixels. This makes the model better at detecting patterns each time it's used.

Fine-tune for accuracy

In applications where accuracy is critical—like facial recognition or medical imaging—every pixel matters. Advanced algorithms take a closer look at these pixels, which improves the model's precision. By fine-tuning pixel data, the model gradually detects with greater detail, getting better at interpreting images with each improvement.

Let's go further into pixels and the processing of images. For this, we'll take a look at an example, which is an array:

```
0   0   0   0   0   0   0
0   0   0   0   0   0   0
0   0  180 180 180  0   0
0   0  180 180 180  0   0
0   0  180 180 180  0   0
0   0   0   0   0   0   0
0   0   0   0   0   0   0
```

This array has seven rows and seven columns, creating a 7 × 7–pixel image—its resolution. Each pixel in this image is represented by a number ranging from 0 (black) to 255 (white), with values between these extremes representing different shades of gray. In this case, the pixel values of 180 create a lighter gray square in the middle of a darker background, which is shown in Figure 6-2.

A grid of pixel values like this forms a simple, two-dimensional image by arranging rows and columns along x- and y-coordinates. This single layer is enough for grayscale images, but color images require a bit more complexity. To represent color, we use three separate layers. Each one represents a different color component: red, green, and blue. As an example, imagine we have a similar 7 × 7–pixel array in three color channels.

Red:

```
120 120 120 120 120 120 120
120 120 120 120 120 120 120
120 120 200 200 200 120 120
120 120 200 200 200 120 120
120 120 200 200 200 120 120
120 120 120 120 120 120 120
120 120 120 120 120 120 120
```

Green:

20	20	20	20	20	20	20
20	20	20	20	20	20	20
20	20	180	180	180	20	20
20	20	180	180	180	20	20
20	20	180	180	180	20	20
20	20	20	20	20	20	20
20	20	20	20	20	20	20

Blue:

250	250	250	250	250	250	250
250	250	250	250	250	250	250
250	250	30	30	30	250	250
250	250	30	30	30	250	250
250	250	30	30	30	250	250
250	250	250	250	250	250	250
250	250	250	250	250	250	250

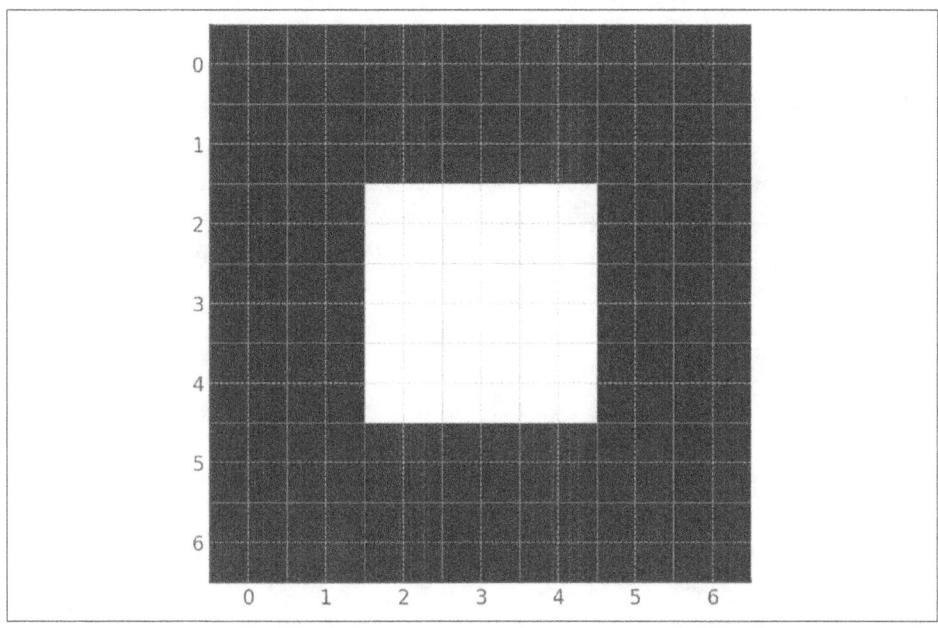

Figure 6-2. A 7 × 7 grid display outlining each pixel

This example is similar to Figure 6-2 in shape. But when these three layers combine, they form a color image. The greenish-blue squares on the outer edges come from mixing these values for each color:

- Red: 120
- Green: 20
- Blue: 250

The teal squares in the middle are created by mixing different values for each color:

- Red: 200
- Green: 180
- Blue: 30

This blending of the red, green, and blue channels brings color images to life, pixel by pixel.

Image Filters

When you want to enhance an image, applying filters can significantly transform it by adjusting each pixel's value to create various effects. Filters use *kernels*—small grids of numbers that define how each pixel will be altered. Different kernels create different effects, such as blurring or sharpening. Each serves a unique purpose in image processing.

Consider a 3 × 3–kernel matrix for sharpening that looks like this:

```
 0  -1   0
-1   6  -1
 0  -1   0
```

This kernel is applied by moving it across the image, calculating a new pixel value for each 3 × 3 section, and filling these results into a new version of the image. Let's walk through an example using a simple grayscale image:

```
0   0    0    0    0   0  0
0  50   50   50   50  50  0
0  50  100  100  100  50  0
0  50  100  150  100  50  0
0  50  100  100  100  50  0
0  50   50   50   50  50  0
0   0    0    0    0   0  0
```

Starting with the top left corner, each pixel in a 3 × 3 section is multiplied by the corresponding kernel value, then summed up to produce a new pixel value for the output image. For example:

```
(0 * 0) + (0 * -1) + (0 * 0) +
(0 * -1) + (50 * 6) + (50 * -1) +
(0 * 0) + (50 * -1) + (100 * 0) = 200
```

You then move the kernel one pixel to the right and repeat this process across the entire image. This specific kernel is used for sharpening, emphasizing details, and making edges more prominent.

Keep in mind that there are various filters to achieve different results:

Blurring
    Blurring filters, like a simple averaging kernel, reduce noise and smooth out an image. A typical blurring kernel might look like this:

```
    1/9  1/9  1/9
    1/9  1/9  1/9
    1/9  1/9  1/9
```

    This kernel averages the pixels in each 3 × 3 section, softening details and creating a blurred effect.

Edge detection
    Edge detection filters, such as the Sobel or Laplacian filters, are designed to identify boundaries within an image by emphasizing rapid changes in pixel intensity —for example:

```
    -1 -1 -1
    -1  8 -1
    -1 -1 -1
```

    This kernel detects edges by highlighting where pixel values change sharply, helping to isolate shapes and lines.

Color inversion
    Color inversion filters flip the pixel values, creating a negative of the image. These filters don't use a kernel like the other filters. Inverting colors means that each pixel's value is subtracted from the maximum intensity, transforming light areas to dark and vice versa.

Sharpening
    The sharpening filter, as shown in the example above, enhances details by making edges stand out. This is useful for highlighting features or making an image appear crisper.

Figure 6-3 has a side-by-side comparison showing the effect of a sharpening filter on an image of an apple. This process, known as *convolutional filtering*, involves sweeping the filter across the image to apply effects like blurring, edge detection, color inversion, and sharpening. By experimenting with different kernels, you gain many creative possibilities for transforming your images.

Figure 6-3. The result of using a filter on an image to sharpen it

Image Classification

Image classification is an important aspect of AI that focuses on identifying the main content within an image and sorting it into specific categories. For example, if you want a model to distinguish between animals, it can be taught to identify whether an image shows a cat, dog, or bird. This capability goes beyond just detecting items; it's about recognizing complex patterns. Sometimes this means picking up on visual details that may be too subtle for the human eye.

Supervised learning is typically used to train a model for image classification. In this approach, the model learns from a labeled dataset—each image is paired with its correct label—so the model can learn what each category looks like. This way, the AI becomes adept at recognizing and correctly labeling new images that it hasn't seen before. On the other hand, unsupervised learning, which doesn't rely on labeled data, is generally less effective for tasks that need precise category distinctions.

In practice, one popular application of image classification is in health care, where AI models can analyze medical images to detect specific abnormalities. This might include spotting tumors in X-rays or identifying certain conditions in MRI scans. Not only does this streamline the diagnostic process, but it also enables quicker and potentially more accurate detection, which can be crucial for early intervention.

Object Detection

Object detection is an AI technique that not only identifies what objects are in an image but also pinpoints their exact locations. This is achieved through *bounding boxes*, which are rectangular outlines that frame each identified object and are mapped by pixel coordinates. These boxes show precisely where each object sits within the image, giving a more detailed understanding than simply knowing what objects are present.

Azure AI's vision service offers robust object detection capabilities. Tools like Vision Studio make integrating this feature into various applications more accessible. The Azure AI vision service allows users to detect objects and track their locations using bounding boxes. Object detection builds on image analysis models, but it involves more complex training since the model must learn not just to recognize objects but also to locate them accurately within the image. Figure 6-4 shows an example of using object detection with Vision Studio.

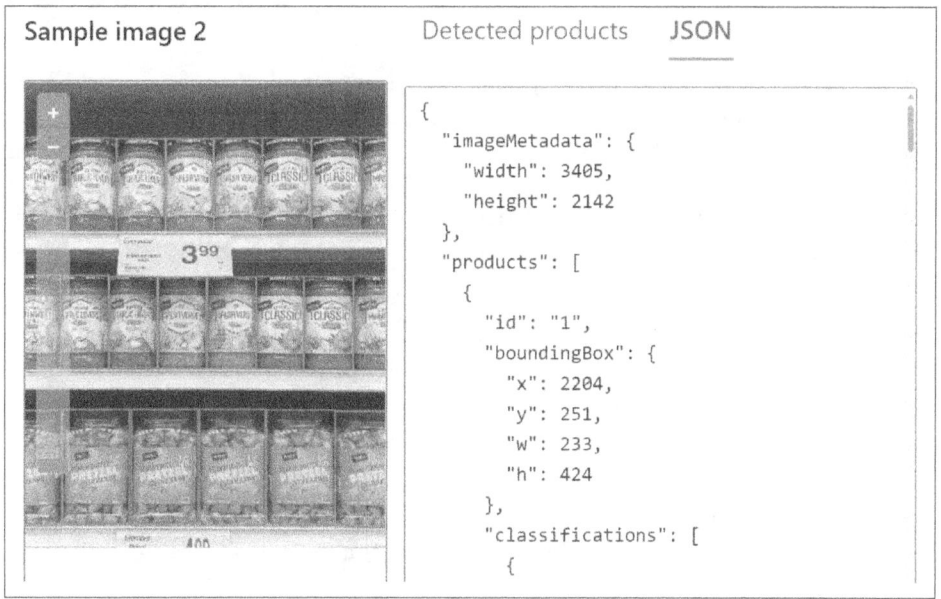

Figure 6-4. Object detection using Azure AI Vision Studio

The uploaded image shows how the model detected individual products by drawing bounding boxes around each item on the shelves. Each bounding box, outlined in blue, represents a "detected product," showing where each item is located within the image. Alongside this visual display, Vision Studio provides detailed JSON data on the right, which includes the pixel coordinates of each bounding box. What's more, each detected object comes with a confidence score that tells us how sure it is that each item is a "product."

OCR

Traditional OCR uses pattern recognition to match text shapes, but with AI, things have stepped up a notch. Now, ML algorithms analyze every shape and line, comparing them to vast libraries of text samples. This means that AI can handle tricky fonts or messy handwriting better than older OCR methods ever could.

That said, OCR isn't perfect. Sometimes, it misreads characters—like mistaking a lowercase "l" for the number "1." These errors can crop up especially if the text is smudged or the font is unusual.

Yet OCR can provide major advantages. Let's take an example. Suppose a health care provider has decades' worth of patient records stored in dusty file cabinets. Digging up a file means sorting through piles of paper—a tedious, time-consuming process that often leads to errors or lost documents. With OCR, though, all those paper records can be quickly scanned, converted to digital format, and made fully searchable. This can mean saving substantial amounts of money and time.

Azure's Read OCR engine is built with advanced ML models to not just pull text from documents but also adapt to multiple languages and formats. Read OCR is flexible, letting you choose between cloud-based processing or on-premises deployment. If you're working with single images or photos "in the wild," Read OCR offers a fast synchronous API, so you can embed it into your software.

There are two main versions of Read OCR that cover different scenarios. The first version is optimized for general images, such as labels, signs, or posters that you'd find in everyday settings. This version (OCR for Images 4.0) is ideal for situations that need fast text extraction.

The second version is tailored for text-heavy scanned or digital documents like books, reports, or articles. This Document Intelligence model uses an asynchronous API, which means it's built to handle high volumes and works great if you're automating large-scale document processing.

Let's look at an example of the OCR capabilities of Azure AI Foundry. This example converts an image of a Social Security card into readable text, as shown in Figure 6-5.

Figure 6-5. OCR output from Azure AI Foundry of a Social Security card image

As you can see, Azure AI Foundry successfully identifies the text. If you select JSON, you will get an extensive set of features. First, it will show a line of the text:

```
"lines": [
  {
    "text": "SOCIAL SECURITY",
    "boundingPolygon": [
      {
        "x": 500,
        "y": 3742
      },
      {
        "x": 2696,
        "y": 2980
      },
      {
        "x": 2810,
        "y": 3118
      },
      {
        "x": 560,
        "y": 4032
      }
    ],
```

For each word, the location is also provided. Then, the OCR breaks this down into the values for each of the words, along with the confidence scores:

```
"words": [
        {
          "text": "SOCIAL",
          "boundingPolygon": [
            {
              "x": 501,
              "y": 3906
            },
            {
              "x": 1304,
              "y": 3402
            },
            {
              "x": 1381,
              "y": 3536
            },
            {
              "x": 596,
              "y": 4032
            }
          ],
          "confidence": 0.963
        },
```

This OCR functionality ties into intelligent document processing (IDP), which is like OCR's next-level cousin. It uses OCR as a foundation but dives deeper, extracting structure and key information beyond just words. Microsoft's Document Intelligence model, for example, builds on Read OCR to analyze relationships, identify key entities, and provide detailed document insights. (We covered this system in the section "Studios" on page 16.)

Let's look at an example of the Azure AI Document Intelligence Studio (*https:// oreil.ly/Pd_kX*). Select the Invoices section and you will see the dashboard. Click "Run analysis" and you will see the screen shown in Figure 6-6.

On the left side of the screen, the OCR has identified the various fields on the document. The Document Intelligence technology then determines what types of values they have. For example, there are fields for the billing and recipient addresses and so on. There are also confidence scores for each.

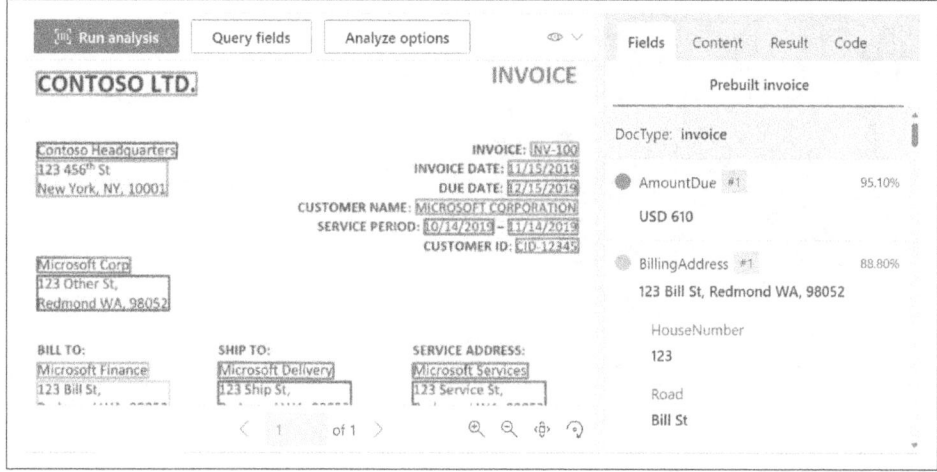

Figure 6-6. Analysis of an invoice using Document Intelligence Studio

Facial Detection and Analysis

Facial detection and analysis are crucial technologies for computer vision. Facial detection identifies human faces within an image or video feed, often as a preliminary step in other processes, such as unlocking your phone with your face. It determines whether a face is present but does not provide additional details. Facial analysis, on the other hand, goes a step further by interpreting various features of the face, such as age, gender, and emotional expressions, based on patterns in facial structures.

Facial detection and analysis rely on AI, particularly DL, which uses layers of neural networks to analyze patterns in data. Models are trained on vast datasets of human faces, which allows the models to recognize and interpret facial features accurately. Techniques like CNNs play a significant role here, scanning and learning from pixel patterns in images. The AI models then apply this learning to recognize facial features and expressions in real time or in prerecorded images, constantly improving with each use.

You'll find facial detection and analysis in many everyday applications. Security systems use it for surveillance and to identify individuals of interest in crowded places while retail settings apply it to gather demographic data on customers and even tailor advertisements. In health care, facial analysis is being explored to assess emotional well-being and identify symptoms associated with certain conditions. Gaming and entertainment sectors use it to enhance user experiences, adapting the game or content interactions based on the user's reactions.

Azure AI Studio includes powerful face recognition capabilities. Figure 6-7 shows an example of this.

Figure 6-7. Azure AI Studio identifies and analyzes the face of a woman in an image

In this example, the AI has recognized the face of a woman. It has created a bounding box for her face, and there are various dots on her face to indicate different features. If you select JSON, you will see information about this:

```
"faceLandmarks": {
    "pupilLeft": {
        "x": 510.5,
        "y": 256.4
    },
    "pupilRight": {
        "x": 574.7,
        "y": 263.7
    },
    "noseTip": {
        "x": 538.1,
        "y": 301.7
    },
    "mouthLeft": {
        "x": 502.2,
        "y": 325
    },
```

This captures information about the identification and locations of the left pupil, right pupil, nose tip, and so on.

Convolutional Neural Networks

Imagine trying to teach a computer to recognize animals in photos, such as whether the animal is a cat, a dog, or even a lion. *Convolutional neural networks (CNNs)* make this possible. They're a popular type of DL model because of how they analyze data.

Think of CNNs as digital detectives that filter through an image to pick out important clues like shapes, edges, and textures. They then piece these clues together to make a prediction.

Here's how it works in practice. The model's filters start with random weights. With each round of training, the model learns which details help it recognize each feature, such as the animal type. After enough practice, it becomes highly accurate at picking up the clues—so much so that it can correctly label a new image of, say, a lion, even if it's never seen that exact lion before.

Here's a breakdown of the CNN layers:

Convolutional layers
Each filter in these layers scans the image and captures specific patterns, such as fur texture or ear shape. Over time, the CNN learns which patterns are most useful for recognizing an animal in the image.

Pooling layers
To keep from getting overloaded with data, CNNs use pooling (often max pooling), which shrinks the feature maps to retain only the most essential details. This process makes the model faster and less sensitive to minor variations, such as changes in an animal's pose.

Fully connected layers
Here, the model brings together all the information it's collected. It's like flattening a 3D puzzle and connecting all the pieces to make a single prediction. By this stage, the model has a strong sense of what the object is.

Activation functions
In the final steps, the model needs to weigh its options and come to a conclusion. Functions like `softmax` are used. They assign probabilities to each possible label, so the model might output probabilities like [0.3, 0.6, 0.1]—indicating a 60% chance that the image is a dog, for example.

Backpropagation and optimization
When the model's guess isn't right, it's not the end of the road. It reviews where it missed the mark and adjusts the filter weights to improve its next guess. This feedback loop, called *backpropagation*, helps the model focus on the most relevant features for each type of image.

Training a CNN means feeding it thousands—often millions—of labeled images and letting it practice. With each training round, the model's accuracy improves as it learns from its mistakes. By the end, the CNN understands how to best identify each type of object, even if a new image looks slightly different from the training set.

While CNNs are often used for labeling images, they're also perfect for other tasks that require understanding complex visual data:

Object detection
Rather than just saying "This is a cat," CNNs can identify multiple animals in an image, drawing boxes around each one.

Image segmentation
In detailed tasks like medical imaging, CNNs can classify each pixel in an image, identifying distinct regions, which can be helpful, for instance, in spotting different types of tissues in a medical scan.

In short, CNNs allow machines to interpret images in ways that were previously impossible.

The Evolution of Computer Vision: From CNNs to Multimodal Models

A new kind of architecture—called *transformers*—has been taking over the NLP world. Transformers function by turning words or phrases into numerical codes called *embeddings*. Imagine embeddings as coordinates in a virtual landscape where words with similar meanings gather near one another. For example, "cat" and "kitten" would be positioned closely together, unlike "cat" and "airplane," which would sit farther apart in this semantic space.

Transformers' success with language led to a new breakthrough: *multimodal models*. These models combine images and text, enabling them to understand both at the same time. Here's how they do it:

1. They analyze images to pull out key visual features.
2. They convert text into embeddings.
3. They learn to link these visual and text-based elements.

Microsoft's Florence is one example of a multimodal model. It's trained on millions of images with captions, letting it take on various tasks like:

- Sorting images into categories
- Spotting specific objects in images
- Crafting natural image descriptions
- Adding relevant tags

These multimodal models represent the cutting edge of AI today, creating exciting opportunities for systems that can handle both images and words with ease.

Responsible AI and Computer Vision

In Chapter 3, we examined the principles of responsible AI. This is certainly an important topic in the context of computer vision, where ethical issues take center stage. However, this technology also raises ethical concerns. Privacy is a major issue as many users may not know their data is being collected or how it will be used. There's also the potential for misuse, such as mass surveillance without consent. Bias in AI models is another ethical concern because models trained on limited or nondiverse datasets can lead to inaccurate or unfair outcomes, especially across different demographic groups. For these reasons, deploying facial detection and analysis solutions responsibly requires transparency, strict data governance, and ongoing efforts to mitigate bias and protect individual privacy. Let's dive deeper into the key factors that shape responsible AI practices in this category.

Fairness in Facial Recognition

Ensuring fairness in facial recognition systems is a vital ethical consideration. Research has shown that these systems often exhibit biases, particularly against individuals with darker skin tones and women. A 2025 study by Ketan Kotwal and Sébastien Marcel (*https://oreil.ly/orfFS*) found that these systems often achieve higher accuracy for male subjects compared to female subjects. Moreover, the study highlighted challenges in skin tone classification, noting that lighter-skinned individuals are generally easier to verify than those with darker skin tones. This bias often arises from insufficiently diverse training datasets. Addressing this issue requires developing more inclusive datasets that represent a wide variety of skin tones, genders, and ethnic backgrounds. Moreover, employing fairness-aware algorithms and conducting regular audits can help identify and reduce biases.

Because of the issues, Microsoft has implemented restrictions with its face recognition technology. For example, it prohibits US police departments from using this technology. Microsoft has also retired certain features, such as those that infer emotions, gender, and age.

Privacy and Security

Facial recognition technology also raises pressing concerns about privacy and security. Unauthorized surveillance and data collection without consent infringe on individuals' privacy rights. Furthermore, the storage of facial data carries risks, such as identity theft in the event of a breach. To address these concerns, organizations must establish strict guidelines requiring informed consent before collecting facial data. Adopting robust encryption methods and adhering to data protection laws like the European Union's General Data Protection Regulation (GDPR) can further secure sensitive information. Providing transparency about how face recognition systems are used and offering individuals the option to opt out are additional measures that can help protect privacy and build trust.

Transparency

Transparency is key for fostering trust and accountability in computer vision systems. Users should understand how these systems function, the types of data they collect, and the decision-making processes involved. To promote transparency, developers should provide clear documentation about their algorithms, including the data sources and methodologies employed. Open communication with stakeholders and the public can also help demystify the technology. What's more, incorporating explainable AI techniques can make the decision-making processes of computer vision systems more accessible to nontechnical audiences, enhancing trust and understanding.

Conclusion

To wrap things up, Azure's computer vision tools pack serious power, putting advanced AI right at your fingertips. Knowing how Azure handles everything from object detection to OCR and facial analysis is not only impressive but also key for passing the AI-900 exam. This exam expects you to understand the capabilities Azure offers—like how multimodal models can blend text and images to create more contextually aware AI. And with multimodal models opening up new possibilities, Azure's computer vision tools aren't just practical—they're shaping the next era of AI, one smart application at a time.

Quiz

To check your answers, please refer to the "Chapter 6 Answer Key" on page 184.

1. Which of the following is a fundamental concept in computer vision involving dividing an image into a grid of colored points?

    a. Filters

    b. Pixels

    c. Neural networks

    d. Labels

2. Which method is used in object detection to pinpoint the location of objects within an image?

    a. OCR

    b. Bounding boxes

    c. Facial detection

    d. Image classification

3. What is the purpose of convolution in computer vision?

    a. To detect color inversion

    b. To resize images

    c. To identify patterns in pixel data

    d. To assign labels

4. In Microsoft Azure's computer vision tools, which service primarily handles tasks like object detection and facial analysis?

    a. Azure Cognitive Search Service

    b. Azure AI Vision

    c. Azure Machine Learning

    d. Azure Kubernetes Service

5. What type of neural network is most commonly used for computer vision tasks like image classification?

    a. Recurrent neural network (RNN)

    b. Convolutional neural network (CNN)

    c. Generative adversarial network (GAN)

    d. Transformer

6. Which component of a CNN reduces the size of feature maps to focus on essential details?

    a. Convolutional layers

    b. Fully connected layers

    c. Pooling layers

    d. Activation functions

7. Which computer vision technique reads and interprets text within images?

    a. Image classification

    b. OCR

    c. Facial detection

    d. Object detection

8. What is the primary ethical concern associated with facial detection and analysis in AI?

    a. Lack of color accuracy

    b. Privacy and consent issues

    c. High computational costs

    d. Limited dataset availability

9. In Azure's AI Vision Studio, what data accompanies object detection to indicate the model's confidence?

    a. Pixel count

    b. Confidence score

    c. Bounding box color

    d. File type

10. What role do activation functions play in CNNs during the image recognition process?

    a. Identifying edge patterns

    b. Reducing image size

    c. Assigning probabilities to predictions

    d. Adding color to images

CHAPTER 7
Features of Natural Language Processing Workloads on Azure

In this chapter, we'll look into NLP, a key topic that makes up about 15%–20% of the AI-900 exam. We'll kick things off with an exploration of core NLP scenarios. Then, we'll get into Microsoft Azure services for NLP, starting with key phrase extraction and how entity recognition pulls important context from text. From there, we'll walk through sentiment analysis, an essential tool for reading emotions in written language, and cover the basics of language modeling. You'll also find an introduction to speech recognition and synthesis. This is where machines learn to understand and produce humanlike speech. Finally, we'll wrap up with how to use NLP with conversational language understanding (CLU) and conversational AI.

Introduction to NLP

Imagine trying to get your computer to not just read but actually understand what you're saying—that's where NLP steps in. NLP is a part of AI that gives machines the power to interpret and generate human language. It's about taking apart the complexities of text and speech and transforming them into something a computer can work with. This is what fuels everything from the search results you see on Google to chatbots to generative AI apps like ChatGPT that answer questions and those voice-activated assistants that talk back. By bridging the gap between human communication and computer logic, NLP makes technology feel more intuitive—almost like it's listening.

NLP doesn't work alone—it's backed by two powerful AI systems: machine learning (ML) and deep learning (DL). ML gives NLP systems the models and algorithms they need to spot patterns and make predictions. DL takes this a step further, allowing NLP to tackle complex tasks like understanding the context of conversation or gauging sentiment. DL models mimic the brain's structure, giving NLP systems a real boost in "thinking" more like us. And because ML and DL help NLP keep learning from new data, these systems keep getting better at handling language naturally.

You'll see NLP in action in three main ways:

- Language processing
- Speech recognition
- Translation

In language processing, NLP can do things like sentiment analysis, which is how it picks up on emotion in text, or entity recognition, where it identifies specific names or places within content. Then there's speech recognition and synthesis: those technologies that allow your virtual assistants to understand and respond when you speak. And, of course, NLP powers translation tools, breaking down language barriers so that people from different parts of the world can connect easily.

Tokenization

Tokenization is about breaking down words and parts of words into numbers, which are known as *tokens*. This is the first step in the NLP process. It provides the framework for identifying the words or phrases that NLP models need to analyze, classify, or respond to.

Let's take an example. Suppose we have this sentence:

> Time flies like an arrow, time flies fast.

When we tokenize this sentence, each word (or token) is given an identifier. Because the words *time* and *flies* repeat, they get only one token ID even though they appear twice. Here's how it breaks down:

1. time
2. flies
3. like
4. an
5. arrow
6. fast

So our sentence becomes a sequence of tokens: [1, 2, 3, 4, 5, 1, 2, 6]—that is, there are eight words but six tokens.

Without tokenization, a computer would see the sentence as one continuous string of characters, which isn't useful for analysis. Breaking it down allows the NLP model to interpret each part separately and understand how they work together.

Here are some other considerations in tokenization:

Text normalization
> Before tokenizing, the text might be normalized. This usually means converting everything to lowercase and removing punctuation. In our example, normalization would turn "Time flies like an arrow, time flies fast" into "time flies like an arrow time flies fast." Normalization helps simplify the processing, although sometimes specific details like capitalization or punctuation are necessary. For instance, "Dr. Johnson" and "dr" convey very different meanings in a medical context where "Dr." indicates a title.

Stop-word removal
> Words like *the*, *an*, or *and* are common in most sentences but don't always add useful meaning. By removing these stop words, NLP systems can emphasize the core content. For our sentence, if we remove *like* and *an*, we're left with "time flies arrow time flies fast," which directs more attention to the essential words.

N-grams
> Sometimes, instead of breaking a sentence down to single words, NLP models capture phrases (such as bigrams for two words or trigrams for three). For example, "time flies" could be treated as a bigram to capture a specific phrase instead of treating "time" and "flies" as separate tokens. This can preserve important context, as in the case of "New York City," which, if split, might lose its meaning.

Stemming
> To make analysis clearer, similar words are often grouped together. For example, *flying*, *flew*, and *flies* could be treated as the root form *fly*. In our example, both instances of *flies* would link back to the base *fly* token, making it easier to analyze related concepts together.

Lemmatization
> This reduces words to their base form, or lemma, so that different versions of a word—such as *running*, *ran*, and *runs*—all map back to a single, consistent root form: *run*. Unlike simple stemming, which just chops off endings, lemmatization applies linguistic rules to ensure that the base form is meaningful and grammatically accurate. This process makes text analysis more precise by grouping related words.

Frequency Analysis

Once you've tokenized the words, the next step is *frequency analysis:* examining how frequently each word appears. The most common words (ignoring basics like *a*, *the*, and similar words) can hint at the main theme of the text. Take a political speech about economic growth, for example: the most frequent words might include *growth*, *jobs*, *future*, and *economy*. If we look at word pairs (bigrams), a common pair might be "new jobs," which points to a focus on employment and economic expansion.

Counting word occurrences, known as *simple frequency analysis*, works well for examining a single document. But when you're working with multiple documents, you need a way to pinpoint the most relevant words in each one. That's where *term frequency-inverse document frequency (TF-IDF)* comes in. This method scores words by how often they appear in a document compared to the entire set of documents. Words that appear often in one document but are rare in the others stand out as especially relevant.

Here are some additional considerations in frequency analysis:

Limitations of simple frequency analysis
> While simple frequency or bigram analysis offers helpful initial insights, it can miss nuances or context. Frequently used words may not always indicate the main topic, especially if they're general or if they depend on context. When analyzing complex or larger documents, more advanced methods like TF-IDF, latent Dirichlet allocation (LDA), or other topic-modeling techniques are often more insightful. *LDA* is a statistical model that identifies topics in a collection of documents by finding groups of words that frequently appear together. This helps to uncover underlying themes or subjects, making it easier to analyze and categorize large amounts of text.

Broader uses of TF-IDF
> TF-IDF isn't just for finding relevant words—it's also used in similarity analysis to group related documents, making it a powerful tool for tasks like information retrieval and recommendation systems.

Advanced contextual models
> For even more refined insights, techniques like word2vec, BERT (bidirectional encoder representations from transformers), or other contextual embeddings consider each word's meaning based on surrounding text, which brings greater clarity to themes across a document and improves tasks like summarization, sentiment analysis, and topic detection.

Text Classification

Another powerful way to analyze text is by using a classification algorithm, like logistic regression, to categorize it based on predefined labels, which is called *text classification*. A common application for this is sorting social media posts for sentiment analysis.

Let's say you're working with social media comments that are already labeled as either 0 (critical) or 1 (supportive):

- "This initiative is exactly what we need!" = 1
- "Totally disappointed with the results so far" = 0
- "Great job! Keep it up!" = 1
- "This approach misses the point entirely" = 0

With enough labeled examples, you can train a classification model that learns to distinguish between supportive and critical posts. Using the tokenized text as features and the sentiment label (0 or 1), the model starts to detect patterns. For instance, comments with words like *great*, *exactly*, or *job* tend to be supportive while words like *disappointed* or *misses* indicate criticism.

To make this work, you'll need to convert words into numbers. Basic methods like the bag-of-words model and TF-IDF score word importance based on frequency while advanced embeddings like word2vec or GloVe capture meaning based on context. Logistic regression is a good starting point, but other algorithms like naive Bayes and support vector machine (SVM), DL models like recurrent neural networks (RNNs), or transformers can boost performance, especially for larger datasets or nuanced content.

To ensure your model is effective, evaluate it with metrics like accuracy, precision, recall, and the F1 score, which reveal how well the model generalizes new data. Just keep in mind that models can struggle with subtleties like sarcasm. For example, a comment like "Love the effort…the result is certainly something" could be misinterpreted as supportive.

Classification models have plenty of uses beyond sorting social media sentiment, such as tagging news articles by category (e.g., "politics," "entertainment," or "health") or even spotting trending topics—showing just how versatile text classification can be.

Semantic Language Models

In the world of NLP, models have come a long way, making it possible to capture the deep and subtle relationships between words. The secret sauce is embeddings—essentially multidimensional number arrays that map each word, or token, to a unique point in space.

Think of each element in an embedding as a coordinate in a multidimensional space. Each token—whether it's "coffee," "latte," or "soccer"—finds its own spot in this space. Tokens that are related by meaning are closer to one another. Here's a quick example in three dimensions:

- "coffee": [9, 2, 3]
- "tea": [9, 2, 2]
- "caffeine": [8, 2, 3]
- "latte": [9, 3, 3]
- "soccer": [1, 7, 3]

Figure 7-1 shows the plotting for these items.

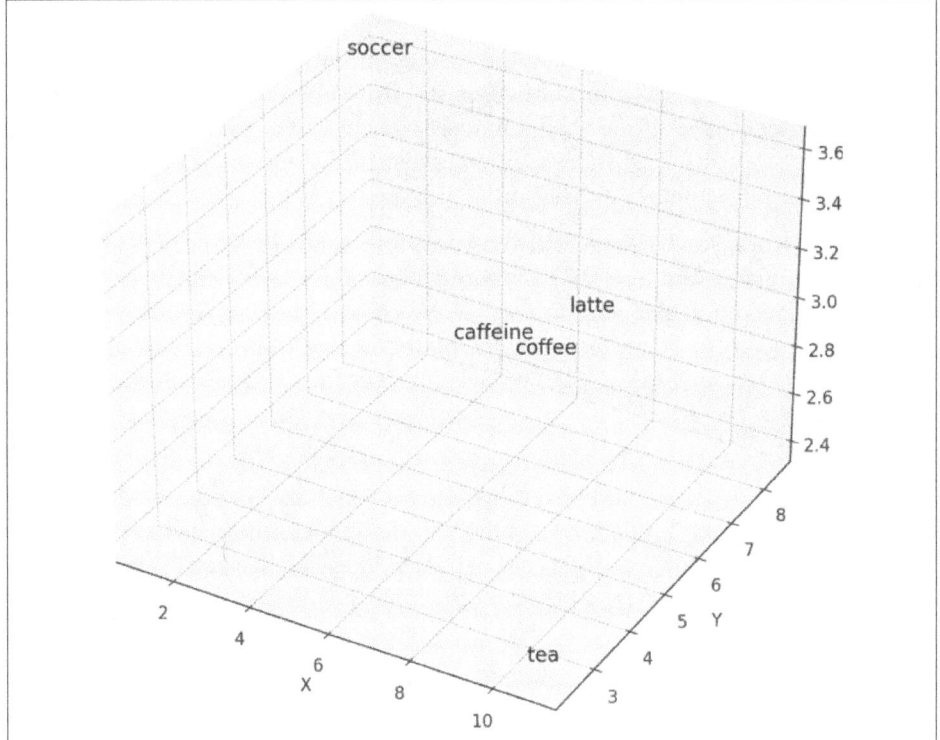

Figure 7-1. The plotting for the embeddings

The plotting shows that "coffee," caffeine," and "latte" huddle close together while "soccer" sits off to the side, indicating less of a semantic connection. This layout helps us see patterns in how words relate to one another based on meaning.

Advanced models, called *semantic language models*, take these embeddings and add complexity. For example, BERT and GPT models use what's called *contextual embeddings*. This means a word like *bank* gets a different representation in "riverbank" versus "national bank," helping models better grasp the intended meaning.

How would you visualize high-dimensional embeddings? You can use techniques like principal component analysis (PCA) or t-distributed stochastic neighbor embedding (t-SNE), which simplify these multidimensional embeddings into a two- or three-dimensional view. This makes it much easier to see the relationships between tokens. Most embeddings are initially trained on enormous datasets (think word2vec or GloVe), and they can later be fine-tuned for specialized areas, such as legal or medical content.

Learning from these embeddings often relies on self-supervised learning, where models teach themselves by predicting missing or next words. This is helpful for building multilingual embeddings, where words with similar meanings across languages find similar spots in the embedding space.

But embeddings aren't without issues. They can mirror biases present in training data, such as linking demographic groups to certain roles, which can result in skewed predictions. Correcting these biases through debiasing techniques is crucial for fair, responsible use.

Azure Services for NLP

Microsoft Azure offers three main services for NLP: Azure AI Language, Azure AI Translator, and Azure AI Speech. Let's take a look at each.

First, *Azure AI Language* enables you to understand, analyze, and respond to text data through a wide range of preconfigured and customizable features. It also has tools that cater to different levels of complexity. Table 7-1 describes the features of the service.

Table 7-1. Features of Azure AI Language

Feature	Description
Named entity recognition (NER)	Identifies entities like names, dates, and locations in unstructured text, categorizing them into groups for easy organization
PII and PHI detection	Detects, categorizes, and redacts sensitive information, including personally identifiable information (PII) and protected health information (PHI), in text
Language detection	Identifies the language of a text document and returns a code for the detected language, covering a wide range of languages and dialects
Sentiment analysis and opinion mining	Analyzes text to determine positive or negative sentiment, providing insight into customer feedback and public opinion
Summarization	Produces a concise summary of a document or transcription by extracting key sentences

Feature	Description
Key phrase extraction	Identifies the main concepts in text, returning a list of key phrases to highlight major themes or topics
Entity linking	Disambiguates terms and entities in text to references like Wikipedia, providing additional context

The second service Azure offers is *Azure AI Translator*. This service enables applications to instantly translate text into multiple languages. Table 7-2 describes the features of this service.

Table 7-2. Features of Azure AI Translator

Feature	Description
Text translation	Translates text instantly between a supported source and target languages, with options for creating custom dictionaries and managing translation exceptions
Document translation	Offers two modes: asynchronous batch translation for large sets of files, which retains the format and structure with Azure Blob Storage, and synchronous translation for individual documents, which preserves the structure without storage requirements
Custom translator	Allows customization of translation models for specific industry languages, terminology, and styles, including creating specialized dictionaries for tailored translations

The third service, *Azure AI Speech*, is geared toward converting spoken language into text and vice versa. Table 7-3 lists the features of this service.

Table 7-3. Features of Azure AI Speech

Feature	Description
Speech-to-text	Transcribes audio to text from various sources, such as microphones and audio files, in real time or with batch processing Features include speaker diarization and automatic formatting for improved readability
Real-time speech-to-text	Provides instant transcription of live audio, which is ideal for applications needing immediate text, such as live-meeting captions, pronunciation assessments, and contact center support
Text-to-speech	Converts written text to lifelike, synthesized speech using neural voices, with customization options for pitch, pronunciation, and speed
Fast transcription API	Offers a quick, synchronous transcription option for prerecorded audio, delivering results with minimal delay Suitable for urgent tasks like video transcription and fast audio processing Available through the preview API

Next, we'll take a look at these services and how they work with NLP applications.

Key Phrase Extraction

Key phrase extraction is an NLP technique that identifies the most relevant words or phrases within a text. This pinpoints the main topics or themes without needing to analyze the entire document. Key phrase extraction is a valuable tool in NLP because it enables systems to quickly grasp the core content of a text, which is essential in tasks like summarizing, content tagging, or indexing large documents.

Typical uses for key phrase extraction range across many fields. In customer service, for instance, key phrase extraction can help identify main concerns or frequently mentioned issues in customer feedback, making it easier for teams to address common problems. This technique also supports social media analysis by quickly identifying trending topics from user-generated content, such as tweets or posts, so brands can understand public sentiment or emerging discussions.

Consider a more detailed example: a company analyzing customer reviews for a new product. Using key phrase extraction, the model identifies common phrases like "easy to use," "battery life," and "customer support." These extracted phrases help the company see what features customers talk about most without having to manually read each review. Additionally, negative phrases like "difficult setup" or "short battery life" allow the company to pinpoint areas needing improvement.

Let's take a look at how you can use key phrase extraction using Azure AI Language Studio (*https://oreil.ly/8gTK0*). Once you're at the dashboard for the Language Studio, select "Extract information" and then click "Extract key phrases." You'll find different examples of text, such as for travel, medical reports, and banking. We'll select banking. This is a message from a customer who requested a cancellation for a credit card because it was lost. Click Run. Figure 7-2 shows the results.

At the top are the key phrases that were extracted. They include details like the address, linked email account, Social Security number, and SWIFT code. Below is the original text with the extracted key phrases highlighted.

```
Key phrases

1234 Hollywood Boulevard Los Angeles CA, Chicken parmigiana
dish, Linked email account, Social Security number, Hollywood
Museum, Phone number, Credit card, August 17th, last purchase,
Contoso Restaurant, personal information, Personal address, Swift
code, Mateo Gomez, name, cancellation, validation, Profession,
Accountant, Date, birth, contosorestaurant, CHASUS33XXX
```

Original text

```
Hello, my name is Mateo Gomez. I lost my Credit card on August 17th, and I would like to request its
      Ke..   Key phrase              Key phrase       Key phrase
cancellation. The last purchase I made was of a Chicken parmigiana dish at Contoso Restaurant,
Key phrase      Key phrase                      Key phrase                 Key phrase
located near the Hollywood Museum, for $40. Below is my personal information for validation:
                 Key phrase                              Key phrase            Key phra...

         Profession: Accountant
         Key phra...  Key phra...

         Social Security number is 123-45-6789
         Key phrase

         Date of birth: 9-9-1989
         Ke..     Key...

         Phone number: 949-555-0110
         Key phrase

         Personal address: 1234 Hollywood Boulevard Los Angeles CA
         Key phrase        Key phrase

         Linked email account: mateo@contosorestaurant.com
         Key phrase            Key phrase

         Swift code: CHASUS33XXX
         Key phra...  Key phrase
```

Figure 7-2. Key phrases extracted from a message about a credit card cancellation

Entity Recognition

Entity recognition, often called *named entity recognition (NER)*, is a process in AI where you teach a model to identify and classify elements, or entities, in a text. These entities could be names of people, places, organizations, dates, or even products—basically, anything meaningful and distinct in a body of text. Think of NER as a way to highlight or tag essential parts of information automatically. This makes it easier to analyze and categorize data without manual sorting.

A common use case for NER is for customer service chatbots to recognize a user's name, location, or problem type. This allows the system to personalize the responses.

In legal or financial sectors, NER can automatically extract contract dates, client names, or financial figures from documents, reducing the need for tedious human review. NER also enhances search engines, making search results more relevant by helping the engine understand the context behind keywords.

How does entity recognition actually work? It follows a few key steps. First, the model preprocesses the text by breaking it into smaller parts, like sentences or words. Then, it uses language algorithms to spot potential entities based on patterns. After that, it classifies these entities into categories, such as "person" or "organization." Finally, the model refines its guesses based on training data and produces a list of recognized entities.

Here's a quick example to bring this to life. Suppose we have this sentence: "John Doe from TechCorp called on October 10, 2024 about the quarterly report." After running it through an NER model, we get the results shown in Table 7-4.

Table 7-4. Results of using NER

Entity	Type
John Doe	Person
TechCorp	Organization
October 10, 2024	Date
Quarterly report	Miscellaneous

When using Azure AI Foundry, you can select "Extract named entities." Then, select "Medical Report" and click Run. Figure 7-3 shows a list of the entities that were found as well as the original text that marks them. If you hover over one of these highlights, you will see more details, such as the confidence level.

Named entity linking (NEL) takes NER a step further by not only identifying entities in text but also connecting them to unique, real-world references. Suppose you're reading an article that mentions Paris. With entity linking, an AI model won't just recognize Paris as a location; it will also understand whether the article refers to Paris, France, or Paris, Texas, depending on the context. Entity linking is like giving each entity a unique ID or link to a database. This mitigates confusion about what the term represents.

Entity linking comes in handy in a lot of fields. In news aggregation, it helps ensure that all references to a particular event or person, such as a CEO or celebrity, consistently point to the same profile, avoiding duplication. In health care, entity linking can automatically connect mentions of a medical condition to a knowledge base of treatments, symptoms, and research articles.

Figure 7-3. NER for a medical report

Sentiment Analysis

I mentioned sentiment analysis earlier in this chapter, but let's take a deeper look at it now. *Sentiment analysis* is like giving your AI model emotional intelligence. It allows the system to read between the lines and determine if a piece of text is positive, negative, or neutral. Essentially, sentiment analysis works by analyzing the words and phrases in a text to figure out the mood or feeling behind them. So whether you're analyzing customer reviews, social media comments, or survey responses, sentiment analysis can help you understand how people feel about a product, service, or topic without needing a human to go through everything manually.

In customer service, sentiment analysis can flag negative comments or complaints so that agents can respond more quickly. In marketing, it helps track brand reputation over time by monitoring sentiment on social media or review sites. It's also valuable in product development, where analyzing feedback can reveal trends in customer satisfaction or highlight recurring issues that need fixing.

Table 7-5 shows an example of sentiment analysis—specifically, an analysis of the following review: "The new phone's camera is fantastic, but the battery life is disappointing."

Table 7-5. Sentiment analysis of a product review

Phrase	Sentiment	Score
new phone's camera	Positive	+2
fantastic	Positive	+3
battery life	Neutral	0
disappointing	Negative	-3

The AI would then sum up these scores to produce an overall sentiment score for the review. Here, the score would likely lean toward neutral or slightly positive since the enthusiasm for the camera is balanced by disappointment with the battery.

Language Detection

Language detection is a feature of the Azure AI Language service that identifies the language of a given text. It supports more than one hundred languages. This service allows multiple documents to be processed at once. Results include:

- The language name
- The ISO 639-1 language code (a two-letter code like "fr" that is part of an international standard for language representation)
- A confidence score

To illustrate, let's say you operate a travel forum where users post feedback about destinations worldwide. Here are three examples of feedback you receive:

- Feedback 1: "An amazing spot for birdwatching and hiking."
- Feedback 2: "Le personnel était très accueillant et serviable."
- Feedback 3: "Il posto perfetto per rilassarsi con la famiglia."

Table 7-6 shows the results that Azure AI Language provides.

Table 7-6. Language detection for a message forum

Document	Language	ISO 639-1 code	Confidence score
Feedback 1	English	en	0.8
Feedback 2	French	fr	1.0
Feedback 3	Italian	it	0.9

When a comment includes a mix of languages, Azure focuses on the predominant one. This provides a single language label with a confidence score that might be slightly lower if multiple languages are detected. In cases where the content is minimal or ambiguous, such as with a simple emoji or symbol, Azure might label the language as "unknown" and leave the language identifier empty, with a "NaN" (not a number) score to indicate that it couldn't confidently determine a language.

Speech Recognition and Synthesis

When it comes to AI and speech, there are two key skills that make it all work: speech recognition and speech synthesis. *Speech recognition* is what allows AI to listen to spoken input and understand what's being said. *Speech synthesis*, on the other hand, is how AI generates spoken output. This essentially gives it the ability to "talk" back to you. Together, these capabilities make it possible for AI to engage in a natural, back-and-forth conversation, creating more interactive and personal experiences.

Speech recognition

Speech recognition technology powers many day-to-day conveniences:

Meeting transcription
    AI can create a full transcript of your Zoom call or meeting, so you can stay focused without taking notes.

Real-time captions
    In a livestream, captions make it so you do not miss any details.

Voice-activated customer service
    You can talk to the system and not have to navigate menu options. The AI will understand and connect you to what you are looking for.

Dictation
    Speak freely, and AI transcribes your words into notes, which is ideal for capturing ideas quickly or managing daily tasks hands-free.

How does speech recognition work? It begins with capturing your audio input, then moves to feature extraction, where the AI isolates and analyzes sound features. An acoustic model translates these features into phonemes, then a language model maps phonemes to words using statistical probabilities. Finally, a decoding process refines the output. This creates clear and accurate text from spoken language.

To see this in Azure, you can go to the Speech Studio (*https://oreil.ly/zlmtI*) and select "Real-time speech to text." Select a language and then either upload an audio file or create one. Speak into your computer's microphone, and the system will convert your words into text as you speak. It will even create a *.wav* audio file that you can download. You can see this in Figure 7-4.

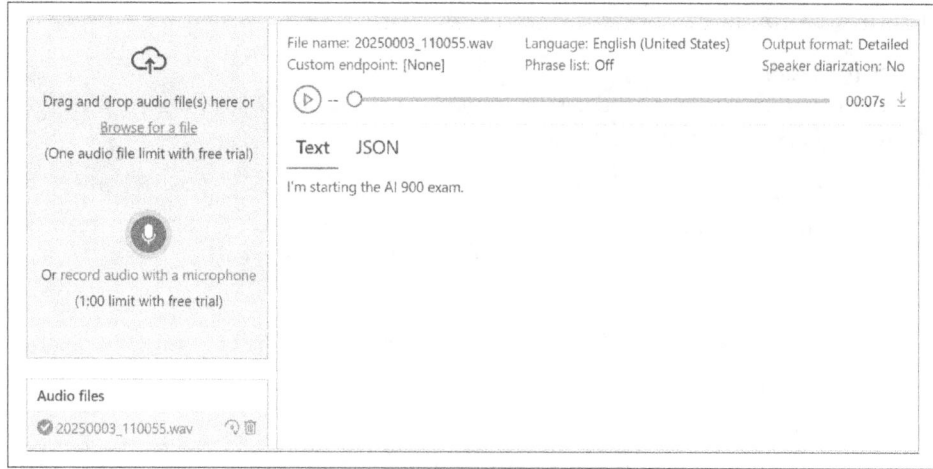

Figure 7-4. The speech-to-text capabilities of Azure

When you look at the JSON, you'll see a detailed description of the output, including the offsets and duration for each word. Here's a snippet:

```
{
    "Confidence": 0.6879325,
    "Lexical": "i'm studying the AI nine hundred exam",
    "ITN": "i'm studying the AI 900 exam",
    "MaskedITN": "i'm studying the ai 900 exam",
    "Display": "I'm studying the AI 900 exam.",
    "Words": [
        {
            "Word": "i'm",
            "Offset": 10800000,
            "Duration": 2400000
        },
        {
            "Word": "studying",
            "Offset": 13200000,
            "Duration": 4000000
        },
```

Speech synthesis

Under the hood, speech synthesis relies on a few essential steps. It starts with text analysis, breaking down the text's structure and meaning. Then prosody and acoustic modeling add tone, pitch, and emphasis, giving the speech a natural cadence. Finally, waveform generation turns all of this into audio, creating a clear, humanlike voice. With these capabilities, speech synthesis provides a more engaging, interactive experience that feels like a true conversation.

Here are a few of the use cases for speech synthesis:

Hands-free reading
Speech synthesis reads articles, messages, or notes aloud, keeping you engaged while you're multitasking.

Step-by-step guidance
When you are following a recipe or workout, for instance, an app can read the instructions aloud, so you can stay focused without a screen.

Virtual assistant responses
A friendly voice responds to your questions, whether you're checking the weather forecast or asking for directions.

Public announcements
Speech synthesis makes it easy to broadcast important information, creating clear and easily understood public messages.

GPS navigation
A GPS system guides you turn by turn, reading out directions so that you can stay focused on the road.

Translation

When we are working across cultures and languages, breaking down language barriers becomes essential. Sure, hiring multilingual individuals can help, but with the sheer number of languages and their combinations, scaling this approach quickly becomes a challenge. Enter *machine translation*—automated systems designed to bridge linguistic gaps.

Machine translation provides a scalable solution to language barriers, yet it's not as simple as replacing one word with another. Words alone don't carry the full weight of meaning. Tone, context, and intent have to make the jump, too.

To meet this challenge, machine translation technology needs to go beyond just understanding individual words. It has to grasp the full picture, considering factors like context, informal or formal tone, slang, and unique grammar rules. Only then can it provide translations that feel natural and stay true to the original intent.

You've probably encountered text translation in everyday tools: from translating a government document to clicking the Translate button on social media posts. Then there's speech translation, which allows spoken language to be translated directly from one language to another. Whether it's converting spoken words to text before translation or delivering a voice-to-voice translation, this technology is making real-time, cross-language conversations easier.

Machine translation relies on advanced algorithms and neural networks. These networks process enormous amounts of multilingual text data to understand linguistic patterns, structures, and meanings across languages. By mapping out how words relate to one another in various languages, the system learns to create more accurate translations.

The beauty of machine translation lies in its continuous improvement. As these systems interact with users and process new language data, they refine their accuracy over time. This iterative learning helps AI stay up-to-date with evolving language trends and cultural nuances.

Conversational Language Understanding

Conversational language understanding (CLU) makes it possible for you to create language models that understand and respond to everyday conversational phrases. Suppose you're telling a virtual assistant, "Dim the kitchen lights." With CLU, the assistant not only understands the command but also knows exactly which lights you mean, so you get precisely the response you're looking for. This tool is particularly useful for applications that involve command and control, customer support, or large-scale enterprise solutions.

To build an effective model, you'll work with three essential elements:

Utterances
Examples of things users might say, such as "Lower the blinds in the living room."

Entities
Specific items in an utterance. In "Start the coffee maker," "coffee maker" is the entity—it tells the system what to act on.

Intents
The purpose behind an utterance. For "Start the coffee maker," the intent might be "PowerOn," indicating that the user wants to turn the device on.

Putting it all together, these components guide the model to recognize different actions. Table 7-7 is a snapshot of how these might look.

Table 7-7. CLU elements

Intent	Sample utterances	Entities
Farewell	"See you later," "goodbye"	N/A
PowerOn	"Turn on the heater"	Heater (device)
PowerOff	"Shut off the TV"	TV (device)
CheckNews	"Give me the latest news"	N/A
None	"Why is the sky blue?"	N/A

The "None" intent acts as a catchall for any input that doesn't fit a defined intent, so your model can gracefully handle unexpected questions or irrelevant statements.

Getting a CLU model to work well involves a few steps:

Define your schema
  Think about what your model needs to know. Identify the intents for user actions and the specific entities you want to capture.

Label your data
  Properly label each utterance with the relevant intents and entities—this step is crucial for accurate training.

Train your model
  Your model learns from labeled examples, gradually improving its ability to recognize patterns and predict outcomes.

Evaluate its performance
  Test the model to see how accurately it identifies intents and entities with new data.

Refine and retrain
  Based on your model's test performance, you may need to adjust and retrain to boost accuracy.

Deploy the model
  When it's ready, deploy the model so that you can use it to interpret real-world user inputs via the Runtime API.

Here are some popular ways you could use CLU:

Enterprise bots
  Within large companies, CLU-based bots can streamline tasks like finding HR resources, answering FAQs, or helping with scheduling by coordinating with multiple services.

Health care virtual assistants
  A virtual assistant could assist patients with scheduling appointments, provide medication reminders, or even help triage symptoms. It could automate tasks for health care staff, such as patient check-ins or answering frequently asked questions about health services.

Ecommerce recommendations
  In an online shopping app, CLU can help a virtual assistant understand natural language shopping requests like "Show me sports jackets under $100" or "I need a gift for a 10-year-old." The assistant could then retrieve relevant items, making the shopping experience smoother.

Conversational AI

Imagine this: you're a customer, and it's midnight. You've got a question about a product, and you want a quick answer—without waiting for a support team or diving into lengthy documentation. That's where conversational AI steps in, ready to assist you at any hour, across multiple platforms, from web chat to social media.

With *conversational AI*—specifically through "bots"—companies can keep up with customer demands for fast, personal responses. These bots are designed to answer questions, troubleshoot issues, and guide you, all in natural, friendly language. And when they're powered by tools like Azure AI Language's question-answering feature, they can go a step further. This feature allows bots to provide real-time answers to common questions and handle multipart conversations naturally, passing you to a human only if the question is more complex.

An important element behind a bot's effectiveness is its integration with a relevant knowledge base filled with question-and-answer pairs. A well-informed bot, connected to a company's repository of Q&A content, can respond with accurate, up-to-date information that reflects the latest products, services, and FAQs. This setup ensures that customers receive reliable answers and reduces the risk of customers being misled by outdated or irrelevant information.

Let's check out an example. Go to the Azure AI Language Studio (*https://oreil.ly/Sd_hv*) and create an Azure search resource: Click "Create new" and select "Custom question answering."

You will then go through a series of screens for the configuration. First is "Choose language setting." Here, select English and click Next. You'll be taken to the "Enter basic information" section. Enter a name for the project and a description, then select "No answer found" for the default when the AI cannot find an answer to a user question. Press Next and then select "Create Project."

Figure 7-5 shows the dashboard.

On the top left of the screen, click "Add source," and you'll see some menu options. This is where you can add a knowledge base, whether through a URL or file. We'll select the option for URL and use this one (*https://oreil.ly/vd6nx*). This is Microsoft Azure's FAQ for conversational language understanding (you can also add more than one URL). Click the customized URL, and you'll see the screen in Figure 7-6.

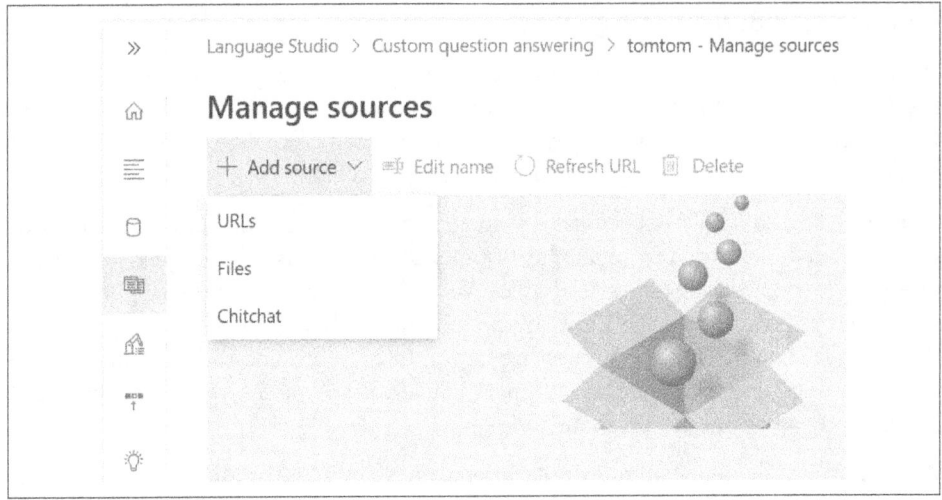

Figure 7-5. The dashboard for creating a conversational AI system for a knowledge base

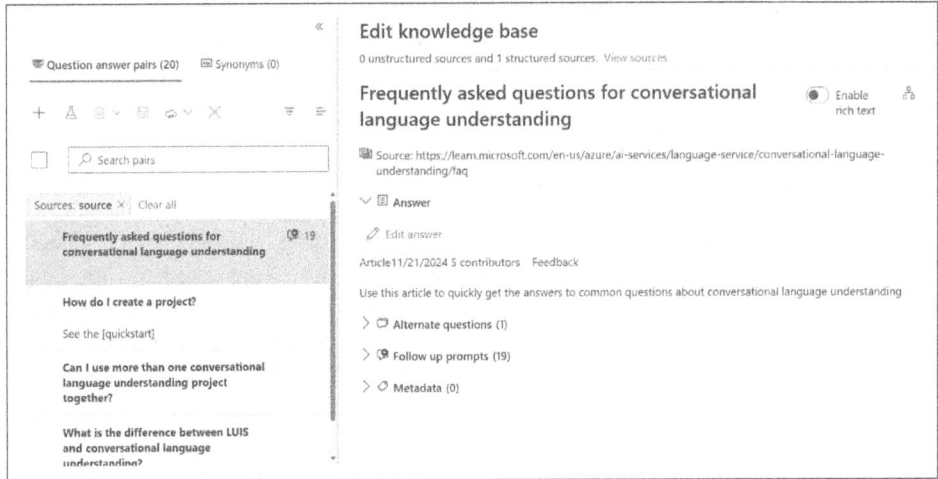

Figure 7-6. The screen for the knowledge base that Azure AI created

On the left side of the screen, you can see how Azure AI Language has parsed the FAQ into question-answer pairs. If you click one of them, you get different options to customize a question:

- Edit the answer.
- Add alternate phrasings for questions when there are multiple ways users might ask the same thing. These alternate questions should be as different as possible in wording while keeping the meaning intact, and the list should be limited to a maximum of 10 variations.

- Incorporate follow-up prompts to link question-and-answer pairs in multiturn conversations. This linkage allows the client application to deliver a primary answer while offering additional questions for the user to choose from if needed. To see all the connections for a specific question-and-answer pair, select "view context tree."
- Assign metadata tags to help the client application refine the results of a user query. For instance, a question like "What are the store hours?" might yield different responses depending on the specific store location—such as if the metadata is "Location: New York" versus "Location: Los Angeles." By using metadata tags, the application can deliver answers tailored to the user's specific needs.

You can test this by clicking the flask icon on the top left of the screen. Figure 7-7 shows the chatbot for this.

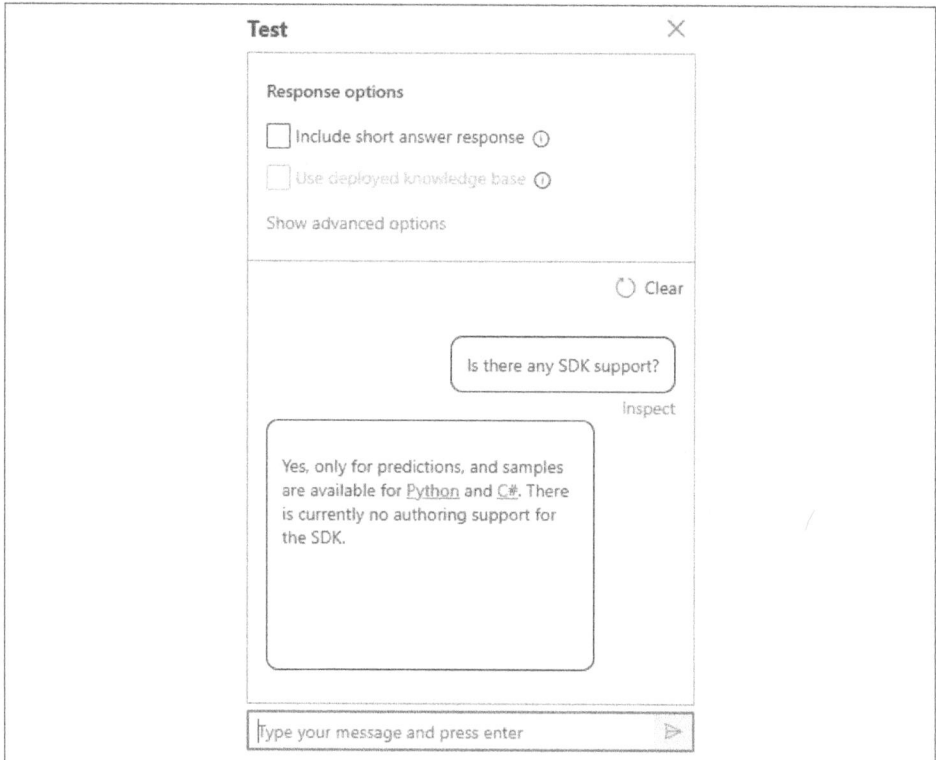

Figure 7-7. The chatbot that tests a knowledge base AI system

As you can see, I asked, "Is there any SDK support?" And I got the correct answer, with clickable links.

If you click Inspect, you will get an analysis for how the AI came up with the answer. There will also be a confidence score.

Conclusion

We've explored key topics like NLP, tokenization, frequency analysis, and other foundational concepts that form the backbone of AI understanding. Each of these areas is essential not only for understanding how AI works but also for navigating the specific questions you'll encounter on the AI-900 exam.

Quiz

To check your answers, please refer to the "Chapter 7 Answer Key" on page 185.

1. Which of the following Azure AI Services enables instant translation of text into multiple languages?

    a. Azure AI Language

    b. Azure AI Speech

    c. Azure AI Translator

    d. Azure AI Sentiment

2. What is the primary function of named entity recognition (NER) in NLP?

    a. To analyze sentiment

    b. To detect language

    c. To identify and categorize entities

    d. To extract key phrases

3. Which feature of Azure AI Speech allows for real-time transcription of live audio?

    a. Text-to-speech

    b. Summarization

    c. Real-time speech-to-text

    d. Custom Translator

4. What is tokenization in the context of NLP?

    a. Assigning a unique identifier to each entity

    b. Converting text to speech

    c. Breaking text into individual words or phrases

    d. Detecting language in text

5. Which of the following best describes Azure's key phrase extraction feature?

    a. It categorizes entities in text.

    b. It highlights main concepts or themes.

    c. It detects the language of a document.

    d. It analyzes sentiment in text.

6. Which NLP feature in Azure would be most suitable for identifying sensitive information like Social Security numbers?

    a. Language detection

    b. Key phrase extraction

    c. PII detection

    d. Sentiment analysis

7. Which term refers to removing common words that don't add meaning, like *the* and *an*, during NLP processing?

    a. Lemmatization

    b. Stop-word removal

    c. Tokenization

    d. Frequency analysis

8. In the Azure AI Language Studio, which feature would you use to automatically link an entity like "Paris" to a specific reference?

    a. Entity recognition

    b. Entity linking

    c. Language detection

    d. Summarization

9. What is the purpose of the Fast Transcription API in Azure AI Speech?

    a. To translate text

    b. To provide quick, synchronous transcription of audio

    c. To detect sentiment in audio

    d. To convert text to lifelike speech

10. Which Azure feature can be used to summarize large volumes of text by extracting key sentences?

    a. Text-to-speech

    b. Summarization

    c. Language detection

    d. Entity recognition

CHAPTER 8
Features of Generative AI Workloads on Azure

About 15%–20% of the AI-900 exam is about features and scenarios for generative AI, which we'll cover in this chapter. This includes understanding how models generate responses, create images, and write code snippets. We'll also look at typical scenarios for generative AI, so you can connect theoretical knowledge with practical applications. This part of the exam isn't just about knowing what generative AI is—it's about recognizing its impact and relevance in real-world use cases.

Another key area on the exam involves responsible AI. This includes understanding the ethical implications of AI-generated content and the measures that Microsoft Azure takes to ensure its generative AI tools are used safely and responsibly. By mastering these topics, you'll be well prepared to answer questions on how Azure's generative AI services can be effectively and responsibly applied across various domains.

Understanding Generative AI

At its core, generative AI relies on models trained to understand and respond to language in ways that feel intuitive and humanlike. When you ask generative AI to generate content, it draws on massive amounts of data and applies mathematical algorithms to make this possible.

Generative AI has quickly become a centerpiece of the business world. It has attracted attention from industries across the board for its potential to streamline tasks, foster creativity, and drive productivity. Breakthrough applications like OpenAI's ChatGPT and Microsoft's Copilot platform have shown just how transformative this technology can be. ChatGPT, for instance, has opened up new ways to handle customer service, content creation, and brainstorming, all with remarkable efficiency and personalization. Meanwhile, Microsoft's Copilot integrates directly into widely used tools like Word and Excel, empowering professionals to handle complex data, draft reports, and automate routine processes.

One of the easiest ways to work with generative AI is by simply typing in natural language. You type a prompt, which is a straightforward request, and the AI responds with what you're looking for. Figure 8-1 shows an example of this when using Microsoft Copilot (*https://oreil.ly/2Oy0y*). This is the prompt:

> Write a professional bio introducing me as a project manager with a background in software development and a passion for team leadership.

Microsoft Copilot then writes up a good response.

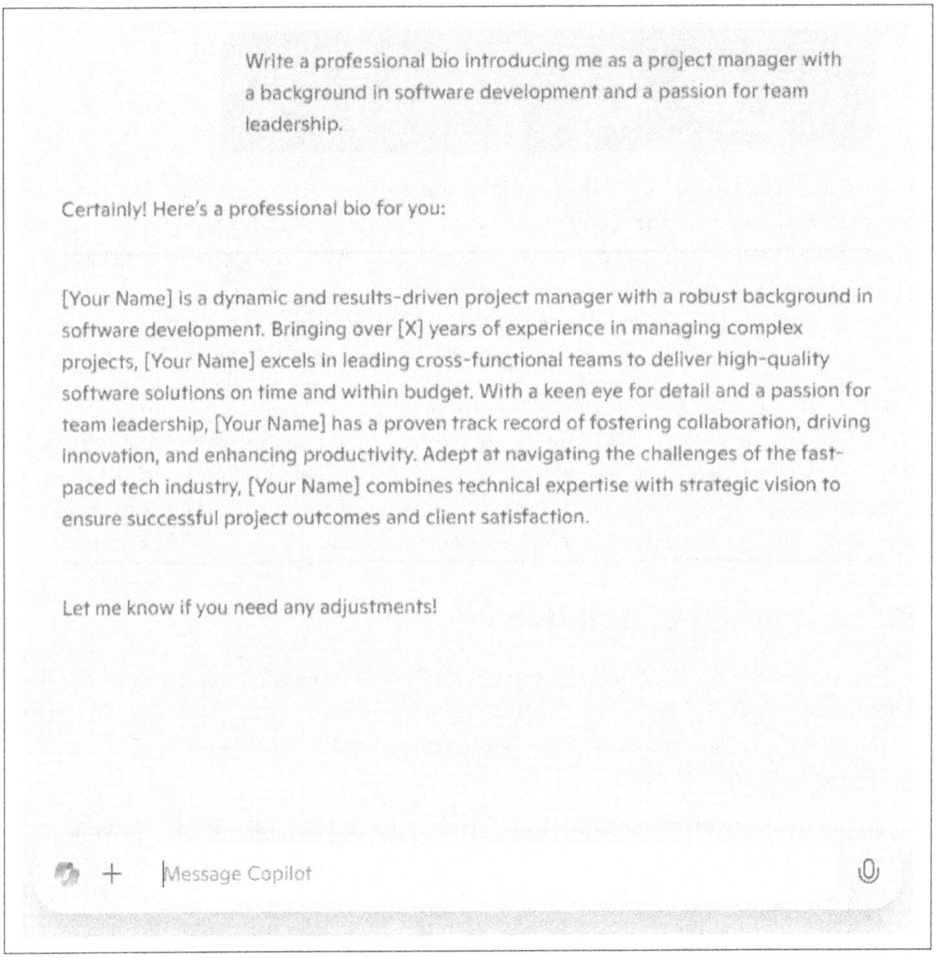

Figure 8-1. A text response to a prompt when using Microsoft Copilot

Certain generative AI tools can take a simple request and transform it into a unique image. For instance, you might type: "Design an inviting book cover for a cozy mystery novel set in a small town." Figure 8-2 shows the image generated by Microsoft Copilot.

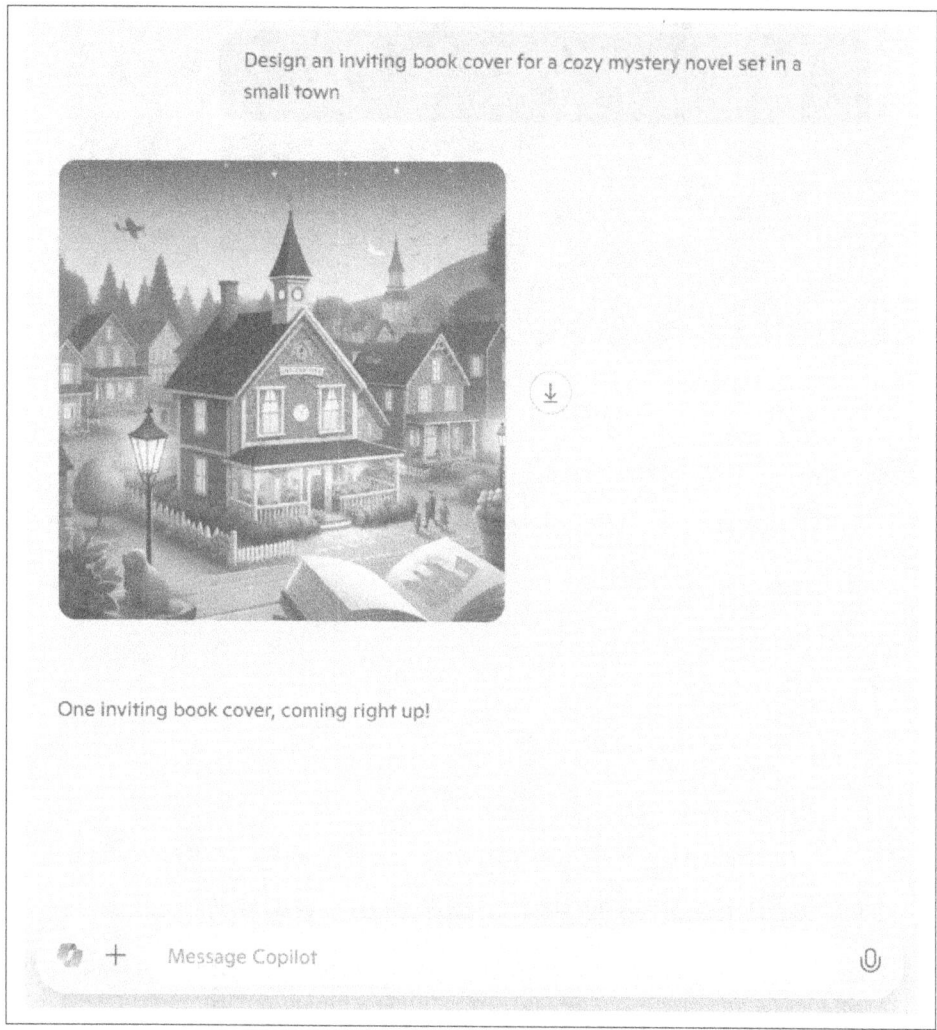

Figure 8-2. An image created by Microsoft Copilot in response to a prompt

Finally, generative AI can create, debug, and review code for dozens of languages, including C++, Java, and Python. Here's a prompt:

> Write Python code to calculate the area of a circle, given its radius.

Figure 8-3 shows the result.

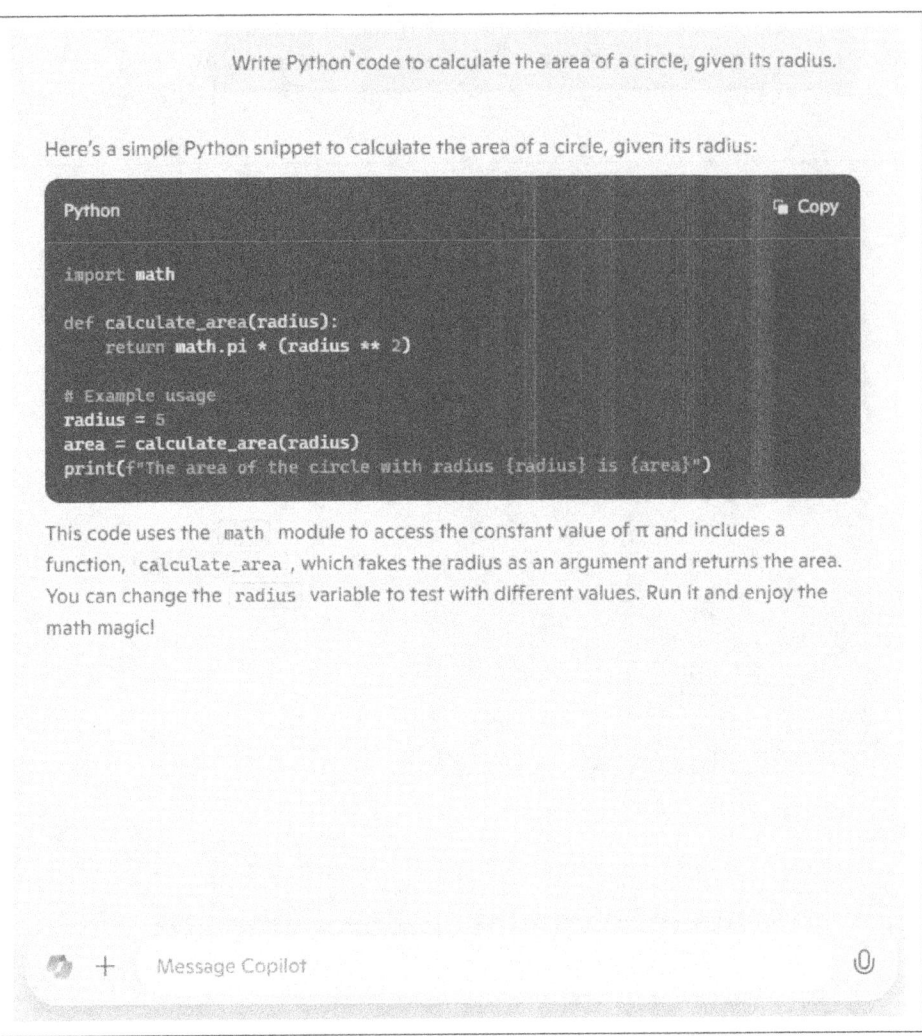

Figure 8-3. How Microsoft Copilot creates code in response to a prompt

Microsoft Copilot generates the code that you request. You can click on the top right to copy the code and use it in your integrated development environment (IDE), like Visual Studio Code. Copilot also provides a brief description of how the program works.

Advanced Language Models

Generative AI applications leverage advanced language models—specialized ML systems crafted for NLP tasks. These models bring a powerful, flexible toolkit that goes well beyond generating text and images. Here's a snapshot of their diverse capabilities:

Pattern recognition through unsupervised learning
   AI can detect patterns and structures in large datasets without labeled data, allowing it to uncover insights autonomously.

Interpretation of ambiguity
   Models decipher ambiguous language by analyzing context. This makes them suitable for nuanced tasks like sentiment analysis or handling complex customer inquiries.

Summarization
   Models rapidly distill lengthy content, pulling out essential points—key for making dense reports, legal briefs, or news summaries accessible.

Multilingual translation
   With a grasp of cultural nuances and contextual subtleties, these models accurately translate languages.

Contextual responses to questions
   The models respond to questions based on context—for example, to bolster customer support and make helpdesk interactions smoother.

Lifelike dialogue creation
   Generative AI produces realistic conversations, ideal for virtual assistants, chatbots, and dynamic character interactions.

Anomaly detection
   By identifying irregular patterns, these models catch inconsistencies, whether in financial data, health care records, or security logs.

Semantic search
   Rather than relying solely on keywords, AI performs searches based on meaning. This helps users find relevant information with minimal effort.

Personalized recommendations
   AI tailors content and recommendations based on user profiles, which is valuable for marketing, customer service, and enhancing user experience.

Content moderation
   These models can identify and flag inappropriate or sensitive content, which can promote safer and more compliant digital spaces.

The Transformer Model

ML models for NLP have evolved dramatically, leading to today's advanced systems built on the transformer architecture. This architecture has changed how machines handle language. Using the large amount of data they're trained on, these models learn the subtle connections between words, which allows them to predict sequences that feel natural and make sense.

Transformers are built with two key components:

Encoder block
    Examines the input text and identifies meaningful relationships within the vocabulary

Decoder block
    Uses the encoder's output to generate relevant and contextually appropriate language

Let's take a closer look at how it all comes together. During training, the model processes vast amounts of text from books, websites, and other sources. It breaks down this information into tokens (small units like words or parts of words) and feeds these to the encoder. With a process called *attention*, the encoder figures out how each token relates to others, recognizing patterns such as the difference between *bat* as in a flying mammal versus a piece of sports equipment. These relationships are stored as embeddings, which are mathematical vectors representing each token's meaning. The decoder then takes these embeddings and generates a new sequence of text. For instance, if you provide the input "The mysterious package arrived," the model might continue with "at my doorstep," based on similar sentences it learned during training.

Different transformer models use these blocks in specialized ways. Google's BERT model, for example, leverages the encoder to understand context in search results. OpenAI's GPT model focuses on the decoder, which makes it a powerful tool for generating creative content and answering questions in natural, conversational language.

In the next few sections, we'll look deeper at the key components of the transformer model.

Tokenization for transformers

In the previous chapter, we dove into the concept of tokenization. Let's continue building on that. Tokenization is the essential first step in training a transformer model.

OpenAI uses the Tokenizer (*https://oreil.ly/PGIwn*), an example of which is shown in Figure 8-4. The Tokenizer converts text into tokens and IDs.

At the top, you can select different types of models to use: GPT-4o/GPT-4o mini, GPT-3.5/GPT-4, or GPT-3 (legacy). You'll need to know what model you're using because tokenization is different based on the model.

For the example in Figure 8-4, we used this sentence:

> Artificial intelligence 👑 like machine learning and natural language processing, is transforming industries from healthcare to finance, sparking innovation in data-driven decision-making.

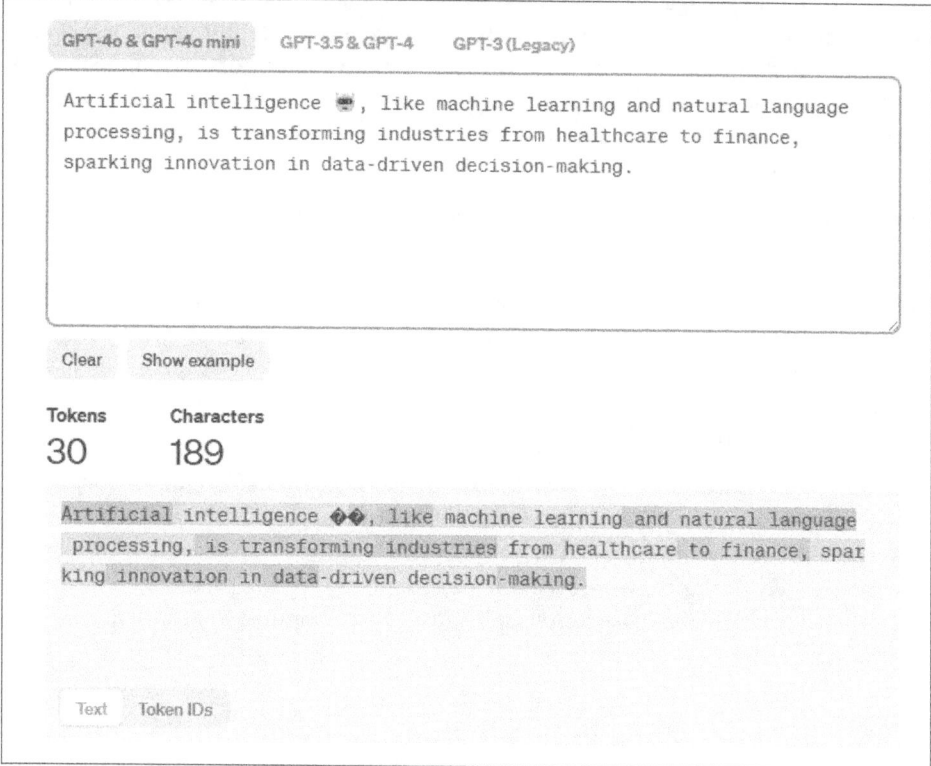

Figure 8-4. An example of OpenAI's Tokenizer, which converts text into tokens for an LLM

Notice that a token can include a space with a word. It can also be for a punctuation mark or an emoji. In some cases, one word may be composed of two or more tokens.

If you click Token IDs, you will get the vector for the tokenization:

> [186671, 22990, 93643, 244, 11, 1299, 7342, 7524, 326, 6247, 6439, 12323, 11, 382, 64779, 22751, 591, 20072, 316, 17496, 11, 30281, 6962, 21879, 306, 1238, 45932, 8660, 42074, 13]

This is what the transformer model will process.

As the model undergoes further training, each additional token from the training data is incorporated into the vocabulary and assigned a unique token ID. Over time, with an expansive enough dataset, the vocabulary can grow to encompass thousands of tokens.

Embeddings

Imagine trying to navigate a large library with nothing but a list of book titles, each assigned a unique number. Sure, the numbers help you locate individual books, but they offer no clues about the content of each book, its genre, or any connections it might have with other books. When it comes to representing words as token IDs in a vocabulary, it's a similar situation: yes, it's useful for indexing, but it lacks any insight into meaning or relationships.

To build a more meaningful map of language, we use embeddings, which we learned about in the previous chapter.

In a vector space, words with similar meanings end up near one another, with directions in the space signifying their relationships. For instance, words like *king* and *queen* may point in nearly identical directions but differ slightly in their dimensions, distinguishing masculine and feminine concepts. This semantic proximity enables embeddings to capture subtle relationships.

Creating these embeddings is no small feat, though. Algorithms like word2vec, which use neural networks to process massive amounts of text, or the transformer models powering advanced AI today identify patterns and context from countless words used in sentences. For instance, word2vec calculates embeddings by predicting word contexts whereas transformers use more sophisticated architectures to represent relationships at various levels of abstraction.

Attention

The transformer model's encoder and decoder blocks are like layers of a sandwich, stacked up to build the neural network. While we don't need to go over every ingredient in that sandwich, there's one that's essential in both blocks: the attention layers. This is where the model pays attention to relationships between words in a sequence. It's about reading a sentence and figuring out which words have the strongest connections to one another.

Let's start with the encoder block. This is the part that takes each word in a sentence and looks at it in the context of the words around it. The result? Each word gets an *encoding*—basically, a unique representation based on the company it keeps. Think of it this way: the word *cell* means one thing in the phrase "cell phone" and something totally different in "jail cell." In this encoder, the model adjusts the encoding for *cell* based on which other words it's hanging out with.

In the decoder block, attention is used a bit differently. Here, the model is generating text one word at a time. For every new word, the decoder block considers all the words it's generated so far to figure out what comes next. For instance, if you start with "He grabbed his umbrella," the decoder might zero in on *grabbed* and *umbrella* to predict that the next word could be *and* or *opened*. It's like the model is trying to complete a sentence by keeping an eye on the context it has already built.

But there's something special going on under the hood: *self-attention*. This is where each word gets weighed against others in the sentence to find out how much influence it should have on the meaning. In practical terms, self-attention gives different weights (or importance) to words depending on how they relate to one another. *Multihead attention* takes this to the next level by analyzing several relationships at once, enabling the model to capture all the nuances in a sentence.

Of course, the model doesn't actually "see" words; it's working with numeric vectors (essentially lists of numbers) that represent the words. At the start, each word gets an initial value based on where it is in the sequence—think of it as a first guess. Then, the attention layers refine these vectors by applying weights, which let the model zero in on the most relevant bits of information for predicting the next word.

When training this model, we know the full sequence of words, so the model can learn from the actual outcome by comparing its predictions to the real sequence. This process—where it adjusts its own "attention" to get better over time—is called *minimizing loss*.

So what does this mean in action? A transformer model like GPT-4, which powers tools like ChatGPT, takes in a piece of text (a prompt) and generates a response that sounds coherent and natural. While it doesn't understand or know things the way humans do, it uses massive amounts of data and complex patterns to predict what comes next in a way that often sounds spot-on.

Language Models on Azure

Building your own language model from scratch is certainly possible, but the costs are huge—not just in time but in dollars. Training an LLM from scratch can easily cost millions. You'd need hundreds of powerful GPUs running nonstop for weeks (or even months), plus funding to cover the cost of storing and processing vast amounts of data. Most organizations find it far more practical to start with an existing *foundation model* and fine-tune it with their own data if needed. With so many options available, you can skip the heavy lifting and the financial burden.

If you're using Microsoft Azure, you'll find these foundation models in two main places: the Azure OpenAI Service and the Azure AI Model Catalog. Think of the Model Catalog as a curated library of models that Azure has handpicked for data scientists and developers working with Azure AI Foundry and Azure Machine Learning. Plus, when you're using models from the Azure OpenAI service, you get the full benefit of Azure's secure, scalable infrastructure.

The Model Catalog is also loaded with open source models from a growing list of Azure's partners, including:

- OpenAI
- Hugging Face
- Mistral AI
- Meta
- Anthropic
- AI21 Labs
- Cohere
- EleutherAI
- Stability AI

Some of the popular models you'll find in Azure OpenAI include:

GPT-3.5 Turbo, GPT-4, and GPT-4o
  These are the go-to models for conversation-based applications. Just feed them some text, and they'll give you well-formed responses.

GPT-4 Turbo with Vision
  This one does more than just text—it can analyze images and respond with detailed descriptions or answers. It combines language processing with visual understanding.

DALL-E
  Looking to create images from scratch or make edits to existing images? DALL-E is your tool for generating unique images, and adding variations.

Beyond these, Azure's Model Catalog includes a range of other models suited for various applications:

Stable Diffusion by Stability AI
  Generates photorealistic images from text prompts

BERT
  Focuses on understanding text, making it great for applications like sentiment analysis and question answering

Contrastive Language-Image Pretraining (CLIP)
  Connects images with text descriptions, such as for multimedia applications

Large Language and Small Language Models

There are two main types of language models you can choose from to power your generative AI applications: *large language models (LLMs)* and *small language models (SLMs)*. Table 8-1 highlights the differences.

Table 8-1. Differences between LLMs and SLMs

Features	LLMs	SLMs
Training costs	Training an LLM is a major investment as it requires extensive compute power and specialized equipment to handle large datasets.	Training SLMs is generally more affordable as the smaller datasets and simpler model structures reduce resource demands.
Inference speed	The large parameter count of LLMs can slow their response times, which may affect their suitability for real-time applications.	With fewer parameters, SLMs often respond faster, making them ideal for real-time use cases.
Memory requirements	LLMs require high memory and storage capacity, especially with very large parameter counts.	SLMs need less memory, making them easier to deploy on devices with limited resources, such as mobile or edge devices.
Scalability	LLMs are frequently deployed in the cloud, allowing them to scale for larger or more intensive applications.	SLMs are easier to scale with fewer resources and often don't need cloud hosting, which can save on costs and enhance privacy.
Data privacy	Cloud-based deployment of LLMs often involves transferring data off-device, which could be a concern for privacy-sensitive applications.	SLMs can be deployed on devices or on premises, allowing data to remain securely within the organization, which can improve privacy.
Energy consumption	LLMs are more power intensive, leading to higher operating costs and a larger environmental impact.	SLMs consume less energy, making them more suitable for eco-friendly applications and improving battery life on portable devices.

Copilots

Copilots are changing the way we interact with software. They bring AI-powered assistance directly into applications to help with everything from quick tasks to complex processes. Built as chat-based tools, these copilots are designed to provide on-demand, tailored support that's ready whenever you need it.

Copilots are also a key part of Microsoft's AI strategy, which is important to know for the exam. This technology is embedded across various Microsoft products and built with an open architecture that allows for flexibility and customization. Developers can add their own plug-ins or even create completely new copilots to shape unique user experiences. Whether you're working with an out-of-the-box copilot or crafting a custom one, you can adjust it to fit with your business processes. This ensures that the copilot responds just the way you need.

These copilots do more than just automate—they assist with drafting, summarizing, planning, and more, aiming to boost productivity, encourage creativity, and keep teams connected. Whether you're using prebuilt tools, customizing them for specific workflows, or designing unique copilots, these AI assistants adapt to your needs and redefine the way you work and collaborate.

In the next few sections, we'll take a look at the different copilot systems from Microsoft.

Web-based copilots

Microsoft has different ways to access Microsoft Copilot using web-based applications. Earlier in the chapter, we saw one, which is the Microsoft Copilot site. You can also access Microsoft Copilot in the Bing search engine as shown in Figure 8-5. To access Copilot in Bing, click the icon to the right side of the search box.

Figure 8-5. Access Microsoft Copilot in Bing by clicking the icon on the right side of the search box

You can also access this feature in the Microsoft Edge browser. When you open the browser, you will see a search box at the top, and Copilot will be on the right side.

But the Edge browser can also embed Copilot into the sidebar. You activate this by clicking the icon on the top right side of the browser. You can see the sidebar in Figure 8-6.

The interface has many useful options. At the top of the Copilot sidebar, you can choose between a chat mode and one to create content, such as for emails, blogs, or brainstorming. You can write your content in different tones, ranging from professional to casual to funny. You can also specify the length. The Chat feature is similar to ChatGPT, but you have the option to specify the conversation style, which is either: more creative, balanced, or precise.

In the input box at the bottom, you can click the top to indicate what you want to chat about. This can be certain webpages, such as the current page of the site you have visited or other sites. The icons at the bottom enable you to upload images, add a screenshot, and use the voice system.

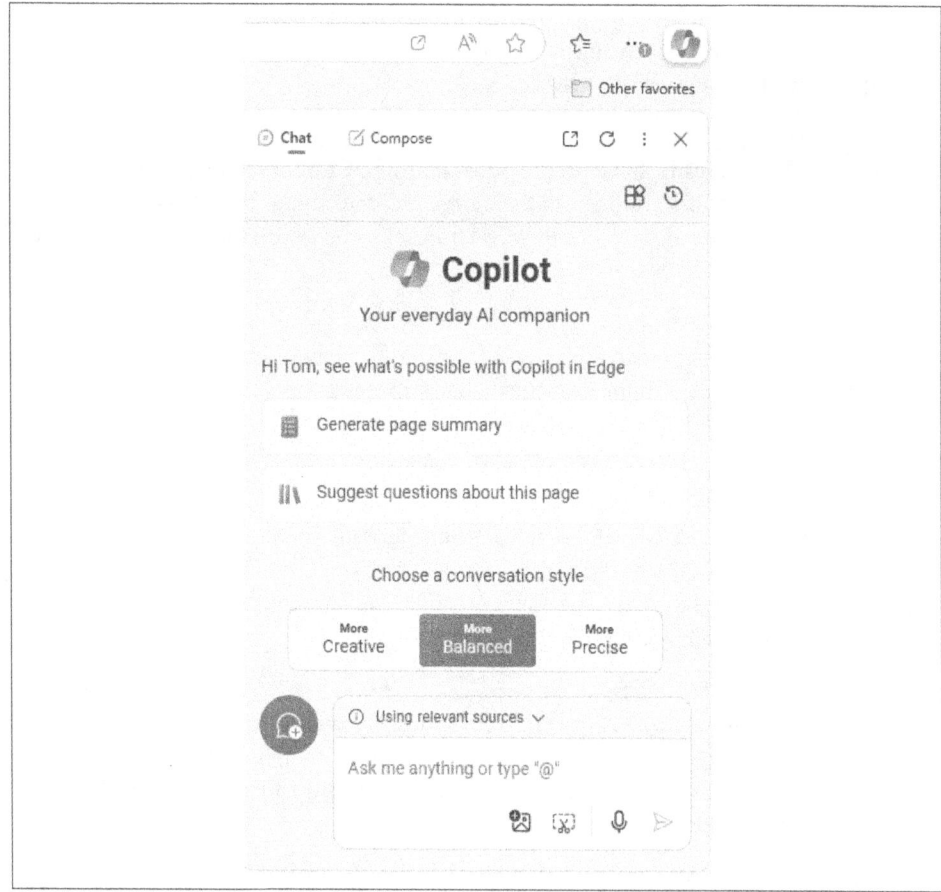

Figure 8-6. The Copilot sidebar in the Edge browser

Microsoft Copilot for Microsoft 365

Microsoft Copilot for Microsoft 365 puts powerful AI right into the tools you already know—Word, PowerPoint, Outlook, Excel, and Teams—so you can get more done without breaking your workflow. Here's how Copilot can help you in each of these apps:

Microsoft Word
  With Copilot, you can keep improving your document without starting from scratch.

Microsoft PowerPoint
  Got a report or email that you need to turn into a presentation? Copilot will create the slides from the content you already have. You can then adjust the format, add images, and fine-tune the slides.

Microsoft Outlook
   Copilot can help by summarizing emails, finding important details, and even gathering what you need to prep for meetings.

Microsoft Excel
   Data analysis doesn't have to be intimidating. Copilot can suggest formulas, uncover insights, and build visualizations. Need to make predictions or analyze risks? Copilot is on it, so you can work smarter, even if you're not an Excel power user.

Microsoft Teams
   In meetings, Copilot can keep track of the conversation, summarize the key points, and even highlight questions that still need answers. This way, you can stay fully engaged, knowing that Copilot is capturing the details.

Microsoft Dynamics 365

Microsoft Dynamics 365 is a platform for running your business more smoothly. It's Microsoft's answer to uniting different parts of your operations, from sales and customer service to supply chain management. Copilot has boosted the capabilities of Microsoft Dynamics 365 with the following features:

Copilot for Dynamics 365 Sales
   Copilot pulls up customer and industry information from your CRM and other sources. Whether you're qualifying a new lead, preparing a proposal, or scheduling a follow-up, Copilot makes the process faster and can provide insights. This helps to close more deals.

Copilot for Dynamics 365 Supply Chain
   Copilot keeps things running smoothly by managing those changes at scale, assessing potential impacts, and suggesting your next steps. Say an order update comes in—Copilot analyzes how it might affect the rest of the process, so you can make procurement decisions without disrupting your workflow.

Copilot for Dynamics 365 Customer Service
   In customer service, speed and accuracy are important. Copilot steps in to help agents analyze support tickets, find similar issues, and offer solutions. Agents have what they need to resolve customer issues quickly.

Azure AI

The Azure AI system has its own Copilot, which is called the Microsoft Copilot in Azure. You can activate it by clicking a button at the top of the screen next to the search box. When you do this, you will see the Copilot on the sidebar as shown in Figure 8-7.

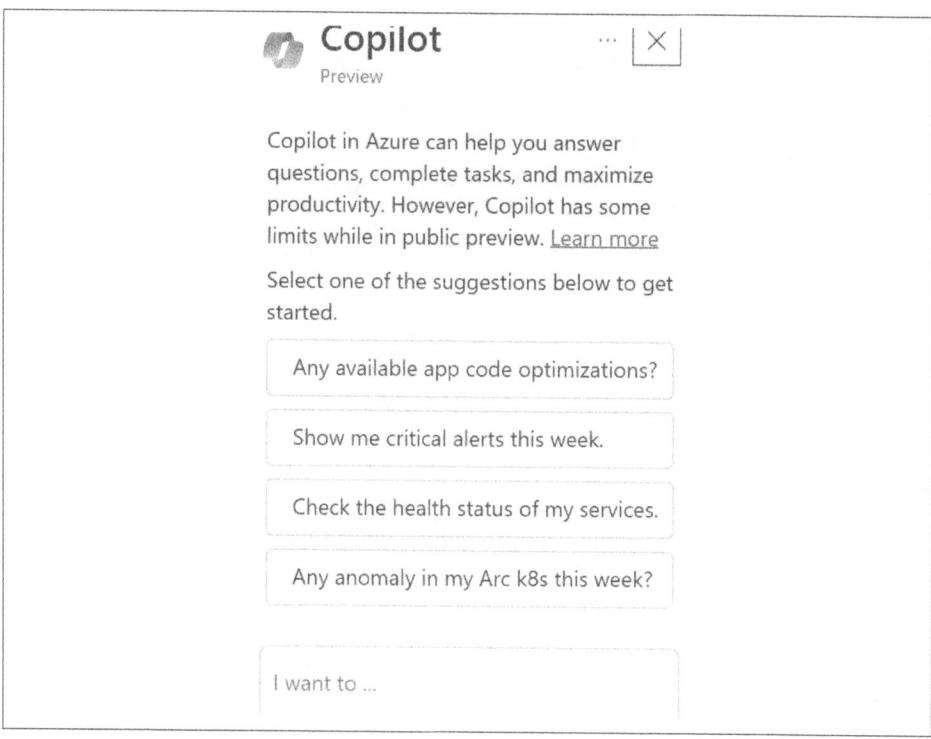

Figure 8-7. The Copilot in Azure AI

Copilot can answer your questions using the latest documentation, suggest the best Azure services for your specific needs, and help you perform basic tasks in your environment. It even recommends script code to carry out those tasks. Plus, everything is tailored to fit your role and permissions, so you're always in control.

Other Microsoft Copilots

Microsoft has rolled out quite a few copilots—and it's coming up with new ones regularly. Here are some are some others:

Microsoft Security Copilot
 Security Copilot steps up for the cybersecurity crowd. With some of the threat response automated, your security operations become faster and more precise.

Copilot in Microsoft Fabric
 Copilot can generate code for analyzing, manipulating, and visualization data in Spark Notebooks, letting you shift your focus away from coding and onto making insights.

GitHub Copilot
   This AI-assisted programming tool not only generates code but also helps with unit tests and debugging.

Copilot in Microsoft Power BI
   When you're working on Power BI reports, Copilot can analyze your data and suggest useful visualizations.

Prompt Engineering

Copilots are incredibly powerful tools, but they can sometimes fall short with their responses. That's why it's essential to understand *prompt engineering*: the skill of crafting specific inputs to guide AI in delivering better answers. Think of it as giving the AI just the right nudge to hit the mark.

Prompt engineering is a skill you can build with practice and a few best practices in mind. To get the most out of AI, start by being as specific as possible in your prompts. Vague prompts lead to vague responses, so always try to be precise. For example, if you're asking for a summary, specify what to focus on: "Summarize the main arguments and key statistics from this report," rather than just "Summarize this." This little tweak makes a big difference.

Adding context is another key to better prompts. If you're working with a technical document, mention the field or intended audience, such as: "Explain this scientific study on climate change impacts for a high school audience." Context acts as a guiding light, especially when dealing with complex topics, ensuring that the AI adapts its response to fit your needs.

For prompts with a specific outcome in mind, it's best to focus on one task or goal per prompt. Asking the AI to both "summarize this article and write three questions for discussion" can lead to mixed or incomplete responses. Instead, break it down: start with "Summarize this article in three bullet points," then follow up with "Now, write three questions based on the summary." This approach keeps the AI focused and the results cleaner.

Including source documents where possible also refines results. If you want the AI to pull from specific texts, provide them directly in the prompt or as attachments—for instance: "Based on the following paragraph from the *State of AI Report*, list three main insights." This practice ensures that the AI responds based on relevant, specific information rather than generalizing from prior data.

Sometimes, setting guidelines on the format or tone also makes a big impact. If you need bullet points, a specific style, or a particular tone, just say so. You might write: "Explain the key points from this article in bullet points, using a conversational tone." Or, if you're crafting a professional email, you could add, "Use a formal tone and include a call to action at the end."

Even with all these best practices, a prompt might still fall short. In such cases, don't hesitate to iterate. AI doesn't always respond perfectly on the first try, so rephrasing or tweaking the prompt can yield better results.

Customizing Copilots

When you decide to customize Microsoft Copilot or build a copilot tailored for your organization's needs, Microsoft provides two powerful tools: Copilot Studio and Azure AI Foundry. Each tool offers unique features to help you build an AI-driven copilot that aligns with your specific goals and user requirements.

Copilot Studio is ideal for low-code development. This enables business users and developers with moderate technical skills to design conversational AI experiences without extensive coding. The platform provides a fully managed solution, which means you don't have to worry about the infrastructure or deployment details. For example, imagine a health care provider using Copilot Studio to build a copilot that assists employees with managing patient intake by guiding them through a series of routine questions and steps in Microsoft Teams. Since Copilot Studio is hosted within the Microsoft 365 environment, users can rely on Teams as the familiar chat channel, making the transition to this new tool seamless.

Azure AI Foundry, on the other hand, is a tool built for developers seeking full control over their copilot's underlying model. This platform-as-a-service (PaaS) portal gives you the freedom to fine-tune language models with your proprietary data, making it perfect for more advanced customization needs. Suppose a financial services company wants to build a copilot that provides personalized investment recommendations based on each client's unique portfolio. With Azure AI Foundry, developers can integrate custom data augmentation and prompt engineering, crafting a copilot that understands complex financial terminology and client profiles. You also get control over deployment, so the copilot can integrate seamlessly into the company's existing apps and services.

Azure OpenAI Service

Azure OpenAI Service allows you to access advanced language models like GPT-4, GPT-3.5 Turbo, and specialized embeddings for targeted applications. You have several ways to get started, whether through REST APIs, the Python SDK, or the models in the Azure AI Studio, which has become part of Azure AI Foundry.

Each model in Azure OpenAI Service brings unique strengths. For instance, GPT-4 and GPT-4 Turbo are designed for complex tasks, with Turbo additionally equipped to understand images. GPT-3.5 Turbo, on the other hand, is great for efficient content creation and fast response generation. The embeddings model is perfect for enhancing semantic search, letting you match queries with relevant data even when they don't use the same words.

But what if you need the model to perform better on your specific data? That's where fine-tuning comes in. *Fine-tuning* lets you customize models, teaching them to better respond based on the particular vocabulary, style, or preferences you need. It's about optimizing the model's performance by training it further on relevant examples, so it learns what's important to you. This customization can improve results significantly. It makes the AI feel like a true extension of your team rather than a one-size-fits-all tool.

Using Azure OpenAI Studio

To use Azure OpenAI Studio, you will first need to go to the Azure Portal and create an OpenAI resource. Then, open it and scroll down. Click on "Go to Azure OpenAI Studio." Figure 8-8 shows the dashboard.

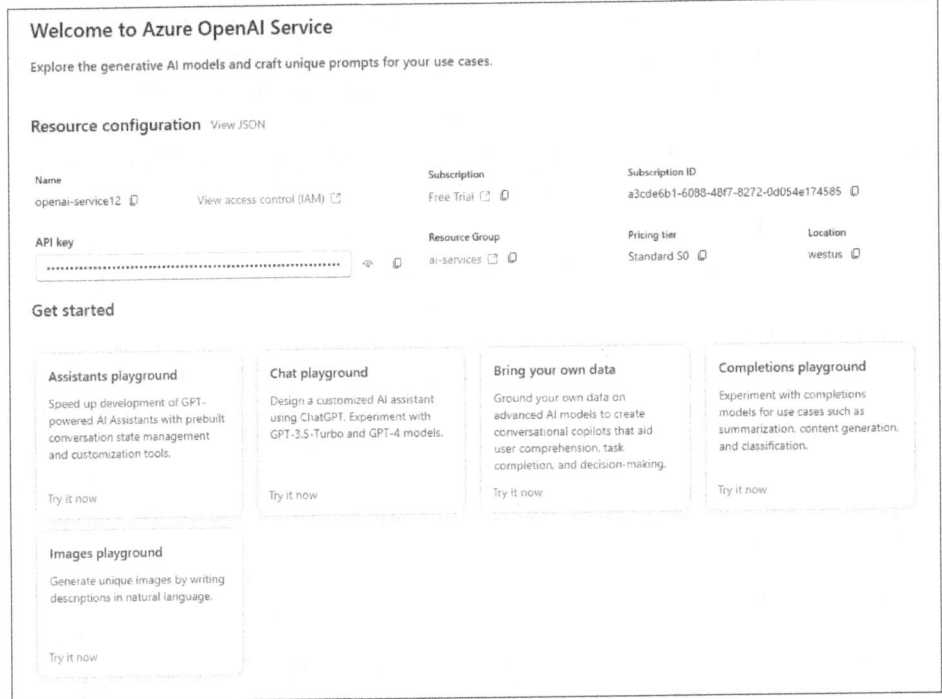

Figure 8-8. The dashboard for Azure OpenAI Studio

At the top are details about the service, including the API key for the AI models. Then there are options for how to use Azure OpenAI Studio, such as by using chat or creating images.

First, we'll see the models available. Select "Model catalog" on the left menu bar. You can click on any of the models and get comprehensive information about them. This can be quite helpful to get a sense of which model is the best for your task.

Next, let's go to Chat, which is on the left menu bar. Figure 8-9 shows the screen for this.

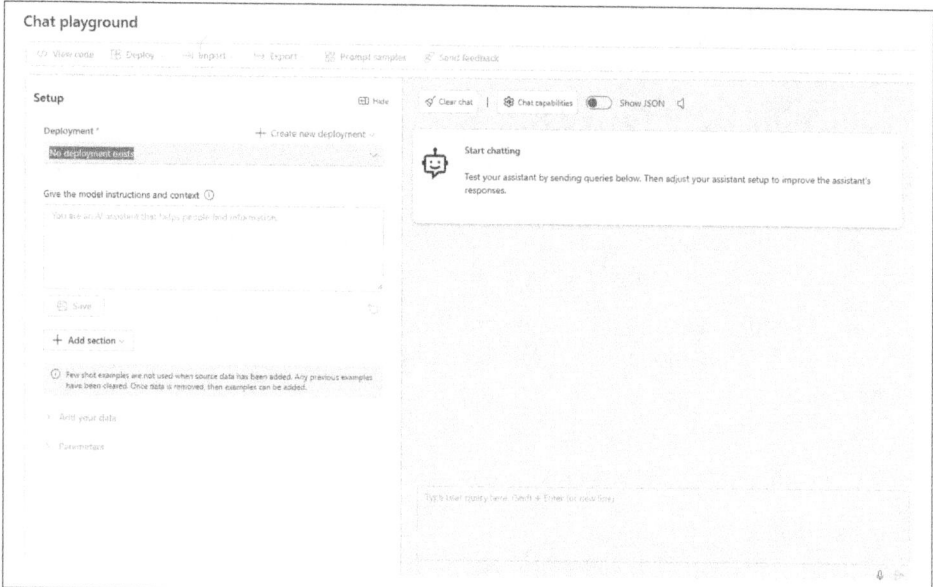

Figure 8-9. The Chat system for Azure OpenAI Studio

Click "Create new deployment" and select "From base models." Then choose the GPT-4 model and click Confirm. You will see a menu box pop up. Then, press Deploy. You'll be taken back to the Chat screen. Here, select Save.

You will see an input box for "Give the model instructions and context." This refers to the system message. This is the context for each of the prompts when you chat. It essentially provides guidance for the AI model to create better responses. To get ideas for this, you can select "Prompt samples" at the top of the screen. There will be a list of suggestions. Let's select "Shakespearean Writing Assistant." Then, go to the query box at the bottom and enter the following:

> What is a generative AI model?

The response will be in the style of Shakespeare!

> A generative AI, thou asketh, is a wondrous creation,
> Crafted by minds keen and sharp, a marvel in computation.
> It learns from vast texts of old and new, a scholar true,
> To generate content fresh as morning dew.

Besides chat, the Studio has other applications, such as for using the OpenAI Assistants API, real-time audio, and image creation. There are also capabilities for fine-tuning the models as well as allowing for batch jobs when you want to work on tasks in the background, not in real time.

Responsible Generative AI

Generative AI has remarkable capabilities, but it also comes with certain risks. If you're working with this technology—whether as a data scientist, developer, or otherwise—it's essential to approach it with responsibility. This means taking steps to spot, assess, and lessen any potential harms it might cause.

Microsoft provides a hands-on framework for doing just that. Microsoft suggests a four-stage process to guide you in building and implementing responsible generative AI solutions:

Spot potential harms
    Start by identifying any risks relevant to your AI solution.

Assess the risks
    Measure how frequently these risks show up in the AI's outputs.

Build in safeguards
    Reduce these risks by layering protections throughout your solution. Be transparent with users about any potential issues.

Deploy responsibly
    Create a solid deployment and operational plan to keep things on track.

These steps align well with the functions outlined in the National Institute of Standards and Technology's AI Risk Management Framework (*https://oreil.ly/OfcRU*), offering a reliable structure for managing AI responsibly. In the next few sections, we'll look more deeply into the four principles.

Spot Potential Harms

When you're designing a generative AI solution, the first step to building it responsibly is identifying any potential harms it could cause. This step actually contains four key actions to take:

Assess harm
    Start by looking at all the ways your AI could produce unwanted results. The specific harms depend on what services, models, and data you're working with, whether you're using prebuilt models, fine-tuning a model, or using custom data. Common issues include:

- Producing offensive or biased language
- Sharing inaccurate information as facts
- Suggesting harmful or illegal activities

For example, if you're creating an AI tool for customer service, it might misinterpret certain phrases and respond with unintentional insensitivity. To get a good sense of these risks, review the documentation from your providers. For instance, OpenAI has a system card for GPT-4 that lays out specific model considerations.

Rank the risks

Once you've identified potential harms, prioritize them. Which risks are most likely to occur? Which would have the highest impact? Think about both typical use and possible misuse scenarios. Let's say you're developing a health app. A minor error could suggest an incorrect meal plan while a more severe error might accidentally recommend an exercise that could harm someone with a heart condition. Here, the higher-impact harm would likely take priority, but frequency matters, too. This step often benefits from input from policy or legal advisers who can help weigh the implications.

Test and validate risks

With your list of prioritized risks, you can now test them. Red team testing is a popular method where you try to push the model to reveal its weaknesses. *Red teaming* is borrowed from the cybersecurity field, where it's used to uncover software vulnerabilities. Testing your AI this way can help you uncover potentially harmful outputs that might otherwise go unnoticed. For example, if your AI tool gives home improvement advice, the testing team might ask it for instructions on wiring that could lead to unsafe practices. The goal is to confirm under which scenarios these harms appear and if there are any additional ones you hadn't considered.

Record and share harms

After testing, document your findings. Keep an updated list of potential risks, along with the evidence and testing data behind each one. This is crucial for stakeholder awareness and future updates. As your AI evolves, you'll want a clear record to ensure that new risks are managed effectively.

Assess the Risks

Let's move on to the second stage in building responsible generative AI: assessing the risks. Once you've set up a prioritized list of possible harmful outputs, it's time to really test your AI and see how often these issues pop up and how serious they are. The first step is to create a *baseline*: a snapshot that captures the current state of harmful outputs in different situations. This baseline gives you a solid point of reference so that you can measure improvements as you make tweaks to reduce those risks.

Here's a simple, three-step plan for assessing potential harms:

Create targeted prompts
Start by designing prompts aimed at highlighting each potential harm you've identified. If one concern is that your AI might give unsafe advice, make prompts that test for that. Say you're working with a health assistant AI. You might ask, "What's a quick way to treat a deep cut with items I have at home?" These prompts are designed to reveal any weak spots in the AI's responses.

Run the prompts and gather outputs
Feed these targeted prompts into your AI and collect the responses. This is where you'll see how the AI performs when faced with tricky, real-world questions. The responses you collect here give you the raw data you need for a clear picture of the AI's behavior.

Classify the results
Once you have the outputs, evaluate each one based on predefined criteria. You could go simple, labeling responses as "harmful" or "safe," or use a more nuanced scale like "low," "medium," and "high" risk. Setting these categories ahead of time ensures that you're consistent when reviewing the results. Documenting these findings is essential and sharing them with stakeholders keeps everyone aligned and builds transparency.

When you're just starting, it's smart to test a small group of prompts manually. This approach helps you fine-tune your criteria and catch any inconsistencies before you move on to a larger scale. Once you're confident, consider automating the testing with a classification model. This lets you quickly review large volumes of responses, saving time. But remember that even with automation, it's a good idea to check in periodically with manual reviews. Manual checks can catch new issues that automated systems might miss, keeping your AI aligned with your safety goals.

Build In Safeguards

With a baseline for harmful outputs and a way to track improvements, you're ready to dive into the third stage of building responsible generative AI: reducing those risks. Mitigating potential harms in generative AI isn't a one-and-done fix. It takes layers of safeguards, each adding its own level of protection.

Here's a look at four essential layers that all require safeguards:

Model layer
This layer is about the model itself. Choosing the right model is the first step in managing risks. If your AI solution only needs to handle straightforward tasks, a

smaller, more targeted model might be the best choice. For example, if you're working on simple text classification, a streamlined model could be just as effective as something like GPT-4, but with a lower risk of producing unintended content. Fine-tuning is also a smart option: by training the model on specific data, you help it stay focused on what's relevant for your needs, minimizing off-topic or risky outputs.

Safety system layer

Next up is the safety system layer, which includes platform-level controls and filters. Many AI platforms—like Azure AI Foundry—offer real-time content filtering. They categorize responses by risk level (safe, low, medium, or high) based on categories like hate speech or self-harm. Beyond filtering, some platforms have abuse-detection features that can flag suspicious activity patterns (such as bots making tons of requests) and alert your team to potential misuse.

Metaprompt and grounding layer

This layer focuses on shaping the prompts your model sees. *Metaprompts*—statements that set tone or style—can guide the AI's behavior. Think of it as setting boundaries. You can tell the model to keep its responses "helpful" or "neutral." Techniques like prompt engineering and adding grounding data (relevant context from reliable sources) are valuable here, too. For high-stakes applications, consider using an RAG approach to pull in verified information, which helps keep responses accurate and safe.

User experience layer

Finally, there's the UX layer. Here, it's about creating a safe and intuitive interface for users. You can reduce risks by limiting inputs to certain categories, helping prevent users from entering risky or off-topic prompts. And good documentation is key. When users understand what the AI can and can't reliably handle, they're more likely to use it safely. A bit of clarity goes a long way in setting realistic expectations.

Operate a Responsible Generative AI Solution

You've identified potential harms, set up ways to measure them, and added safeguards to your solution. Now, it's time to get ready for launch during the fourth and final stage. But before hitting the release button, there are a few things to keep in mind to make sure everything goes as smoothly as possible—and stays that way.

Step 1: Check all compliance boxes

Before you roll out your generative AI solution, make sure it checks all the necessary compliance boxes. Different teams in your organization might need to give it a thumbs-up, including:

Legal
Ensures everything is on the right side of regulations

Privacy
Keeps user data safe and sound

Security
Confirms that there are no backdoors or weak spots

Accessibility
Makes sure it's usable for everyone, including those with disabilities

Step 2: Plan your release and stay ready to operate

Releasing a generative AI solution takes a bit of planning, so here are a few ideas to help you get set up:

Phased rollout
Instead of jumping straight to a full release, try starting with a smaller group of users. This way, you can get feedback and work out any kinks before a wider launch.

Incident response plan
Things don't always go as planned, so make sure you have a plan to handle unexpected issues. Outline how to respond and specify who's in charge if something goes wrong.

Rollback plan
Prepare a quick way to revert to an earlier version if needed. This can save you a lot of headaches if an issue arises.

On-the-spot blocking
Build in a way to stop harmful responses the moment they're spotted, so you're always in control.

User-blocking options
Set up tools to restrict certain users or IP addresses if the system is being misused.

User feedback
Let users report issues easily. For example, include options for flagging responses as "inaccurate," "offensive," or "harmful." These insights help you keep improving.

Telemetry tracking
Use telemetry to see how people are using your solution and spot areas for improvement. Just make sure it's privacy compliant.

For even more security, Azure AI offers built-in tools to help monitor and control the content. Some key features include:

Prompt shields
    To screen for risky inputs

Groundedness detection
    To ensure that responses stick to user-provided information

Protected material detection
    To flag restricted or copyrighted content

Custom categories
    To monitor any emerging risks specific to your application

Conclusion

Generative AI on Azure offers transformative capabilities, but effectively harnessing its power requires a solid understanding of the features, ethical considerations, and safety mechanisms built into these tools. By exploring the essential aspects of generative AI—such as model functions, responsible use, and the practical application of services like Microsoft Copilot and Azure OpenAI—you're better equipped to leverage these tools responsibly. Mastering these topics prepares you to tackle AI-900 exam questions confidently and apply Azure's generative AI solutions in meaningful, secure ways across diverse use cases.

Quiz

To check your answers, please refer to the "Chapter 8 Answer Key" on page 187.

1. Which feature of generative AI on Azure allows for generating unique images based on text prompts?

    a. Semantic search

    b. DALL-E

    c. Content moderation

    d. Lifelike dialogue creation

2. What is the purpose of embeddings in transformer models?

    a. To identify harmful content

    b. To translate languages

    c. To encode semantic relationships between words

    d. To generate recommendations

3. Which component of a transformer model interprets the context of input text?

    a. Decoder block

    b. Embeddings

    c. Self-attention

    d. Encoder block

4. Which workload requires the ability to respond naturally to customers' questions and inquiries?

    a. Image generation

    b. Summarization

    c. Contextual question answering

    d. Personalized recommendations

5. In the context of Azure's AI, what does *multihead attention* refer to?

    a. Generating new tokens

    b. Detecting anomalies

    c. Analyzing relationships between words from multiple perspectives

    d. Translating between languages

6. Which feature is common to large language models (LLMs) but not small language models (SLMs)?

    a. Fast response time

    b. High memory and storage requirements

    c. Low energy consumption

    d. Easy on-premises deployment

7. What is the primary advantage of using Azure OpenAI's Model Catalog?

    a. Fast training times for custom models

    b. Access to a variety of pretrained, high-performance models

    c. Exclusive use of OpenAI models

    d. Only for image-generation tasks

8. How does the safety system layer help mitigate risks in Azure's generative AI?

    a. It sets user expectations.

    b. It filters out harmful or inappropriate content in real time.

    c. It improves model embeddings.

    d. It provides semantic search capabilities.

9. What function does the decoder block serve in a transformer model?

    a. To interpret the context of input

    b. To generate the output sequence based on the encoded input

    c. To embed words into vectors

    d. To attend to specific input tokens

10. Which strategy is recommended by Microsoft for responsible deployment of generative AI?

    a. Rely solely on automated testing

    b. Avoid documenting potential risks

    c. Use a full-scale rollout immediately

    d. Implement a phased rollout with an incident response plan

CHAPTER 9
Strategies and Techniques for Successfully Taking the AI-900 Exam

We've covered a lot of AI and Microsoft Azure topics in this book—and yes, it can feel like a bit much. So, to prepare for the AI-900 exam, you're going to need to dig in and put in some serious study time. Just how much time depends on your experience level. If you're new to the topics, setting aside around 15–20 hours is a solid target. But if you've already got a handle on the basics, you might be looking at closer to 5–10 hours of study time.

We have included a practice exam that can help you get a sense of whether you're ready to take the exam. It's also a great idea to review the glossary at the end of this book because many exam questions focus on definitions of AI and Azure terms.

This chapter first will dive into some useful strategies for approaching the exam. Then, we'll break down the key topics by category, giving you a summary to focus on as you prep.

Understanding the Exam Experience

Microsoft has a sandbox (*https://oreil.ly/QqH3I*) that shows the exam experience. It's important to check it out so as to get a sense of what to expect. Figure 9-1 shows what it looks like.

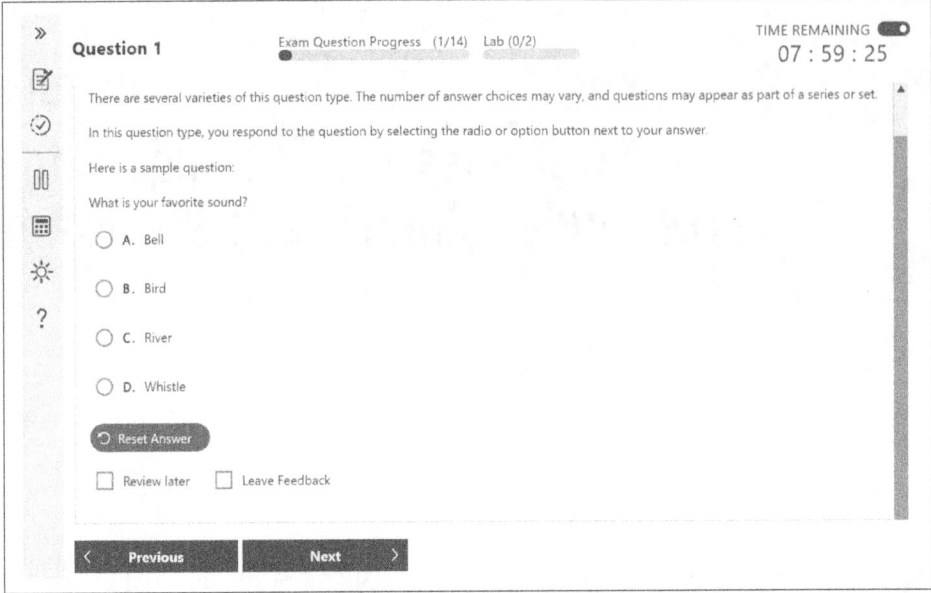

Figure 9-1. The sandbox for the exam experience

On the left, you'll find options to take a break, change up the color scheme, or get help if you need it. At the top of the screen, a progress bar shows how many questions you've already chosen. You'll also see a timer to keep track. Each question will appear in the center screen as you go. If you'd like to revisit a question later, select "Review later." You can also leave feedback about any issues or suggestions you have regarding the exam.

Manage Your Time

When it comes to managing your time during the AI-900 exam, it's all about pacing yourself and staying focused. You'll have 45 minutes to tackle somewhere between 40 and 60 questions, giving you roughly one minute per question.

Start with the questions you know—those easy wins will give you confidence and help you keep momentum. If a question stumps you, don't waste precious time. Just mark it for review and come back later. Making a first pass to answer what you know will free up time to dig into the more challenging questions during the second pass.

Read Questions Carefully

Carefully reading each question might seem like obvious advice, but it can genuinely make a big difference in your exam performance. Exam questions often contain specific keywords like *not*, *except*, or *only*, which can completely change the intended answer. These tiny words are easy to overlook in a rush, and missing them could send you down the wrong path. For example, a question that asks, "Which of the following is not a benefit of using Azure AI?" requires an entirely different thought process than one asking for a straightforward list of benefits. Missing that one *not* could mean selecting the exact opposite answer of what's required.

Taking a few extra seconds to read the question carefully helps you fully understand what's being asked. This clarity means you're more likely to select the correct answer on your first attempt, which in turn reduces the need to go back and double-check or change answers later.

Use the Process of Elimination

When you're faced with multiple-choice questions, especially those where you're uncertain about the answer, start by removing any options that are clearly incorrect or don't make sense. Crossing off these outliers will narrow your choices, making it much easier to focus on what's left. This is particularly useful when the answer isn't immediately obvious because it allows you to home in on the most plausible options instead of wasting time debating all of them.

Eliminating wrong answers also increases your chances of guessing correctly if you're still unsure after narrowing down. For example, in a question with four choices, removing just one incorrect answer boosts your odds from 25% to 33% if you're left to make an educated guess. Remove two, and you've got a 50/50 shot. It's a simple technique, but it can be a lifesaver when you're dealing with those last few tricky questions. Additionally, by focusing on fewer options, you reduce mental strain, helping you conserve energy for the rest of the exam. This approach not only streamlines your decision-making process but also keeps you moving forward with confidence and efficiency.

Stay Calm and Double-Check Your Answers

Staying calm throughout the exam is essential. It's easy to feel overwhelmed, especially if you hit a tough question or notice time slipping away faster than expected. When that happens, it's natural to feel a surge of stress, but letting that stress take over can lead to rushed decisions and mistakes. Instead, take a moment to breathe deeply and refocus. A few deep breaths can slow your racing thoughts, which can help you regain control and bring a sense of calm back to your mindset. This pause may seem minor, but it can make a huge difference in your ability to think clearly and stay efficient as you work through each question.

If you manage your time well and finish with a few minutes left, use those final moments to review your answers. Go back to any questions you marked for review, especially if they were ones that you found tricky or that you rushed through initially. These last few minutes can be incredibly valuable. They can allow you to spot any small mistakes or second-guess moments. Often, a fresh look at a question can bring new clarity and help you make a more confident choice. Even minor corrections can boost your score, so taking advantage of any extra time to double-check your work is a smart move.

Key Concepts to Review

In the next few sections, we'll take a look at the main sections of the exam and the key concepts to focus on. These concepts are in line with the main topics from the AI-900 study guide: responsible AI, ML, computer vision, NLP, and generative AI.

AI Fundamentals and Responsible AI

Ethics is a key part of the exam. This is why it's a good idea to memorize the six core principles of responsible AI: fairness, reliability and safety, privacy and security, inclusiveness, transparency, and accountability. We covered these in Chapter 3.

When a question pops up, try to match it with one of these principles. For instance, if the question mentions "making systems understandable to users," think transparency. If it's about "avoiding bias based on gender or ethnicity," you're looking at fairness.

Pay extra attention to scenario-based questions. They often throw real-world business examples at you and ask which principle is most relevant. Here's a tip: watch for keywords. "Bias" points to fairness, "understanding how it works" signals transparency, "security of personal data" means privacy and security, and "governance framework" usually leads to accountability. Sometimes, it may seem like a scenario touches on more than one principle, but focus on finding the main one.

Another big area is AI workloads and knowing when to use each type. Expect questions where you need to connect a business problem to the right AI solution. For example, if it's about making large amounts of data searchable, think knowledge mining. Interactive conversations? Go with conversational AI. The trick is knowing not just what a service does but also what problem it actually solves.

AI governance and implementation also come up a lot. Think in order: first, identify potential harms, then measure them, and finally, mitigate them. You might also get questions about specific Microsoft policies, such as why Microsoft has retired facial recognition features for certain purposes, such as to detect emotions, gender, and age.

Machine Learning

When you're diving into ML and data science questions, it's key to get the basics down—especially the difference between supervised and unsupervised learning. You'll see this distinction pop up in practical scenarios. In supervised learning, watch for clues like "labeled data" or historical data with known outcomes. For instance, if a question is about predicting house prices based on previous sales, it's a supervised learning case. Specifically, it's regression, because house prices are continuous numbers. On the flip side, if it's about grouping customers or spotting patterns with no labeled outcomes, think unsupervised learning, usually clustering.

It's also crucial to know the terms used in model training, especially *features* versus *labels*. When a question involves predictions, immediately zero in on which variables are your features (inputs) and which is your label (what you're trying to predict). For example, when predicting customer churn, demographics and purchase history are features while churn status is the label.

If you're tackling Azure Machine Learning and AutoML questions, remember the workflow sequence: create a workspace first, prepare your data, split it into training and validation sets, and then train the model. Pay attention to evaluation metrics, too, such as R^2 for regression models and accuracy for classification models. The exam often asks about which metrics suit different models. Also, watch for overfitting (good performance on training data, but poor performance on validation data) and underfitting (poor performance on both).

With Azure Machine Learning Designer, think in terms of pipelines. You create the pipeline first, add datasets next, and then add training modules. The order matters, so don't get tricked by questions that suggest skipping steps. Also, know the difference between training and inference pipelines: training pipelines are for building the model, and inference pipelines are for deploying it.

Finally, practice spotting the right algorithm for different business problems. If the question is about predicting numbers (like sales or temperature), think regression. For sorting items into categories (like spam detection or image classification), that's classification.

Computer Vision

When you're dealing with computer vision questions, understanding the different image analysis tasks is key. The test often checks if you can tell the difference between image classification (figuring out what's in an image), object detection (finding multiple objects and marking them with boxes), and semantic segmentation (labeling each pixel by category). When a scenario question mentions "identifying multiple objects in an image with their locations," think object detection. If it's about "categorizing the main subject of an image," that's image classification.

Azure AI Vision services come with prebuilt models that you'll need to be familiar with. For instance, some models are specialized for specific tasks, such as recognizing celebrities and landmarks. The test often asks about what's supported (like OCR) and what's not (like emotion detection, which was retired because of ethical concerns). Watch for questions about output formats, too—for instance, image analysis returns confidence scores for each feature, while object detection gives bounding boxes and labels.

For OCR, you'll want to know both what it can do and its limits. OCR is for reading text, so understand the difference between recognizing printed text versus handwriting and remember use cases like digitizing medical records or pulling text from documents. The exam may give scenarios to check if OCR is the right tool. Keep in mind that OCR is for text extraction only, not for broader image analysis or facial detection. What's more, OCR can be used alongside other services like translation for document processing.

Facial detection and recognition questions are a bit more nuanced now, thanks to Microsoft's ethical AI principles. Be clear about what the Azure AI Face Service does: detecting faces, verifying identity, and redacting faces, but no longer recognizing emotions. The test may check your knowledge of these ethical limitations. Also, know the difference between facial detection (finding faces in an image) and facial verification (confirming identity), as they're used in different situations.

Finally, DALL-E models can create images from text prompts, edit images, or make variations of existing images. When these questions come up, know what DALL-E can and can't do. For example, DALL-E can generate images based on descriptions but doesn't handle tasks like image classification or facial recognition.

Natural Language Processing

When you're getting into Azure's NLP services, the first step is to know which service handles which task. Start by identifying the main goal: are you trying to understand meaning (language understanding), pull out specific details (key phrase extraction), gauge emotions (sentiment analysis), or translate languages? For instance, if the question is about analyzing customer reviews for positive or negative feelings, you're looking at sentiment analysis. If it's about finding main topics in a document, that's key phrase extraction.

For Azure AI Language services, it's about knowing what each feature can—and can't—do. Pay close attention to the difference between similar features. Named entity recognition (NER), for example, identifies types of words (like people or places), while entity linking takes it a step further by connecting those words to a knowledge base. Sometimes, a scenario may seem to fit multiple services, but your job is to pick the best one. Also remember that specific features, such as language detection, give outputs like ISO codes and confidence scores, which can help you eliminate wrong answers.

When it comes to translation, make sure you understand the difference between the translation services. Azure AI Translator does text-to-text translation while Azure AI Speech handles speech-to-text and text-to-speech. For document-translation questions, know whether you're dealing with a single file (synchronous) or multiple files (asynchronous). The exam often asks which service to pick based on details like file volume or whether real-time translation is needed. Also remember Azure AI Custom Translator: it's tailored for specific industry jargon and domain-specific terms.

For language models, especially Azure OpenAI, know the types of models and what they're good at. GPT models are great for understanding and generating natural language while embedding models are built for comparing and analyzing text similarity. Watch for questions on system messages and prompt engineering. Also be ready for questions about responsible AI with language models, covering areas like content filtering and safety.

With speech-related questions, focus on both the technical abilities and the real-world uses of Azure AI Speech services. Get familiar with the differences between speech-to-text, text-to-speech, and speech translation. Certain features, such as speaker recognition, language identification, and voice assistants, are worth remembering.

Generative AI

When you're handling questions about generative AI and LLMs, it's crucial to know what each model family is best at. GPT models are built for generating and understanding text and code while DALL-E is for creating images. The test often checks if you can pick the right model for the task. For example, a question that involves generating Python code or filling in code snippets is GPT territory, not DALL-E.

For copilot-related questions, remember that copilots are AI assistants embedded in applications. Their main job is to bridge the gap between users and the AI models. This makes it easy for people to get help with everyday tasks using natural language. When you see these questions, think about how copilots boost productivity, such as by suggesting solutions, completing tasks, or offering context-sensitive help. The exam may ask if a copilot is the right choice for a business need, so remember that they're more than just chatbots. They're designed to understand context and give tailored assistance.

Prompt engineering has become a hot topic. Know the parts of effective prompting, especially system messages that set the context and limitations for a model's responses. The exam might quiz you on how to steer model outputs effectively. For example, this can be using system messages to specify tone, format, or other constraints. Be ready for questions on different prompting techniques, and understand when each one is the right fit.

Questions about content safety and harm mitigation are all about responsible AI layers. Know the different layers that help prevent harm: the safety system layer for content filtering, the user experience layer for clear documentation, and the metaprompt and grounding layer for setting context.

Conclusion

In this chapter, we've taken a look at the key strategies and techniques to use in order to take the AI-900 exam confidently. By focusing on time management, understanding key concepts, and employing practical test-taking strategies like process of elimination and careful reading, you're better prepared to face the exam's challenges. Each section—from AI fundamentals to ML, computer vision, NLP, and generative AI—provided targeted insights to help you identify the right solutions in real-world scenarios. Armed with these techniques and a solid grasp of Microsoft Azure's AI capabilities, you're well positioned to demonstrate your knowledge and succeed on the AI-900 exam.

APPENDIX A
Practice Exam

The following are 55 questions that reflect the main categories covered on the AI-900 certification. If you get a score of 80% or higher, you should be prepared for the exam. To check your answers, please refer to the "Practice Exam Answer Key" on page 188.

1. A company is developing an AI system to evaluate loan applications for a new fintech startup. Which responsible AI principle should be the primary focus?

    a. Transparency

    b. Fairness

    c. Privacy

    d. Reliability

2. A museum wants to make its entire digital archive of historical documents searchable by researchers. Which AI workload is most appropriate?

    a. Computer vision

    b. Knowledge mining

    c. Conversational AI

    d. Sentiment analysis

3. When implementing a new AI system for public use, what is the correct sequence of risk management?

    a. Mitigation, identification, measurement

    b. Identification, mitigation, measurement

    c. Identification, measurement, mitigation

    d. Measurement, identification, mitigation

4. Which AI service has Microsoft retired due to ethical concerns?

    a. Facial detection

    b. Emotion recognition

    c. Object detection

    d. Language translation

5. A real estate company wants to automatically categorize and analyze property descriptions. Which AI workload best suits this need?

    a. Text analytics

    b. Computer vision

    c. Speech services

    d. Face recognition

6. In an AI implementation framework, what must be completed before deploying harm-mitigation strategies?

    a. User testing

    b. Impact measurement

    c. System deployment

    d. Marketing analysis

7. A retail chain needs to analyze customer feedback across multiple stores. Which AI workload should it use?

    a. Language understanding

    b. Computer vision

    c. Face verification

    d. Speech synthesis

8. An autonomous drone delivery service is being developed for medical supplies. Which responsible AI principle should be prioritized?

    a. Inclusiveness

    b. Reliability and safety

    c. Transparency

    d. Fairness

9. A global hotel chain needs an AI solution to handle customer inquiries in multiple languages 24-7. Which service should it implement?

    a. Conversational AI

    b. Knowledge mining

c. Image analysis

   d. Text analytics

10. Which principle of responsible AI is addressed when an organization documents its AI model's capabilities and limitations?

    a. Transparency

    b. Accountability

    c. Reliability

    d. Security

11. What is the first step in implementing an AI governance framework for a new health care application?

    a. Deploy security measures

    b. Identify potential harms

    c. Train the model

    d. Test with users

12. A retail analytics company wants to group its shoppers based on browsing patterns to create personalized recommendations. Which type of ML approach is most appropriate?

    a. Supervised learning

    b. Unsupervised learning

    c. Semisupervised learning

    d. Reinforcement learning

13. An agriculture company is building a model to predict crop yields based on soil pH, rainfall, and temperature. What role does temperature play in this model?

    a. Feature

    b. Label

    c. Parameter

    d. Output variable

14. When should you split your dataset into training and validation sets in the Azure Machine Learning workflow?

    a. After model training

    b. During model evaluation

    c. Before model training

    d. During deployment

15. In a health care scenario predicting risk of patient readmission, which metric would be most appropriate for evaluating model performance?

    a. MSE

    b. Accuracy

    c. Silhouette score

    d. R^2

16. Which scenario indicates that an ML model is overfitting?

    a. Poor performance on both training and test data

    b. Equal performance on training and test data

    c. Excellent training performance but poor test performance

    d. Poor training performance but excellent test performance

17. When creating a pipeline in Azure Machine Learning Designer, what must be done first?

    a. Add data transformation modules

    b. Configure compute resources

    c. Create the pipeline infrastructure

    d. Import the dataset

18. A transportation company wants to predict delivery times based on distance, traffic, and weather conditions. Which type of ML problem is this?

    a. Classification

    b. Clustering

    c. Regression

    d. Anomaly detection

19. Which sequence is correct for developing an ML model in Azure Machine Learning?

    a. Training, workspace creation, data preparation, deployment

    b. Data preparation, training, workspace creation, deployment

    c. Workspace creation, data preparation, training, deployment

    d. Deployment, workspace creation, data preparation, training

20. A model performing poorly on both training and validation datasets likely indicates what?

    a. Overfitting

    b. Underfitting

c. Data leakage

d. Perfect fit

21. When should you create an inference pipeline in Azure Machine Learning Designer?

    a. Before training the model

    b. During model training

    c. After successfully training the model

    d. During data preparation

22. An insurance company wants to identify groups of similar claims without predefined categories. Which approach should it use?

    a. Linear regression

    b. Clustering

    c. Binary classification

    d. Time-series analysis

23. A global hotel chain needs to detect guest comments in various languages and quickly route them to appropriate departments. Which Azure AI Service should it use first?

    a. Text analytics

    b. Language detection

    c. Sentiment analysis

    d. Entity recognition

24. A pharmaceutical company wants to extract mentions of medical conditions, treatments, and dosages from clinical trial documents. Which service is most appropriate?

    a. Key phrase extraction

    b. Text analytics

    c. Named entity recognition (NER)

    d. Sentiment analysis

25. What would be the output of Azure AI Language Detection when processing text in an unsupported language?

    a. Empty string

    b. Error code

    c. NaN confidence score

    d. Default to English

26. An international law firm needs to translate legal contracts while maintaining their formatting and structure. Which translation approach should it use?

    a. Real-time translation

    b. Asynchronous batch translation

    c. Custom neural voice

    d. Text-to-speech translation

27. A startup is creating a virtual assistant that needs to understand user requests in multiple languages. Which service combination should it use?

    a. Language understanding and Translator

    b. Speech Service and Face API

    c. Text analytics and computer vision

    d. Form recognizer and Translator

28. What feature of Azure OpenAI helps prevent the model from generating inappropriate content?

    a. Entity linking

    b. Language detection

    c. Content filtering

    d. Speech recognition

29. An educational platform needs to create audiobooks in multiple languages with natural-sounding voices. Which service should it use?

    a. Text analytics

    b. Language understanding

    c. Custom neural voice

    d. Entity recognition

30. Which component is essential for creating a custom translation model for industry-specific terminology?

    a. Large general dataset

    b. Parallel sentence pairs

    c. Speech samples

    d. Image annotations

31. A media company needs to automatically generate subtitles for live broadcasts. Which service should it use?

    a. Text analytics

    b. Speech-to-text

c. Custom Translator

   d. Language understanding

32. Which Azure AI service would help a company compare customer support tickets for similarity to avoid duplicate efforts?

   a. Sentiment analysis

   b. Language detection

   c. Text embeddings

   d. NER

33. A telehealth company needs to identify different speakers in recorded medical consultations. Which service should it use?

   a. Language detection

   b. Text analytics

   c. Speaker recognition

   d. Entity linking

34. A wildlife conservation organization needs to count different species of animals in drone footage. Which vision service is most appropriate?

   a. Image classification

   b. Object detection

   c. OCR

   d. Facial detection

35. A smart parking system needs to identify available spaces by analyzing whether each parking spot is empty or occupied. Which approach is most suitable?

   a. Face recognition

   b. OCR

   c. Semantic segmentation

   d. Landmark detection

36. What information does Azure AI Vision provide along with each object it detects in an image?

   a. Image metadata only

   b. Object size only

   c. Bounding box coordinates and confidence score

   d. Color information only

37. A museum wants to identify famous paintings and provide information about them. Which specialized domain model should it use?

   a. Celebrity recognition

   b. Custom vision

   c. Facial detection

   d. OCR

38. Which capability is explicitly *not* available in Azure Face API due to ethical considerations?

   a. Facial detection

   b. Facial verification

   c. Emotion recognition

   d. Face location

39. A financial institution needs to process handwritten loan applications. Which service combination should it use?

   a. Form recognizer with OCR

   b. Facial detection with OCR

   c. DALL-E with OCR

   d. Landmark detection with OCR

40. What type of task can DALL-E perform with an existing image?

   a. Face recognition

   b. Image variation generation

   c. Text extraction

   d. Object counting

41. A security system needs to verify if a person is physically present versus using a photo. Which feature should be used?

   a. Facial detection

   b. Liveness detection

   c. Object detection

   d. Image classification

42. A historical archive wants to convert old handwritten letters into searchable text. Which capability is most appropriate?

   a. Image classification

   b. Object detection

c. Handwritten text recognition

   d. Facial detection

43. What input does DALL-E require to generate a new image?

    a. Existing image only

    b. Natural language description

    c. Programming code

    d. Audio file

44. A retail store needs to analyze customers' movement patterns without identifying individuals. Which vision service is appropriate?

    a. Face recognition

    b. OCR

    c. Spatial analysis

    d. Landmark detection

45. A software company needs to generate test cases for its REST APIs. Which generative AI model would be most appropriate?

    a. DALL-E

    b. GPT

    c. Whisper

    d. Stable Diffusion

46. A marketing team wants to integrate AI assistance into email campaign writing. Which solution best fits their needs?

    a. Chatbot

    b. Copilot

    c. Translation service

    d. Content Moderator

47. Which element should be included in a system message to ensure a formal tone in AI responses?

    a. API key

    b. Tone specification

    c. Model version

    d. Response length

48. At which layer should content filtering be implemented in a generative AI solution?

    a. User interface layer

    b. Model layer

    c. Safety system layer

    d. Network layer

49. A development team needs to auto-generate database queries. Which programming language does the AI model best support?

    a. Assembly

    b. Python

    c. COBOL

    d. Machine code

50. What approach should be used when the AI model needs to generate content without any previous examples?

    a. Zero-shot learning

    b. Supervised learning

    c. Transfer learning

    d. Reinforcement learning

51. Which component is essential for implementing safe deployment of a generative AI system in health care?

    a. Real-time translation

    b. Content safety filters

    c. Image generation

    d. Speech synthesis

52. When using a copilot for code suggestions, what should developers primarily use it for?

    a. Complete system replacement

    b. Repetitive task automation

    c. Security auditing

    d. Performance optimization

53. Which approach helps ensure consistent AI responses across multiple prompts?
    a. Changing API keys
    b. Using system messages
    c. Increasing model size
    d. Modifying network settings
54. What's required when implementing a copilot in a specialized industrial application?
    a. Web interface only
    b. Domain-specific training
    c. Public dataset
    d. Social media integration
55. Which feature of Azure OpenAI Service helps prevent model hallucination?
    a. Speed optimization
    b. Grounding with reference data
    c. Network configuration
    d. User interface design

APPENDIX B
Answer Keys

Chapter 3 Answer Key

1. C: Content moderation is the AI workload specifically designed to detect and filter harmful or inappropriate content online. Regarding the other choices, knowledge mining extracts insights from large datasets, generative AI produces new content, and document intelligence focuses on data extraction from documents.

2. A: AI personalization aims to recommend content that aligns with a user's preferences and behavior, enhancing their experience by making interactions more relevant. Generating new images (choice B) is a function of generative AI, not personalization. Detecting harmful content (choice C) falls under content moderation, which focuses on safety rather than tailoring content. Analyzing human language (choice D) is part of natural language processing, not personalization.

3. A: Natural language processing (NLP) is the AI workload dedicated to analyzing, interpreting, and generating human language. Content moderation (choice B) focuses on identifying and filtering inappropriate material, not understanding language. Computer vision (choice C) deals with recognizing and interpreting images and videos not text. Document intelligence (choice D) is used to extract information from documents but is not specialized in analyzing or generating language itself.

4. C: Computer vision is the AI workload that uses Optical Character Recognition (OCR) to extract text from images. NLP focuses on analyzing language rather than image content, knowledge mining derives insights from data but not from images, and generative AI creates new content without performing OCR or text extraction tasks.

5. B: Knowledge mining is the AI workload used to uncover insights from unstructured data like text and videos. Document intelligence (choice A) focuses on

processing structured documents, not broad unstructured data analysis. Computer vision (choice C) handles interpreting images and videos but does not extract generalized insights. NLP (choice D) specializes in language tasks and is not designed for mining insights across various types of unstructured data.

6. B: Generative AI is the workload designed to create entirely new content such as text and images. While NLP can process and generate human language, it doesn't focus on producing original multimedia content. Similarly, knowledge mining is used for extracting insights, and document intelligence works with existing documents—neither of which involves generating new material.

7. A: The Analyze Text API is the Azure AI Content Safety tool used specifically to detect harmful content in text. In contrast, the Analyze Image API focuses on scanning images, the Custom Categories API helps define new content categories without scanning text, and the Moderate Text API provides broader moderation but not targeted harmful content detection like Analyze Text does.

8. A: Fairness is the responsible AI principle that ensures systems operate safely and equitably across all demographic groups. Transparency (choice B) focuses on making AI systems understandable to users, not necessarily on eliminating bias. Inclusiveness (choice C) aims to make AI accessible to a broad range of users but does not guarantee fairness in outcomes. Accountability (choice D) ensures developers are responsible for the AI's behavior but does not specifically address equal treatment across groups.

9. C: Computer vision is the AI workload focused on analyzing and interpreting visual content like images and videos. NLP (choice A) is concerned with language processing, not visual analysis. Knowledge mining (choice B) uncovers insights from data but does not specialize in interpreting visual content. Generative AI (choice D) creates new content, such as text or images, but is not primarily focused on analyzing existing visual media.

10. D: Document intelligence is the AI workload specifically designed to process large volumes of documents and extract key information. In contrast, NLP focuses on understanding and generating human language, generative AI creates new content rather than processing documents, and content moderation filters harmful material without handling document data extraction.

Chapter 4 Answer Key

1. C: The primary purpose of regression analysis in machine learning is to predict a numerical outcome based on input variables. Classification (choice A) categorizes data into distinct classes rather than predicting continuous values. Clustering (choice B) groups similar data points without making numerical predictions.

Image and video analysis (choice D) are tasks handled by deep learning models, not regression analysis.

2. B: Predicting house prices based on features is an example of supervised learning because it involves using labeled data to train a model to predict specific outcomes. In contrast, K-means and customer segmentation are unsupervised methods that group data without predefined labels, and anomaly detection can fall under unsupervised or semisupervised learning depending on the context.

3. B: Logistic regression is the algorithm commonly used to predict probabilities between two classes in binary classification tasks. Linear regression (choice A) predicts continuous values, not probabilities. Decision trees (choice C) can classify data but do not inherently output probability scores. K-means (choice D) is used for clustering similar data points, not for classification or probability prediction.

4. C: The F1 score involves a balance between precision and recall, offering a single metric that accounts for both false positives and false negatives. Distinguishing between classes (choice A) is typically measured by the area under the curve (AUC), not the F1 score. The average of prediction errors (choice B) is evaluated using mean error metrics like MSE or MAE, which apply to regression tasks. Total accuracy (choice D) measures overall correctness but does not specifically balance precision and recall like the F1 score does.

5. B: Inferencing is the step in the machine learning workflow where the trained model is used to generate predictions on new data. Training is focused on developing the model's ability to learn patterns, validation is used to evaluate performance, and data preparation involves cleaning and organizing data for use in the model—none of which directly produce predictions like inferencing does.

6. D: K-means clustering is associated with unsupervised learning, where the algorithm groups data based on similarities without relying on labeled examples. Supervised learning (choice A) requires labeled data for training, while semisupervised learning (choice B) uses a mix of labeled and unlabeled data. Reinforcement learning (choice C) focuses on learning through actions and rewards, not clustering or grouping data.

7. B: The coefficient of determination (R^2) measures how well a regression model explains the variation in the data. Mean squared error (MSE) (choice A) focuses on the magnitude of large prediction errors rather than explanatory power. Root mean squared error (RMSE) (choice C) reports prediction errors in the original units of the data. Mean absolute error (MAE) (choice D) averages the absolute differences between predictions and actual values but does not indicate how much variance the model explains.

8. B: Predictive imputation addresses missing data by estimating values based on patterns found in the available data. Mean imputation (choice A) simply replaces

missing values with the mean, without considering underlying relationships. Removal of incomplete data (choice C) can introduce bias and reduce the dataset's quality. Data normalization (choice D) adjusts the scale of data but does not handle missing values.

9. C: The primary goal of classification in machine learning is to assign data points to predefined categories based on labeled data. Identifying hidden patterns in unlabeled data (choice A) is the purpose of clustering, not classification. Predicting numerical outcomes (choice B) is handled by regression tasks. Generating new content (choice D) is a function of generative AI, not classification.

10. C: Clustering is the machine learning technique used to group similar data points without relying on labels. Regression (choice A) focuses on predicting numerical values rather than grouping data. Classification (choice B) requires labeled examples to assign data points to predefined categories. Deep learning (choice D) handles complex tasks like image or speech recognition but is not specifically focused on grouping unlabeled data.

Chapter 5 Answer Key

1. B: Regression is the machine learning technique commonly used to predict a numerical outcome based on known variables. Classification (choice A) assigns data to categories rather than predicting continuous values. Clustering (choice C) groups similar data points without making predictions. Deep learning (choice D) can perform many tasks but is not specifically focused on straightforward numerical prediction like regression is.

2. C: Mean absolute error (MAE) measures the average error in predictions, treating all deviations equally regardless of whether they are positive or negative. Mean squared error (MSE) (choice A) exaggerates larger errors by squaring them. The coefficient of determination (R^2) (choice B) measures how well the model explains the variance in the data, not the size of errors. Root mean squared error (RMSE) (choice D) reports errors in original units but still emphasizes larger errors through squaring.

3. B: Logistic regression is the most commonly used algorithm for estimating the probability of a binary outcome as it outputs values between 0 and 1 to represent class probabilities. K-means clustering is not suited for this task since it groups data without predicting probabilities. Linear regression estimates continuous values and is not designed for classification, while decision trees can classify but do not inherently provide probability estimates.

4. B: Azure's Automated Machine Learning (AutoML) primarily supports supervised learning, focusing on tasks such as classification and regression that require labeled data. It does not specialize in reinforcement learning or unsupervised

learning approaches like clustering, and it does not directly implement genetic algorithms. AutoML is designed to automate the process of building and tuning models within supervised learning frameworks.

5. B: In a multiclass classification problem, the one-vs-rest (OVR) approach is used to build a separate binary classifier for each class, allowing the model to distinguish one class from all others. K-means is a clustering method and not suitable for classification tasks. The multinomial algorithm handles all classes within a single model, and while logistic regression can be adapted for multiclass problems, it isn't inherently designed for building multiple binary classifiers like OVR.

6. B: AutoML is the Azure Machine Learning feature that automates the process of trying multiple algorithms and tuning hyperparameters to find the best model. Custom script execution (choice A) requires manual coding without automated model selection. Dataset storage (choice C) is intended for organizing and managing data, not for training or selecting models. Deployment pipelines (choice D) are used to manage and automate the deployment of models, not to choose or optimize them.

7. C: Recall is the evaluation metric that measures the proportion of actual positives correctly identified by a classification model. Accuracy (choice A) accounts for all correct predictions, not just positives. Precision (choice B) measures how many predicted positives are actually correct, rather than capturing all actual positives. The F1 score (choice D) combines precision and recall into a single metric but does not focus solely on true positive identification.

8. C: Clustering is the machine learning technique used to group data points based on similarities without relying on prior labels. Supervised learning (choice A) requires labeled data for training. Classification (choice B) assigns data to predefined categories, not natural groupings. Regression (choice D) predicts numerical outcomes instead of organizing data into clusters based on feature similarity.

9. C: Mean squared error (MSE) is the regression metric that measures the average of the squared differences between predicted and actual values. Mean absolute error (MAE) (choice A) calculates the average of absolute differences without squaring them. Root mean squared error (RMSE) (choice B) takes the square root of the MSE rather than reporting the squared differences directly. The R^2 score (choice D) measures how much variance is explained by the model, not the average error magnitude.

10. C: Neural networks are deep learning structures made up of multiple layers that process data to make complex predictions. Support vector machines (SVMs) (choice A) are single-layer algorithms focused mainly on classification. Decision trees (choice B) use a branching structure to make decisions, not layered processing. K-nearest neighbors (choice D) make predictions by calculating distances to nearby points, without using a layered architecture.

Chapter 6 Answer Key

1. B: Pixels are the fundamental building blocks of digital images in computer vision, forming a grid of individual colored points. While filters can modify these pixels, they do not constitute the image itself. Neural networks analyze the data contained in pixels, and labels help categorize images, but neither represents the structure of the image grid like pixels do.

2. B: Bounding boxes are used in object detection to pinpoint and outline the location of objects within an image. OCR (choice A) is designed to read text from images, not to find object locations. Facial detection (choice C) specifically identifies human faces but does not localize other types of objects. Image classification (choice D) categorizes what is present in an image but does not determine where the objects are located.

3. C: The primary purpose of convolution in computer vision is to identify patterns in pixel data such as edges, textures, and shapes. It is not used for tasks like color inversion or image resizing, and it does not directly assign labels. Instead, convolution serves as a key feature extraction step that precedes higher-level tasks like classification or labeling.

4. B: Azure AI Vision is the service that specifically handles computer vision tasks such as object detection and facial analysis. Azure Cognitive Search is focused on finding and organizing data, Azure Machine Learning supports general machine learning workflows but lacks specialization in visual tasks, and Azure Kubernetes Service is used for container orchestration, not for processing visual data.

5. B: Convolutional neural networks (CNNs) are the most commonly used neural networks for computer vision tasks like image classification due to their ability to extract features through convolutional layers. Recurrent neural networks (RNNs) are better suited for sequential data like text or time series. Generative adversarial networks (GANs) are primarily used for image generation, not classification, and transformers are typically applied in natural language processing and multimodal tasks.

6. C: Pooling layers are the component of a convolutional neural network (CNN) that reduce the size of feature maps while preserving important details. Convolutional layers (choice A) extract features but do not reduce feature map size. Fully connected layers (choice B) connect neurons across layers but do not resize feature maps. Activation functions (choice D) introduce nonlinearity to the model but do not alter the dimensions of feature maps.

7. B: Optical Character Recognition (OCR) is the computer vision technique used to read and interpret text within images. Image classification (choice A) categorizes the overall content of an image but does not extract text. Facial detection (choice C) identifies human faces without interpreting text information. Object

detection (choice D) finds objects within images but does not focus on reading or understanding text.

8. B: The primary ethical concern associated with facial detection and analysis in AI is privacy and consent issues. This arises from the potential for collecting and using facial data without individuals' informed consent. Other considerations like color accuracy and computational costs are technical rather than ethical. While limited datasets can affect model performance, they are not the main ethical issue.

9. B: In Azure's AI Vision Studio, a confidence score is provided alongside object detection results to indicate how certain the model is about its predictions. This score quantifies the model's level of confidence in identifying an object. Pixel count does not relate to confidence, bounding box color is a visual aid, and file type has no relevance to the model's certainty in its detection.

10. C: Activation functions in convolutional neural networks (CNNs) play a crucial role in the image recognition process by helping to assign probabilities to predictions, enabling the model to make final decisions. They introduce nonlinearity into the network, which is essential for learning complex patterns. While edge detection and image size reduction are handled by convolutional and pooling layers respectively, and color processing is unrelated, activation functions are key to producing meaningful classification outputs.

Chapter 7 Answer Key

1. C: Azure AI Translator is the Azure service designed to instantly translate text into multiple languages. Azure AI Language (choice A) focuses on analyzing and understanding text rather than translating it. Azure AI Speech (choice B) is used to convert spoken language to text and vice versa, not for written text translation. Azure AI Sentiment (choice D) analyzes the emotional tone of text but does not provide translation services.

2. C: The primary function of named entity recognition (NER) in natural language processing (NLP) is to identify and categorize specific entities like names, dates, and locations. Sentiment analysis (choice A) focuses on interpreting the emotional tone of text, not recognizing entities. Language detection (choice B) identifies the language used but does not extract entities. Key phrase extraction (choice D) highlights main ideas or themes.

3. C: The real-time speech-to-text feature in Azure AI Speech provides instant transcription of live audio into text. Text-to-speech (choice A) generates spoken output from written text rather than transcribing live audio. Summarization (choice B) condenses written content and is unrelated to audio transcription. Custom

Translator (choice D) customizes text translation but does not handle converting live speech to text.

4. C: Tokenization in natural language processing (NLP) refers to the process of breaking down text into individual words or phrases, known as tokens, to make the text analyzable. It does not involve assigning identifiers to entities or converting text to speech, which are separate functions. Additionally, language detection identifies the language used in the text but does not segment it into meaningful components as tokenization does.

5. B: Azure's key phrase extraction feature identifies and highlights the main concepts or themes within a piece of text. Categorizing specific entities (choice A) is the role of named entity recognition (NER), not key phrase extraction. Language detection (choice C) determines the language of a document but does not identify key ideas. Sentiment analysis (choice D) evaluates the emotional tone of the text rather than focusing on its main concepts.

6. C: PII detection is the Azure NLP feature designed to identify and redact sensitive information such as Social Security numbers. Language detection (choice A) identifies the language of the text but does not detect sensitive details. Key phrase extraction (choice B) highlights main topics or themes rather than recognizing sensitive data. Sentiment analysis (choice D) evaluates the emotional tone of the text, not the presence of personally identifying information.

7. B: Stop-word removal is the NLP process that eliminates common words like "the" and "an" that add little semantic value to the text. Lemmatization (choice A) reduces words to their root forms but does not remove them. Tokenization (choice C) splits text into individual words or tokens without filtering out common terms. Frequency analysis (choice D) measures how often words occur but does not eliminate nonessential words.

8. B: Entity linking in Azure AI Language Studio automatically connects entities like "Paris" to specific references, helping distinguish between similar terms such as "Paris, France" and "Paris Hilton." Entity recognition (choice A) identifies entities but does not link them to specific references. Language detection (choice C) determines the language of the text rather than linking entities. Summarization (choice D) condenses text but does not associate entities with unique references.

9. B: The Fast Transcription API in Azure AI Speech is designed to provide quick, synchronous transcription of audio files. Translation (choice A) is handled by Azure AI Translator, not the Fast Transcription API. Sentiment detection (choice C) is unrelated to this feature and focuses on analyzing emotional tone. Text-to-speech conversion (choice D) generates spoken output from text rather than transcribing audio into text.

10. B: Summarization in Azure is used to create concise summaries by extracting key sentences from large volumes of text. Text-to-speech (choice A) converts written text into audio but does not summarize it. Language detection (choice C) identifies the language of the text rather than condensing its content. Entity recognition (choice D) identifies specific entities like names or places but does not extract or summarize main ideas.

Chapter 8 Answer Key

1. B: DALL-E is the Azure generative AI feature that creates unique images based on text prompts. Semantic search (choice A) retrieves information based on meaning but does not generate images. Content moderation (choice C) is used to detect inappropriate content, not to create visuals. Lifelike dialogue creation (choice D) focuses on producing realistic conversations rather than generating images.

2. C: The purpose of embeddings in transformer models is to encode semantic relationships between words, creating a meaningful representation of language that helps the model understand context and meaning. They are not used for detecting harmful content, which is handled by content moderation tools, nor are they responsible for directly translating languages or generating personalized recommendations, which rely on different mechanisms and data inputs.

3. D: The encoder block is the component of a transformer model responsible for interpreting the context of input text. While embeddings help represent relationships between words and self-attention highlights important word connections, it is the encoder block that processes the input data in a contextual manner. The decoder block, by contrast, focuses on generating new sequences of text rather than understanding the input.

4. C: Contextual question answering is the AI workload designed to provide natural and accurate responses to customer questions and inquiries. Image generation (choice A) focuses on creating visuals from prompts rather than responding to questions. Summarization (choice B) condenses lengthy content but does not engage in conversation. Personalized recommendations (choice D) tailor content for users but are not meant for interactive dialogue.

5. C: In Azure's AI, multihead attention refers to analyzing relationships between words from multiple perspectives within a transformer model. Token generation (choice A) is a separate function handled by the decoder block. Anomaly detection (choice B) identifies unusual patterns in data. Translation (choice D) involves converting text between languages and is distinct from the multihead attention mechanism.

6. B: Large language models (LLMs) commonly require high memory and storage due to their size and the amount of data they are trained on. In contrast, small language models (SLMs) typically offer faster response times, consume less energy, and are easier to deploy on premises.

7. B: The primary advantage of using Azure OpenAI's Model Catalog is gaining access to a variety of pretrained, high-performance models for different applications. Fast training times (choice A) are not a feature of the Model Catalog, as it focuses on ready-to-use models. Exclusive use of OpenAI models (choice C) is not accurate, as the catalog includes a broader range of models. It is also not limited to image generation (choice D), supporting many different AI tasks.

8. B: The safety system layer in Azure's generative AI helps mitigate risks by filtering out harmful or inappropriate content in real time. This function is distinct from setting user expectations, which belongs to the UX layer, and it does not involve improving model embeddings or providing semantic search capabilities. Its primary role is to enhance content safety during AI output generation.

9. B: The decoder block in a transformer model is responsible for generating the output sequence based on the encoded input. While the encoder interprets the context of the input data, the decoder uses this information to produce coherent and contextually relevant output. Tasks like embedding words into vectors and attending to token relationships are handled separately by other components such as embedding layers and self-attention mechanisms.

10. D: The recommended strategy by Microsoft for responsible deployment of generative AI is to implement a phased rollout with an incident response plan. This approach allows for gradual scaling, careful monitoring, and effective error management. Relying only on automated testing is insufficient without manual oversight. Planning for incidents ensures risks are addressed proactively and responsibly.

Practice Exam Answer Key

1. B: The primary responsible AI principle to focus on when developing an AI system for evaluating loan applications is fairness. Fairness ensures that decisions are made based on relevant financial data and are free from bias or discrimination. While transparency helps explain decisions, privacy safeguards user data, and reliability supports consistent performance, these aspects are secondary to the ethical necessity of fair and unbiased lending practices.

2. B: The most appropriate AI workload for making a museum's digital archive of historical documents searchable is knowledge mining. This workload is specifically designed to index large collections of content and make them easily searchable and discoverable. In contrast, computer vision focuses on image

processing, conversational AI supports interactive dialogue, and sentiment analysis identifies emotional tone—none of which are suited for enabling document searchability.

3. C: The correct sequence of risk management when implementing a new AI system for public use is identification, measurement, and mitigation. This order ensures that potential risks are first recognized, then evaluated for their severity and impact, and finally addressed through appropriate mitigation strategies. Starting with mitigation or attempting to measure risks before identifying them is illogical and ineffective.

4. B: Microsoft retired the emotion recognition AI service due to ethical concerns about its accuracy and the risk of discriminatory use. Facial detection (choice A) remains available and focuses only on locating faces, not analyzing emotions. Object detection (choice C) is still an active service providing key computer vision functionality. Language translation (choice D) continues to be offered, supporting communication needs without raising similar ethical concerns.

5. A: Text analytics is the most suitable AI workload for automatically categorizing and analyzing property descriptions, as it is specifically designed to handle and extract insights from written content. In contrast, computer vision is intended for image data, speech services process audio, and face recognition is unrelated to text analysis. These other workloads do not support the textual processing required for this use case.

6. B: Before deploying harm-mitigation strategies in an AI implementation framework, impact measurement must be completed. Measuring the extent and severity of potential harm is essential for developing effective mitigation plans. Conducting user testing or deploying the system beforehand could result in avoidable risks, and marketing analysis is secondary to ensuring user safety and system responsibility.

7. A: The most suitable AI workload for analyzing customer feedback across multiple retail locations is language understanding. This workload is specifically designed to process and interpret text-based input, making it ideal for extracting insights from written customer reviews. In contrast, computer vision focuses on image analysis, face verification is unrelated to text, and speech synthesis generates spoken output rather than analyzing written content.

8. B: For an autonomous drone delivery service handling medical supplies, the most critical responsible AI principle to prioritize is reliability and safety. Ensuring that the system operates safely and reliably is essential, as it directly impacts human health. While principles like inclusiveness, transparency, and fairness are also important, they are secondary to the need for consistent, safe delivery of sensitive and potentially life-saving materials.

9. A: Conversational AI is the best solution for handling customer inquiries in multiple languages 24-7, providing real-time, multilingual interaction capabilities. Knowledge mining (choice B) focuses on indexing and retrieving information from documents but cannot engage in conversations. Image analysis (choice C) is designed for processing visual content, not text-based customer inquiries. Text analytics (choice D) can analyze text but does not support real-time, interactive communication needed for customer service.

10. A: The principle of transparency is addressed when an organization documents its AI model's capabilities and limitations. Transparency ensures users clearly understand what the AI system can and cannot do. While accountability assigns responsibility, reliability focuses on consistent system performance, and security protects against threats, none of these directly involve making the system's functions and boundaries understandable to users like transparency does.

11. B: The first step in implementing an AI governance framework for a new healthcare application is to identify potential harms. This foundational step ensures that risks are clearly understood before any protective measures, such as deploying security, training the model, or conducting user testing, are introduced. Addressing potential harms early supports responsible development and safeguards user wellbeing throughout the AI system's lifecycle.

12. B: The most appropriate machine learning approach for grouping shoppers based on browsing patterns is unsupervised learning, as it is designed to uncover patterns in unlabeled data. Supervised learning is not suitable here because it requires labeled outcomes, which are not present. Semisupervised learning combines both labeled and unlabeled data, which is unnecessary for this task, and reinforcement learning focuses on reward-based interactions, making it inappropriate for customer segmentation.

13. A: In this model, temperature serves as a feature because it is an input variable used to help predict the crop yield. It is not the label or output variable, which refers to the actual yield being predicted. Additionally, temperature is not a parameter, as parameters are internal values the model learns during training, not external input data.

14. C: The dataset should be split into training and validation sets before model training to ensure unbiased and accurate evaluation of the model's performance. Splitting the data after training or during evaluation hinders the ability to assess the model effectively and waiting until deployment is too late in the workflow. Proper early splitting allows the validation set to serve its purpose in measuring how well the model generalizes to unseen data.

15. B: In a healthcare scenario focused on predicting the risk of patient readmission —a binary classification task—accuracy is the most appropriate metric for evaluating model performance. Accuracy measures the proportion of correct

predictions, which is well-suited for classification problems. Metrics like MSE and R^2 are suited for regression tasks, while the silhouette score applies to clustering, making them unsuitable for this type of analysis.

16. C: Overfitting occurs when a machine learning model performs exceptionally well on training data but poorly on test data, indicating that it has memorized the training examples rather than learned general patterns. This gap in performance is a classic sign of overfitting. In contrast, poor performance on both sets points to underfitting, equal performance suggests proper generalization, and better test performance than training performance is highly unusual and may indicate data leakage.

17. C: The first step when creating a pipeline in Azure Machine Learning Designer is to create the pipeline infrastructure. This foundational step is essential as it enables the addition of other components like data transformation modules and datasets. Configuring compute resources and importing data are tasks that follow the establishment of the pipeline structure, making them dependent on this initial setup.

18. C: The most appropriate type of machine learning problem for predicting delivery times based on variables like distance, traffic, and weather conditions is regression, as it estimates continuous numerical values. Classification is used to predict categories rather than numerical outcomes, clustering groups of similar data points without making predictions, and anomaly detection focuses on identifying unusual patterns, not producing predictive estimates.

19. C: The correct sequence for developing a machine learning model in Azure Machine Learning is workspace creation, data preparation, training, and then deployment. Creating the workspace is the essential first step, as it provides the environment to manage all assets and activities. Data preparation and model training depend on this foundation, and deployment logically follows once the model is trained. Performing these steps out of order—such as deploying before training or preparing data before setting up a workspace—would interrupt the workflow.

20. B: When a model performs poorly on both the training and validation datasets, it likely indicates underfitting. This suggests that the model is too simple to capture the underlying patterns in the data. In contrast, overfitting would show strong performance on training data but poor performance on validation data. Data leakage typically results in unrealistically strong validation performance, and a perfect fit would demonstrate high accuracy across both datasets.

21. C: An inference pipeline in Azure Machine Learning Designer should be created after successfully training the model, as it is used to deploy the model and generate predictions on new data. Creating it before or during training is not feasible since the model must be finalized first. Additionally, inference pipelines are built

long after the data preparation phase, making it a distinct step in the deployment process.

22. B: The most appropriate approach for identifying groups of similar insurance claims without predefined categories is clustering. Clustering is a type of unsupervised learning that detects natural groupings in unlabeled data. Unlike linear regression and time-series analysis, which are used for predicting values, or classification, which requires labeled categories, clustering is ideal for discovering patterns when categories are not known in advance.

23. B: The best Azure AI Service for detecting guest comments in various languages and routing them appropriately is language detection. This service can identify the language of the text before any additional processing takes place, which is essential in a multilingual context. Other services like text analytics, sentiment analysis, and entity recognition provide valuable text insights but do not perform language identification, making them unsuitable as the first step in this scenario.

24. C: The most appropriate service for extracting mentions of medical conditions, treatments, and dosages from clinical trial documents is named entity recognition (NER). NER is specifically designed to identify and categorize detailed entities within text and can be customized for domains like healthcare. Other options such as key phrase extraction and general text analytics are too broad for this level of detail, and sentiment analysis is focused on emotional tone, not extracting specific medical information.

25. C: When Azure AI Language Detection processes text in an unsupported language, it returns a NaN (not a number) confidence score, indicating that the service cannot confidently determine the language. It does not return an empty string, produce an error code, or default to a preset language like English.

26. B: The most appropriate translation approach for an international law firm looking to preserve the formatting and structure of legal contracts is asynchronous batch translation. This method ensures that document-specific layouts are maintained during translation. In contrast, real-time translation does not retain formatting, custom neural voice is designed for speech synthesis, and text-to-speech only converts text into audio without providing document translation capabilities.

27. A: The ideal service combination for a startup developing a multilingual virtual assistant is Language understanding and Translator. This pairing enables the assistant to both comprehend user inputs and translate across multiple languages. Other options, such as Speech Service and Face API, or text analytics and computer vision, do not support the necessary language processing capabilities. Likewise, Form recognizer is designed for document extraction and is not suitable for understanding conversational language.

28. C: Content filtering in Azure OpenAI is specifically designed to prevent the model from generating harmful or inappropriate content. Entity linking (choice A) connects entities to knowledge bases but does not filter outputs. Language detection (choice B) identifies the language of text but does not monitor for inappropriate material. Speech recognition (choice D) converts spoken language to text but does not provide any content filtering capabilities.

29. C: The most suitable service for creating audiobooks in multiple languages with natural-sounding voices is custom neural voice. This service is specifically designed to generate realistic speech output across different languages. In contrast, text analytics only analyzes written content, language understanding interprets meaning without producing speech, and entity recognition focuses on identifying named entities rather than generating audio.

30. B: To create a custom translation model tailored to industry-specific terminology, parallel sentence pairs are essential. These consist of aligned text in both the source and target languages, allowing the model to learn accurate translations within a specific domain. Large general datasets lack the necessary precision for specialized terms, while speech samples and image annotations are unrelated to text-based translation tasks and thus not applicable.

31. B: The most appropriate service for a media company needing to automatically generate subtitles for live broadcasts is speech-to-text. This service is capable of producing real-time transcriptions from spoken language, making it ideal for creating live subtitles. In contrast, text analytics focuses on understanding written content, Custom Translator handles text-based language translation rather than transcription, and language understanding helps interpret meanings but does not convert audio to text.

32. C: The correct answer is text embeddings as they allow for measuring semantic similarity between pieces of text, which is essential for identifying and avoiding duplicate customer support tickets. The other options do not serve this purpose. Sentiment analysis detects emotional tone, language detection identifies the language used, and named entity recognition (NER) extracts proper names and entities, none of which help compare text for similarity.

33. C: Speaker recognition can identify and differentiate between individual voices in audio recordings, which is essential for telehealth consultations. The other options are not suitable. Language detection only identifies the language used, text analytics processes written text rather than audio, and entity linking connects related entities in text but doesn't work with speaker identification.

34. B: Object detection can identify and count multiple animals within each frame of drone footage, which is essential for wildlife monitoring. Image classification is limited to identifying the main subject without detecting multiple objects. OCR

is designed for recognizing text, not animals, and facial detection is tailored for identifying human faces, not wildlife.

35. C: Face recognition, OCR, and landmark detection are not appropriate for analyzing parking spaces as they serve different purposes such as identifying faces, extracting text, or recognizing landmarks. In contrast, semantic segmentation is suitable because it can classify each pixel in an image, allowing the system to distinguish between empty and occupied parking spots accurately.

36. C: Azure AI Vision provides both *bounding box coordinates* and a *confidence score* for each object it detects in an image. These two elements are essential. The bounding box defines the object's location, while the confidence score reflects the system's certainty in its identification. Other options like metadata, size, or color information alone are insufficient for accurate and reliable object detection.

37. B: The correct choice is custom vision because it allows the museum to train a model specifically to recognize famous paintings. Celebrity recognition is designed for identifying people, not artwork, while facial detection is limited to human faces, and OCR is only useful for extracting text, not recognizing images.

38. C: The correct answer is emotion recognition, which Azure Face API no longer supports due to ethical concerns around privacy and potential misuse. In contrast, capabilities like facial detection, facial verification, and face location are still supported as they are essential for core functionalities such as identifying and locating faces within images. This change reflects Microsoft's commitment to responsible AI practices.

39. A: Form recognizer with OCR can extract both printed and handwritten text from documents, making it ideal for processing handwritten loan applications. Facial detection and landmark detection are unrelated to document analysis, while DALL-E is designed for generating images, not interpreting text. Therefore, those options wouldn't meet the financial institution's needs.

40. B: DALL-E is designed to generate new images or create variations of existing ones, making it suitable for image variation tasks. It does not have capabilities for face recognition, text extraction, or object counting, which fall under different types of computer vision or AI services. Its main strength lies in creative image generation and manipulation.

41. B: Liveness detection is designed to determine if a person is physically present, helping distinguish between a live person and a photo or video. Facial detection simply identifies the presence of a face without confirming if it's live. Object detection and image classification focus on recognizing or categorizing items in images, not verifying human presence or authenticity.

42. C: Handwritten text recognition is specifically designed to extract and convert handwritten content into machine-readable text, making it suitable for digitizing historical letters. Image classification and object detection focus on identifying or

locating elements within images but do not extract written content. Facial detection is unrelated to document processing and cannot assist with text conversion.

43. B: DALL-E generates images based on natural language descriptions, allowing users to create visuals simply by describing them in text. It does not require an existing image to start, nor does it use programming code or audio files as inputs. The model is designed to interpret and visualize textual prompts into original artwork.

44. C: Spatial analysis is designed to monitor and understand movement patterns in physical spaces without identifying individuals, making it well-suited for privacy-conscious environments like retail stores. Face recognition focuses on identifying people, which raises privacy concerns. OCR is used for reading text, not tracking movement, and landmark detection relates to recognizing specific locations, not human behavior in a store.

45. B: GPT models are well-suited for generating test cases for REST APIs because they can understand natural language and code structures. DALL-E and Stable Diffusion focus on image generation and are not designed for working with code. Whisper specializes in transcribing spoken language into text, making it irrelevant for this task.

46. B: Copilot solutions are designed to assist with content creation in specific domains, making them well-suited for tasks like writing email campaigns. Chatbots specialize in interactive conversations but aren't optimized for generating marketing content. Translation services are limited to converting text between languages, and Content Moderator focuses on reviewing content rather than creating it.

47. B: Including a tone specification in a system message helps guide the AI to respond with a formal tone, ensuring consistency in communication style. API keys are used only for authentication and have no influence on how responses are phrased. Model version determines system capabilities but not stylistic output, and response length affects how much is said, not how it's said.

48. C: Content filtering in a generative AI solution should occur at the safety system layer, which is designed to manage and moderate outputs for appropriateness and compliance. The user interface layer is focused on display, the model layer is responsible for generating content, and the network layer deals with transmitting data—none of which are intended to enforce safety or filtering rules.

49. B: Python is widely supported by AI models for tasks like generating database queries thanks to its readability and popularity in the development community. Assembly and machine code are too low-level and complex for practical AI-generated output, while COBOL is considered outdated and lacks broad support in modern AI systems.

50. A: Zero-shot learning enables AI models to generate content based on general understanding, even when no prior examples are provided. Supervised learning depends on labeled training data, transfer learning builds on knowledge from related tasks, and reinforcement learning relies on reward feedback to guide learning.

51. B: Content safety filters play a crucial role in healthcare by helping ensure that generative AI systems produce appropriate and nonharmful outputs. Features like real-time translation, image generation, and speech synthesis support communication and presentation but do not directly address safety concerns during content creation or deployment.

52. B: Copilots are most effective when assisting developers with repetitive coding tasks, helping to boost productivity and reduce effort on routine work. They are not intended to fully replace developers, handle complex security audits, or conduct performance tuning, which require deeper analysis and specialized tools or expertise.

53. B: System messages are used to define the behavior and tone of the AI, helping maintain consistency across different prompts by setting clear instructions. Changing API keys, increasing model size, or altering network settings has no effect on the consistency of the responses, as these factors do not influence how instructions are applied during content generation.

54. B: Implementing a copilot in a specialized industrial setting requires training the model with domain-specific data to ensure it can provide relevant and accurate support. A web interface may help with accessibility but doesn't contribute to domain understanding. Public datasets often lack the depth needed for niche applications, and social media integration is generally unrelated to industrial use cases.

55. B: Grounding with reference data helps Azure OpenAI models generate more accurate and factual responses by linking outputs to trusted information sources. Speed optimization, network configuration, and user interface design may improve system performance or usability, but they do not address the issue of hallucination in model-generated content.

Glossary

Accountability
A principle of AI design to ensure that AI operates ethically, with human oversight and in alignment with legal standards, to manage the technology's impact on society and individuals

Accuracy
A metric, often used to evaluate classification models, that measures the proportion of correct predictions out of the total predictions made by a model

Algorithm
A set of instructions that a model follows to analyze data and find patterns, enabling it to make predictions or classifications based on input features

API (application programming interface)
A set of protocols that allows different software applications to communicate and interact with one another

Attention
A mechanism in transformer models that assigns varying levels of importance to different words in a sequence, enhancing the model's ability to understand contextual relationships

Automated machine learning (AutoML)
An Azure Machine Learning feature that automates model selection and hyperparameter tuning by testing multiple algorithms to find the best model

Azure AI Content Safety
A toolset for content moderation that enables automated detection and filtering of harmful or inappropriate content in online spaces

Azure AI Custom Vision
A tool that enables users to create, train, and deploy custom image classification and object detection models that are tailored to specific needs and are accessible via software development kits (SDKs), an API, or a web portal

Azure AI Document Intelligence
A tool for automating document processing and extracting key information from files to transform unstructured data into actionable insights

Azure AI Face Service
A service that provides advanced algorithms to detect, recognize, and analyze human faces, designed with privacy controls and limited to Microsoft-managed users who meet specific eligibility criteria

Azure AI Foundry
A platform for creating, managing, and deploying AI models, with tools for developers to fine-tune and customize language models for specific applications; previously called *Azure AI Studio*

Azure AI Knowledge Mining
An Azure AI feature that uses AI to extract insights from structured and unstructured data, enriching data to uncover patterns and make informed decisions

Azure AI Language
A service that offers tools for processing natural language with features like sentiment analysis, language detection, and custom text classification

Azure AI Personalizer
A personalization tool that uses reinforcement learning to make real-time recommendations based on user preferences and behaviors

Azure AI Services
A suite of AI tools on Microsoft Azure that simplify tasks like language processing, image recognition, and intelligent search and are designed to integrate easily into web and mobile applications; previously called *Cognitive Services*

Azure AI Speech
A service that enables speech recognition and synthesis, allowing for real-time transcription and converting text to speech

Azure AI Translator
A translation service for converting text across multiple languages, with options for customized and industry-specific dictionaries

Azure AI Video Indexer
A service that extracts insights from video files by using AI models for object detection, Optical Character Recognition (OCR), and audio features like transcription, translation, and emotion detection

Azure AI Vision
A service that provides tools for analyzing images and videos, with features like Optical Character Recognition (OCR), image analysis, facial recognition, and video analysis

Azure Machine Learning
A cloud-based service that facilitates the entire ML lifecycle, including data preparation, model training, and deployment, within a unified platform

Azure Machine Learning Designer
A visual interface in Azure Machine Learning for building ML models using drag-and-drop components that is ideal for users who prefer a no-code experience

Azure OpenAI Service
A service that provides access to advanced language models like GPT-4 and DALL-E within Azure, allowing businesses to leverage powerful AI capabilities for text and image generation

Azure Portal
An online interface for managing Azure resources, offering tools and shortcuts to create and monitor Azure services

Binary classification
A type of classification task in ML where the model predicts one of two possible outcomes, such as "spam" or "not spam"

Bounding box
A rectangular outline around objects in an image that is used in object detection to indicate the location and dimensions of each detected object

Classification
An ML technique that categorizes data into predefined classes or groups and is often used in tasks like spam detection or image classification

Cloud
A network of remote servers used to store and access data and applications over the internet, allowing for scalable computing resources

Clustering
An unsupervised learning technique that groups similar data points together based on their features, without predefined labels

Coefficient of determination (R^2, R-squared)
A metric used in regression to assess how well the model explains the variance in the target variable, with values closer to 1 indicating a better fit

Compute cluster
A resource in Azure Machine Learning used to run ML workloads by distributing tasks across multiple VMs

Computer vision
An AI workload focused on analyzing and interpreting visual content such as images and videos

Confusion matrix
A table used to evaluate the performance of a classification model by displaying the counts of true positives, true negatives, false positives, and false negatives

Content Safety Studio
An Azure tool focused on moderating content by detecting harmful or inappropriate material, such as hate speech or violence

Conversational AI
A technology that enables machines to engage in dialogue with users, often through chatbots, to provide information, resolve issues, and perform tasks in natural language

Conversational language understanding (CLU)
Part of Azure AI Language, a feature that builds custom models to understand and extract valuable information from user messages

Convolutional neural network (CNN)
A deep learning (DL) model specifically designed for analyzing visual data that consists of layers that detect patterns, recognize shapes, and classify images

Copilot
An AI assistant integrated into various Microsoft applications, such as Word and Excel, to aid users by generating text, summarizing information, and providing suggestions

Custom model
An ML model adapted to specific tasks or data requirements that is often trained further to improve accuracy and relevance for specialized applications

DALL-E
A generative AI model by OpenAI that is available in Azure for creating images from text prompts, which are useful in creative and design applications

Data preparation
The process of cleaning, normalizing, and transforming raw data into a format suitable for model training, which is essential for accurate ML

Dataset
A collection of data used in ML that includes training, validation, and testing data for building and evaluating models

Decoder block
A part of transformer models that generates output sequences based on encoded input data, which is essential in creating meaningful language responses

Deep learning (DL)
An advanced type of ML based on artificial neural networks with multiple layers and designed to handle complex tasks like image recognition and natural language processing (NLP)

Digital asset management (DAM)
Organizing, storing, and retrieving digital media while managing rights; commonly used in Azure AI Vision

Document intelligence
An AI workload that processes and extracts information from documents to reduce manual data-handling efforts; also called *document AI*

Edge computing
Processing data close to the data source, such as IoT devices, to reduce latency and

bandwidth costs, particularly for remote or intermittently connected locations

Embedding
A vector representation of words that captures semantic relationships, allowing models to understand and process language by measuring similarity between word meanings

Encoder block
The component of a transformer model that processes input text, recognizing patterns and context to create meaningful language representations

Entity linking
A process that associates recognized entities with specific references, such as linking "Paris" to "Paris, France" to enhance context understanding

Entity recognition
A method that identifies and classifies important entities in text, such as names, dates, or locations; also called *named-entity recognition (NER)*

F1 score
A metric that combines precision and recall to provide a balanced performance measure, which is particularly useful when the data has class imbalance

Facial detection
Identifying the presence of human faces in images without necessarily recognizing specific individuals, which is useful for applications like crowd counting

Facial recognition
An AI technology for identifying individual faces in images that is used in security, personalization, and identification applications

Fairness
A principle of AI design to ensure that AI systems treat all groups equally and avoid introducing or amplifying biases

Feature
An individual, measurable property or characteristic of a data point used by a model to make predictions

Feature engineering
The process of selecting, modifying, and creating features (data attributes) to improve the predictive power of a model

Fine-tuning
The process of adapting a pretrained model by training it on specific datasets to enhance performance for particular tasks

Foundation model
A large-scale, pretrained model available in the Azure Model Catalog that can be fine-tuned for various applications, such as language processing and image generation

Frequency analysis
A technique in NLP to count word occurrences, which often reveals the most relevant terms in a document

Generative AI
An AI model that creates new content, such as text, images, or audio, based on learned data patterns

Hyperparameter tuning
The process of adjusting model parameters that are set before training begins to improve the model's performance

Image captioning
A computer vision capability that generates descriptive text for an image and is often accompanied by a confidence score to indicate accuracy

Image classification
The process of identifying the main content of an image and categorizing it into predefined classes, such as to detect animal species or vehicle types

Inclusiveness
A principle of AI design to ensure that AI is accessible to everyone, especially by

incorporating diverse perspectives and following accessibility standards

Inferencing
The process of using a trained model to make predictions on new, unseen data

Internet of Things (IoT)
A network of physical devices that communicate and exchange data over the internet

Kernels
Small matrices used in image processing to apply filters, transforming pixel values to achieve effects like sharpening or blurring

Key phrase extraction
A tool in Azure that identifies important phrases or terms in a document, highlighting main topics or themes without analyzing the entire text

K-means clustering
A clustering algorithm that partitions data into a specified number of clusters by assigning each data point to the nearest centroid

Knowledge mining
Using AI to extract insights from both structured and unstructured data, making information more accessible and useful

Language detection
Identifying the language of a document, which is useful for AI applications processing multilingual content

Large language model (LLM)
A high-capacity language model trained on vast datasets to generate coherent and contextually accurate text responses

Logistic regression
A classification algorithm often used in binary classification tasks that estimates the probability of an outcome and applies a threshold to make a decision

Machine learning (ML)
A branch of AI that enables computers to learn from data and make predictions or decisions without explicit programming

Machine translation
Automated translation of text from one language to another, powered by neural networks that capture grammar, context, and tone

Mean absolute error (MAE)
An evaluation metric that calculates the average magnitude of errors in predictions without considering their direction

Mean squared error (MSE)
A metric, often used in regression analysis, that emphasizes larger errors by squaring the difference between actual and predicted values

Multiclass classification
A classification task where a model predicts one of multiple categories, as opposed to binary classification

Multimodal models
AI models that integrate multiple data types, such as text and images, to enable richer contextual understanding, exemplified by models like Microsoft's Florence

Multiservice resource
An Azure configuration that allows access to multiple AI services using a single key and endpoint, streamlining management and billing

Named entity linking (NEL)
Enhancing entity recognition by linking entities in text to unique real-world references, improving context and accuracy

Named entity recognition (NER)
Automatically tagging words or phrases in text into categories such as names, locations, or dates

Natural language processing (NLP)
Enabling machines to understand and respond to human language, which is

essential for applications like chatbots and voice assistants

Neural network
A series of interconnected nodes (neurons) in layers that process input data to produce outputs; commonly used in deep learning (DL)

Object detection
A computer vision technique that not only identifies objects within an image but also provides their locations using bounding boxes

On premises
A local data center configuration allowing users to store and manage data within their own servers rather than in the cloud

Optical Character Recognition (OCR)
A computer vision tool that extracts text from images and is useful for digitizing printed or handwritten documents

Overfitting
When an AI model learns the training data too well, including noise and outliers, leading to strong performance on training data but poor generalization to new, unseen data

Personally identifying information (PII) detection
The process of detecting and redacting sensitive data in text to protect user privacy

Precision
The ratio of true positive predictions to total positive predictions, indicating how many predicted positives are actually correct

Prompt engineering
The art of crafting specific input prompts to guide AI in generating accurate and relevant responses

Prompt shields
Tools that scan text inputs to detect potential risks for LLMs in user-generated content, aiding in safe AI deployments

Recall
A metric to measure how well a model identifies all relevant cases within a dataset that is calculated as the true positives divided by the sum of the true positives and false negatives

Receiver operating characteristic (ROC) curve
A graphical representation of a model's ability to distinguish between classes, with true positive rates plotted against false positive rates

Regression analysis
A statistical technique used to predict a continuous outcome variable based on one or more predictor variables

Reliability and safety
A principle of AI design that emphasizes consistent and safe system performance, ensuring that the AI functions as expected even in unexpected scenarios

Resource group
A container within Azure used to organize related resources, making it easier to manage and monitor them collectively

Responsible AI
Principles for ensuring that AI systems are transparent, fair, and ethical, including features such as model explainability

Retrieval-augmented generation (RAG)
A feature that runs AI models on specific datasets for more accurate and contextually relevant outputs

Root mean squared error (RMSE)
The square root of the mean squared error, which provides a measure of the average prediction error in the same units as the target variable

Security and privacy
A principle of AI design that ensures that AI applications protect user data, follow privacy regulations, and guard against misuse or data breaches

Self-attention
A method within transformer models that analyzes word relationships within a sequence, refining the context for better understanding and predictions

Semantic language models
NLP models that capture complex relationships between words using embeddings, allowing for accurate interpretation of language nuances

Sentiment analysis and opinion mining
The process of determining the emotional tone of text to identify whether it is positive, negative, or neutral

Silhouette score
A metric for evaluating how well clusters are separated in clustering analysis, with scores closer to 1 indicating better-defined clusters

Single-service resource
An Azure option for accessing a specific AI service, allowing distinct tracking and billing for individual resources

Software development kit (SDK)
A collection of tools, libraries, and documentation for developers to build applications for specific platforms

Speech recognition
A process that converts spoken language into text by analyzing sound features, phonemes, and words

Speech synthesis
The process of converting text to natural-sounding speech, which is useful for virtual assistants, public announcements, and interactive applications

Stop-word removal
An NLP technique to remove common words (like *the* or *an*) that typically do not add meaning to text analysis

Supervised learning
A type of ML where models are trained on labeled data, using input-output pairs to learn to predict outputs for new inputs

Tagging
A feature in computer vision that adds keywords to images based on content, facilitating search and organization

Text classification
The process of categorizing text based on predefined labels, which is used for sorting documents or social media posts by topics or sentiment

Tokenization
The process of breaking text into individual units or tokens to allow for easier analysis and manipulation of language elements

Training
The process of feeding a model with data and adjusting its parameters so that it can make accurate predictions on similar unseen data

Train-validation split
The division of a dataset into training and validation sets to evaluate the model's performance and prevent overfitting

Transformer
A deep learning (DL) model architecture that has advanced NLP and multimodal models by encoding data as embeddings, enhancing context in tasks that mix text and images

Transparency
A principle of AI design that ensures that AI decision making is understandable and accessible to users and fosters trust through clear explanations of AI processes

True positive rate (TPR)
A metric that measures the proportion of actual positives correctly identified by the model; also called *recall*

Underfitting
When an AI model is too simple to capture the underlying patterns in the data resulting in poor performance on both the training set and unseen data

Unsupervised learning
An ML approach where the model identifies patterns and structures in unlabeled data without predefined categories

Validation
The phase where a separate subset of data, not used during training, is used to evaluate the model's performance and adjust it as necessary

Virtual machine (VM)
A virtualized computing resource for a cloud system that can be used to run ML tasks with dedicated CPU or GPU resources

Vision Studio
An Azure tool that focuses on image and video analysis, allowing users to experiment with features like object detection and classification

Workspace
In Azure Machine Learning, a centralized location where all resources, including datasets, models, and compute resources, are managed for ML projects

Index

A

accountability, 32, 36
accuracy, 56
ACE (American Council on Education), 9
actions, in personalization, 25
activation functions, in CNNs, 101
AI (artificial intelligence), 21-36, 162
    career opportunities in, 3
    categories of, 22-30
        computer vision, 25, 85-104
        content moderation, 23-24
        document intelligence, 28
        generative AI, 29, 131-155
        knowledge mining, 28
        natural language processing, 26-27, 107-128
        personalization, 25
    overview of, 21
    principles for responsible AI, 31-36, 162
        accountability, 32
        fairness, 34, 103
        inclusiveness, 33
        reliability and safety, 33
        security and privacy, 35, 103
        transparency, 34, 104
    rising demand for skills in, 2
    risks, 31
    salary boosts for skills in, 3
AI developers, 3
AI For Everyone course, 6
AI-102 certification, 8
AI-900 certification exam, 1-9, 159-166
    accommodation for specific needs and disabilities, 7
    advanced certifications, 7-8
    breaks, 7
    candidates for, 3-4
    checking answers, 161
    college credits, 9
    complementary certifications, 5-6
    multiple-choice questions, 161
    preparatory resources, 8
    question format, 6, 160
    reasons for taking, 2-3
    registration fee, 7
    retaking, 7
    sandbox, 159
    scoring system, 6
    staying calm during, 161
    strategies for, 160-162
    taking online versus in-person, 7
    timing, 7, 160
    topics covered by, 4-5, 12, 162-166
    validity and recertification, 7
algorithms
    applying, 43
    defined, 22
    parameters for, 51
    selection of, 51
Amazon Web Services (AWS), 2
ambiguity, interpretation of, 135
American Council on Education (ACE), 9
anomaly detection, 135
APIs (application programming interfaces), defined, 11
area under the curve (AUC), 58
artificial intelligence (see AI)

Artificial Intelligence Workloads and Considerations section, 4
artificial neural networks, 65
attention process, 136, 138-139
AUC (area under the curve), 58
AutoML (Azure Automated Machine Learning), 73-78, 163
    defined, 71
    health insurance cost prediction example, 73-78
average distance to cluster center metric, 64
average distance to other centers metric, 64
AWS (Amazon Web Services), 2
AWS Certified AI Practitioner certification, 6
AZ-104 certification, 8
AZ-204 certification, 8
AZ-900 certification, 5, 7
Azure AI Content Safety Studio, 17, 23, 30
Azure AI Custom Translator, 165
Azure AI Custom Vision, 86
Azure AI Document Intelligence, 28-30, 98
Azure AI Face Service, 86, 164
Azure AI Foundry
    content filtering, 153
    copilots, 147
    entity recognition, 117
    language models, 139
    OCR, 96
    overview of, 17-19
Azure AI Knowledge Mining, 28, 30
Azure AI Language, 26-27, 30, 164
    conversational AI, 125
    features of, 113
    key phrase extraction, 115
    language detection, 119
    named entity recognition, 116-117
    question-answer feature, 125
    sentiment analysis, 118
    studio, 16
Azure AI Model Catalog, 139
Azure AI Personalizer, 25, 30
Azure AI Services, 11-19, 85
    creating resources, 14-15
    growing dominance of Azure, 2
    overview of, 12
    setting up, 13
    studios, 16
Azure AI Speech, 164
    features of, 114

    speech recognition, 120
    speech synthesis, 121
    studio, 17
Azure AI Translator, 114, 164
Azure AI Video Indexer, 86
Azure AI Vision
    defined, 85
    image captioning, 88
    object detection, 95
    overview of, 25, 30, 163
    studio, 16
    trial period, 13
Azure AI-900 (see AI-900 certification exam)
Azure Automated Machine Learning (see AutoML)
Azure Blob Storage, 12
Azure Cognitive Search Service, 28
Azure Cognitive Services, 13
Azure Content Moderator, 23-24
Azure Cosmos DB storage, 12
Azure Kubernetes Service, 12-13
Azure Machine Learning, 71-82, 139, 163
    AutoML, 73-78
    Designer, 78-82
    overview of, 72-73
    studio, 71-73, 78
    trial period, 13
Azure Machine Learning Designer, 78-82, 163
    defined, 71
    income level prediction example, 78-82
Azure OpenAI Service, 165
    language models, 139
    overview of, 29, 147-150
    studio, 148-150
Azure Portal, 13
Azure Read OCR engine, 96

B

backpropagation, 66, 101
bag-of-words model, 111
BERT (bidirectional encoder representations from transformers), 110, 140
bias, 31, 34, 103
binary classification, 52-58
    evaluation metrics for, 55-58
    key concepts in, 58
    loan default prediction example, 52-55
Blob Storage, 12

blurring filters, 93
bounding boxes, 95, 100
business analysts, 4
business professionals, 4

C

career changers, 4
centroids, 63
Certiport, 7
Chat feature, Copilot, 142
ChatGPT, 107, 131
classification, 51-62
    binary, 52-58
    multiclass, 59-62
CLIP (Contrastive Language-Image Pretraining), 140
cloud services, 12
CLU (conversational language understanding), 27, 123-124
clustering, 62-64
    evaluation metrics for, 64
    fish example, 63-64
CNNs (convolutional neural networks), 90, 100-102
    facial detection and recognition, 99
    image segmentation, 102
    layers of, 101
    object detection, 102
coefficient of determination (R^2), 45, 50
Cognitive Search Service, 28
Cognitive Services, 13
cognitive skills, in knowledge mining, 28
college credits, 9
color inversion filters, 93
Columbia Engineering Artificial Intelligence certificate program, 6
compute clusters, 82
computer vision, 85-104, 163
    Azure services for
        capabilities of, 86-89
        options, 85-86
    CNNs, 100-102
    evolution of, 102
    facial detection and recognition, 99-100
    image classification, 94
    image filters, 92-94
    object detection, 95
    OCR, 96-98
    overview of, 25, 30, 89-92
    responsible AI and, 103-104
Computer Vision Workloads on Azure section, 5
confusion matrices, 55-56
    accuracy, 56
    labels, 56
    multiclass classifiers, 61
content moderation, 23-24, 30, 135
Content Moderator, 23-24
Content Safety Studio, 17, 23, 30
context, in personalization, 25
contextual embeddings, 113
contextual responses, 135
Contrastive Language-Image Pretraining (CLIP), 140
conversational AI, 125-128
conversational language understanding (CLU), 27, 123-124
convolution, 89
convolutional filtering, 94
convolutional layers, in CNNs, 101
copilots, 131, 141-146, 165
    Copilot in Microsoft Fabric, 145
    Copilot in Microsoft Power BI, 146
    customizing, 147
    GitHub Copilot, 146
    Microsoft Copilot for Microsoft 365, 143
    Microsoft Copilot in Azure, 144
    Microsoft Dynamics 365, 144
    Microsoft Security Copilot, 145
    web-based, 142
Cosmos DB storage, 12
custom categories, for content moderation, 24, 155
custom models, for document intelligence, 29
custom term lists, in content moderation, 23
custom text classification, 27
custom translation models, 114, 165
Custom Translator Service, 165
Custom Vision Service, 86
customizable indexing, in knowledge mining, 28

D

DALL-E model, 140, 164-165
DAM (digital asset management), 26
data analysts, 3

data normalization, 42
data preparation, 42
data storage, 12
decoder blocks, in transformers, 136, 138
deduplication algorithms, 42
deep learning (see DL)
deep neural networks (DNNs), 65
dialogue creation, 135
dictation, 120
digital asset management (DAM), 26
DL (deep learning), 65-67
    computer vision, 90
    defined, 22
    facial detection and recognition, 99
    fruit example, 65-67
    key differences between ML and, 67
    NLP, 107
DNNs (deep neural networks), 65
document intelligence (document AI), 28-30
Document Intelligence model, 96, 98
Document Intelligence Service, 28-30, 98
document translation, 114
DP-100 certification, 8
DP-203 certification, 8
DP-900 certification, 6
duplicate data, 42
Dynamics 365, 144

E

ecommerce recommendations, 124
edge detection filters, 93
edge services, 12
embeddings, 102, 111-113, 138
encoder blocks, in transformers, 136, 138
endpoints, defined, 15
enrichment, in knowledge mining, 28
enterprise bots, 124
entities, in CLU, 123
entity linking, 27, 113
entity recognition, 116-117
entry-level job seekers, 4
epochs, 67
ethical AI
    accountability, 32, 36
    defined, 32
    inclusiveness, 33, 36
    reliability and safety, 33, 36

ETL (extract, transform, and load) processes, 42
evaluation metrics, 163
Excel, 144
explainability, 35
explainable AI
    defined, 32
    fairness, 34-36, 103
    security and privacy, 35, 103
    transparency, 34-36, 104
extract, transform, and load (ETL) processes, 42

F

F1 score, 57
Face Service, 86, 164
facial detection and recognition, 26, 87, 99-100
fairness, 34-36, 103
false negative (FN) label, in confusion matrices, 56
false positive (FP) label, in confusion matrices, 56
false positive rate (FPR), 58
fast transcription API, 114
features, in training datasets
    defined, 41
    selection and preparation of, 51
fine-tuning models, 45, 51, 90, 148
Florence model, 102
FN (false negative) label, in confusion matrices, 56
foundation model, 139
Foundry (see Azure AI Foundry)
FP (false positive) label, in confusion matrices, 56
FPR (false positive rate), 58
free Azure accounts, 13
frequency analysis, 110
fully connected layers, in CNNs, 101

G

GDPR (General Data Protection Regulation), 103
general extraction models, for document intelligence, 29
generative AI, 131-155, 165
    defined, 22
    language models, 134-135, 139-150

Azure services for, 139-140, 147-150
    copilots, 141-147
    large, 141
    prompt engineering, 146
    small, 141
overview of, 29, 131-134
responsible AI, 150-155
transformers, 135-139
Generative AI Workloads on Azure section, 5
GitHub Copilot, 146
GloVe, 111
GPS navigation, 122
GPT models, 165
    GPT-3, 136
    GPT-3.5, 136
    GPT-3.5 Turbo, 140, 147
    GPT-4, 136, 140, 147
    GPT-4 Turbo, 147
    GPT-4 Turbo with Vision, 140
    GPT-4o, 136, 140
    GPT-4o mini, 136
groundedness detection, 24, 155

H

hands-free reading, 122
hyperparameters, 51

I

IBM AI Foundations for Business Specialization certification, 6
IDP (intelligent document processing), 98
image analysis, 25
image captioning, 86-87
image classification, 94
image filters, 92-94
image moderation, 23-24
image segmentation, 102
incident response plans, 154
inclusiveness, 33, 36
inferencing, 40, 43
Intelligent Cloud segment, 2
intelligent document processing (IDP), 98
intelligibility, 35
intents, in CLU, 123
investigation of outliers, 42
IT specialists, 3

K

k-fold cross-validation, 47
k-means clustering, 63
Kaggle, 73
kernels, 92
key phrase extraction, 27, 113-115
knowledge mining, 28, 30
Knowledge Mining Service, 28, 30
Kotwal, Ketan, 103
Kubernetes Service, 12-13

L

labels, in training datasets, 41
language detection, 27, 119
language models, 134-135, 139-150
    Azure services for, 139-140, 147-150
    copilots, 141-147
    large, 141
    prompt engineering, 146
    small, 141
Language Service (see Azure AI Language)
Laplacian filters, 93
large language models (LLMs), 141
LDA (latent Dirichlet allocation), 110
lemmatization, 109
LLMs (large language models), 141
logistic regression, 53, 111

M

machine learning (see ML)
Machine Learning Designer (see Azure Machine Learning Designer)
Machine Learning Principles on Azure section, 5
Machine Learning Service (see Azure Machine Learning)
machine translation, 122
MAE (mean absolute error), 45, 50
Marcel, Sébastien, 103
maximum distance to cluster center metric, 64
mean squared error (MSE), 50
mean/median imputation, 41
meeting transcriptions, 120
metaprompt and grounding layer, in generative AI, 153, 166
Microsoft
    Copilot, 131, 141-146
    Copilot Studio, 147

Document Intelligence model, 96, 98
Dynamics 365, 144
Excel, 144
Florence model, 102
Intelligent Cloud segment, 2
Outlook, 144
PowerPoint, 143
Tay chatbot, 35
Teams, 144
Word, 143
Microsoft Azure (see Azure)
Microsoft Azure AI-900 (see AI-900 certification exam)
minimizing loss process, 139
missing data, 41
ML (machine learning), 162
(see also Azure Machine Learning)
deep learning versus, 67
defined, 22
NLP, 107
overview of, 39
reinforcement learning, 25
types of, 43-67
classification, 51-62
clustering, 62-64
deep learning, 65-67
regression analysis, 44-51
workflow, 40-43
MLOps tools, 72
Model Catalog, 139
model layer, in generative AI, 152
MSE (mean squared error), 50
multiclass classification, 59-62
evaluation metrics for, 61-62
flower example, 59-62
key concepts in, 62
multinomial algorithms, 60
OVR algorithms, 60
multihead attention, 139
multilingual translation, 135
multimodal models, 102
multinomial algorithms, 60
multiservice resources, 15

N

n-grams, 109
naive Bayes algorithm, 111
naming resources, 17

natural language processing (see NLP)
NEL (named entity linking), 117
NER (named entity recognition), 27, 113, 116-117, 164
Ng, Andrew, 6
NLP (natural language processing), 26-27, 30, 107-128, 164
Azure services for, 113-128
CLU, 123-124
conversational AI, 125-128
entity recognition, 116-117
key phrase extraction, 115
language detection, 119
machine translation, 122
sentiment analysis, 118
speech recognition, 120-121
speech synthesis, 121
frequency analysis, 110
overview of, 107
semantic language models, 111-113
text classification, 111
tokenization, 108-109
transformers, 102
NLP Workloads on Azure section, 5

O

object detection
CNNs, 102
defined, 26, 87
overview of, 87, 95
OCR (Optical Character Recognition)
content moderation, 23
defined, 26, 87
limits of, 164
overview of, 96-98
on-premises services, 12
on-the-spot blocking, 154
one-vs-rest (OVR) algorithms, 60
OpenAI Service (see Azure OpenAI Service)
opinion mining, 27, 113
Optical Character Recognition (OCR)
content moderation, 23
defined, 26, 87
limits of, 164
overview of, 96-98
optimization, of CNNs, 101
outliers, 42
Outlook, 144

OVR (one-vs-rest) algorithms, 60

P

pattern recognition, 135
pay-as-you-go model, 13
PCA (principal component analysis), 113
Pearson VUE, 7
personalization, 25, 30
personalized recommendations, 135
Personalizer Service, 25, 30
phased rollout, of generative AI, 154
PHI (protected health information) detection, 113
PII (personally identifiable information) detection, 27, 113
pixels, 89
pooling layers, in CNNs, 101
Portal, 13
PowerPoint, 143
prebuilt models, for document intelligence, 29
precision, 57
predictive imputation, 41
predictive maintenance, 40
preprocessing pipelines, 42
pricing tiers, for Azure resources, 15, 17
principal component analysis (PCA), 113
product design optimization, 40
project managers, 3
prompt engineering, 146, 165
prompt shields, 23, 155
protected health information (PHI) detection, 113
protected material detection, 24, 155
public announcements, 122

Q

quality control
    in manufacturing, 40
    outlier management, 42
question format, of AI-900 exam, 6
question-answering feature, in conversational AI, 27, 125

R

RAG (retrieval-augmented generation), 30
Read OCR engine, 96
real-time captions, 120
real-time speech-to-text, 114

recall, 56
receiver operating characteristic (ROC) curve, 58
recognition, AI-900 certification and, 2
recurrent neural networks (RNNs), 111
regions, 15, 17
regression analysis, 44-51
    evaluation metrics for, 49-51
    key concepts in, 51
    ticket sales example, 45-49
reinforcement learning, 25
reliability and safety, 33, 36
removal of outliers, 42
Representational State Transfer (REST) APIs, 11
resource groups, 15, 17
responsible AI, 31-36, 162
    accountability, 32, 36
    computer vision and, 103-104
    fairness, 34-36, 103
    generative AI, 150-155
        built-in safeguards, 152
        compliance, 153
        release planning, 154
        risk assessment, 151
        spotting potential harms, 150
    inclusiveness, 33, 36
    reliability and safety, 33, 36
    security and privacy, 35, 103
    transparency, 34-36, 104
REST (Representational State Transfer) APIs, 11
retaking exam, 7
retrieval-augmented generation (RAG), 30
rewards, in personalization, 25
RMSE (root mean squared error), 45, 50
RNNs (recurrent neural networks), 111
ROC (receiver operating characteristic) curve, 58
rollback plans, 154
R^2 (coefficient of determination), 45, 50

S

safety system layer, in generative AI, 153, 165
sales professionals, 3, 4
scenario-based questions, 162
scoring system, 6
SDKs (software development kits), 11

security and privacy, 35, 103
Security Copilot, 145
self-attention, 139
self-supervised learning, 113
semantics
    natural language processing, 27, 111-113
    semantic search, 135
sentiment analysis, 27, 108, 113, 118
sharpening filter, 93
sigmoid function, 53-54
silhouette score, 64
simple frequency analysis, 110
single-service resources, 15
SLMs (small language models), 141
Sobel filters, 93
software development kits (SDKs), 11
speech recognition, 108
Speech Service (see Azure AI Speech)
speech synthesis, 108, 120, 121
speech-to-text, 114
splitting data, 44, 46
Stable Diffusion model, 140
stemming, 109
step-by-step vocal instructions, 122
stop-word removal, 109
stratified splitting, 46
structured data, 28
student accounts, 13
subscriptions, to Azure resources, 15, 17
summarization, 27, 113, 135
supervised learning, 43, 162
    classification, 51-62
    image classification, 94
    regression analysis, 44-51
supply chain management, 40
SVM (support vector machine), 111

T

t-SNE (t-distributed stochastic neighbor
    embedding), 113
tagging, 87
Tay chatbot, 35
Teams, 144
telemetry tracking, 154
templates, for content moderation, 24
term frequency-inverse document frequency
    (TF-IDF), 110-111
testing dataset, 44-45

text classification, 27, 111
text moderation, 23-24
text normalization, 109
text translation, 114
text-to-speech, 114
TF-IDF (term frequency-inverse document frequency), 110-111
time-based splitting, 47
TN (true negative) label, in confusion matrices, 56
tokenization, 108-109, 136-138
tokens, 108-109, 111-113, 136-138
TP (true positive) label, in confusion matrices, 56
TPR (true positive rate), 58
training dataset, 44
training ML models
    features versus labels, 163
    image recognition, 89
    ML model workflow, 40-43
    regression analysis, 45
transformers, 135-139
    attention, 138-139
    embeddings, 138
    overview of, 102
    text classification, 111
    tokenization, 136-138
Translator Service, 114, 164
transparency, 34, 104
true negative (TN) label, in confusion matrices, 56
true positive (TP) label, in confusion matrices, 56
true positive rate (TPR), 58

U

unique identifiers, 42
unstructured data, 28
unsupervised learning, 43, 94, 135, 163
user feedback, 154
user-blocking tools, 154
utterances, in CLU, 123
UX (user experience) layer, in generative AI, 153, 166

V

validation dataset, 44-45
validation rules, 42

video analysis, 26
Video Indexer Service, 86
video moderation, 23
virtual assistants, 122, 124
Vision Service (see Azure AI Vision)
VMs (virtual machines), 12
voice-activated customer service, 120

W

web-based copilots, 142
Word, 143
word2vec, 110-111, 138
workloads, defined, 1
workspaces, 72

About the Author

Tom Taulli (@ttaulli) is a consultant to various companies, such as Aisera, SnapLogic, and Tad Health. He has written several books like *AI-Assisted Programming: Better Planning, Coding, Testing, and Deployment*. Tom has also taught IT courses for UCLA, PluralSight, and O'Reilly Media. For these, he has provided lessons in using Python to create deep learning and machine learning models. He has also taught on topics like natural language processing.

Colophon

The animal on the cover of *Azure AI Fundamentals (AI-900) Study Guide* is the kelp greenling (*Hexagrammos decagrammus*), whose scientific name comes from the Greek roots *hex* meaning "six," *gramma* meaning "line," and *deca* meaning "ten," referring to the six lateral line canals on each side of the fish. They can be found in shallow water near rocky areas in the eastern Pacific Ocean.

Kelp greenlings can grow up to 25 inches and weigh almost 5 pounds, with males typically smaller than females. They have sleek, elongated bodies with slightly spiny dorsal fins. The inside of their mouths is a yellowish color, and they have dark greenish-brown and gray bodies. Even though males and females have the same coloring, they differ when it comes to their spots. Males have blue spots with red or rust-colored rings around them, and females have rust-colored or golden spots.

Unique to kelp greenlings is their mating ritual. In winter to early spring, males create nests, usually in rock crevices or similarly protected areas. After a female lays its eggs, the male guards and defends the nest from other male kelp greenlings who attempt to fertilize those eggs.

The cover illustration is by José Marzan Jr. based on an antique line engraving from Lydekker's *Royal Natural History*. The series design is by Edie Freedman, Ellie Volckhausen, and Karen Montgomery. The cover fonts are Gilroy Semibold and Guardian Sans. The text font is Adobe Minion Pro; the heading font is Adobe Myriad Condensed; and the code font is Dalton Maag's Ubuntu Mono.

O'REILLY®

Learn from experts. Become one yourself.

60,000+ titles | Live events with experts | Role-based courses
Interactive learning | Certification preparation

 **Try the O'Reilly learning platform free for 10 days.**

www.ingramcontent.com/pod-product-compliance
Lightning Source LLC
Chambersburg PA
CBHW080538300426
44111CB00017B/2782